Deleuze and Guattari's
Immanent Ethics

A volume in the SUNY series in Gender Theory

Tina Chanter, editor

Deleuze and Guattari's Immanent Ethics

Theory, Subjectivity, and Duration

TAMSIN LORRAINE

Published by State University of New York Press, Albany

© 2011 State University of New York

For information, contact State University of New York Press, Albany, NY
www.sunypress.edu

Production by Diane Ganeles
Marketing by Anne M. Valentine

Library of Congress Cataloging-in-Publication Data

Lorraine, Tamsin E.
    Deleuze and Guattari's immanent ethics : theory, subjectivity, and duration / Tamsin Lorraine.
        p. cm. — (SUNY series in gender theory)
    Includes bibliographical references (p.   ) and index.
    ISBN 978-1-4384-3663-0 (hardcover : alk. paper)
    1. Deleuze, Gilles, 1925-1995.   2. Guattari, Félix, 1930–1992.   3. Ethics.
4. Feminist ethics.   I. Title.

    B2430.D454L67 2011
    194—dc22   2011003167

10 9 8 7 6 5 4 3 2 1

Contents

Preface

The reading I give here of Gilles Deleuze and Félix Guattari's conceptions of theory, subjectivity, and ethics is inspired by Deleuze and Guattari's innovative approach to two problems with which I have struggled throughout my adult life. The first problem is that of how to be ethical in an age where traditional approaches to grounding transcendent values in God or reason appear to be increasingly suspect, and the second problem is that of how to conceive of the practice of philosophy in a way that manifests its pragmatic importance to living as well as the aesthetic pleasure it can bring to its practitioners.

As a woman and a feminist who came of age in the 1970s, I was drawn to philosophy for its skeptical attitude; it was by taking a philosophical step back in order to reconsider the assumptions informing my conceptions of truth and ethics that I was able to rethink what I had been told about what it meant to be human or what we could hope for as human beings struggling to live with one another in productive harmony. This critical endeavor gave me important tools in investigating and analyzing reality in light of human subjects marginalized in various ways from the mainstream and opened my eyes to more inclusive ways of conceiving what it meant to be human and how we might better work toward a society that could support our collective humanity. My love of philosophy has thus always had a pragmatic edge to it that spoke to my need to resolve the dissonance I experienced in trying to live ethically as I faced particular life problems (Why did the "right" thing sometimes feel so "wrong"? To whom could I turn for answers when neither specific authority figures nor rational argument could supply completely satisfying solutions?). Deleuze and Guattari's emphasis on a pragmatic conception of language always implicated with the situations of embodied subjects of a particular time and place responding to specific problems along with a conception of human beings as evolving creatures struggling to unfold their capacities to live in always novel circumstances in response to life conceived as becoming, spoke to my need to take an ethical approach more creative than that of applying moral rules or transcendent ideals—an approach that was more attuned to the skewed perspectives of embodied subjects facing unanticipated and even unintelligible (at least according to "normal" or "acceptable" ways of understanding social reality) dilemmas.

Deleuze and Guattari's conception of philosophy not only spoke to the way philosophy has enabled me to resolve some of the dissonance of day-to-day living, it also captured the aesthetic pleasure I often derive from the unexpected perspectives arrived at by unfolding lines of thought I would never have otherwise traveled. It has been one of the great pleasures in my years of teaching philosophy (as well as one of my great frustrations when, as I often do, I fail) to communicate to my students the inherent joy of carefully pursuing the intricacies of the webs of beliefs—with all their implicit nuance and affective charge—that structure the meaning of our lives. Deleuze and Guattari's conception of philosophy as a form of thought that creates concepts through a principle of consistency unfolded in attentive pursuit of the nuances of the meaning of concepts in relation to other concepts, not only gave me a way of understanding the pleasure practicing philosophy gives me, but a way of reading philosophy that opens up the unexpected perspectives it can create rather than closing them off as often happens when we, as we all to often do, become more entrenched in marking territory than pursuing ideas.

In my reading of Deleuze and Guattari I not only attempt to present conceptions of an immanent ethics and philosophy as the creation of concepts that are drawn as consistently and rigorously from a reading of their concepts as I can manage, but I also have attempted to enact the conception of philosophy that I draw from their work: an approach that emphasizes the rigor and creativity philosophy can contribute to cultural debates without ever losing sight of our ongoing and embodied immersion in a world to which we must respond. In that spirit, I have refrained from engaging in debates of interpretation and instead deliberately chosen to take from Deleuze and Guattari as well as the secondary commentaries that have inspired me in the pursuit of this particular project what speaks to the pragmatic concerns of individual human beings wondering, from their very specific locations, how to live ethical lives. In doing so, I have, I hope, not only shared some of these implications, but also some of the joy of carefully working through some of their concepts in light of such implications. I thus hope not only to suggest an innovative approach to ethics that I believe could speak to some of our current ethical impasses, but also to introduce some of my readers to the pragmatic and even aesthetic pleasures, as they are described and enhanced by Deleuze and Guattari's characterization of the process of philosophical thinking, of what might at times seem to be the overly careful approach of the philosopher to a set of texts.

The view of philosophy I develop and enact here suggests that multiple theories from multiple locations can and should be read in light of situated problems in order to encourage the cross-fertilization of productive connections.

I have accordingly made some connections between Deleuze and Guattari's work and work that is not inspired by a Deleuze–Guattarian perspective in order to draw out implicit tendencies in both that provoke new insights into ethical forms of being-human. I present my reading of Deleuze and Guattari from the perspective of my own lived experience as a woman and a feminist philosopher with the specific investments of my location and I exemplify my reading as vividly and forcefully as I can through the problems and examples that I draw from that location. I do not mean (nor do I expect) that my own trajectory through the work of Deleuze and Guattari should be taken as an exhaustive rendering of the use of Deleuze and Guattari for an immanent ethics or feminism, or even that some of the positions I elaborate in light of my interests and location will necessarily coincide with that of other ethical or feminist perspectives inspired by their work. In fact, it is part of the understanding of philosophy that I derive from Deleuze and Guattari's work that different readings should instigate different "counter-effectuations" of the philosophical concepts that may be brought to bear on the problems of specific locations. I hope to follow in the footsteps of readings of Deleuze and Guattari given in books like Rosi Braidotti's *Transpositions* (Braidotti 2006) and Todd May's *Gilles Deleuze: An Introduction* (May 2005) by fostering the unfolding of further "transpositional" connections readers of Deleuze and Guattari can make rather than blocking such connections by insisting on and defending any one way of conceiving their work.

Entering and engaging the Deleuzian and Deleuze–Guattarian project set forth in the many books by Deleuze written on his own as well as in partnership with Guattari is an exhilarating as well as sometimes frustrating experience. Exhilarating because of the almost breathless inventiveness of the terrain it opens, frustrating because just as one becomes familiar with one set of concepts, another set is introduced. Although this may be somewhat disorienting at first, what one finds, if one keeps at it, is that the concepts all start to cohere and resonate on a plane of thought that entails a shift in one's perspective. Deleuze and Guattari's concepts unfold and support a way of perceiving a wide range of experience in terms of dynamic process and an intuitive understanding of life as creative evolution where any one life-form is but a partial and fleeting moment of space-time in a larger durational whole. Deleuze and Guattari attempt to introduce not only some new concepts, but also a way of thinking premised on a shift in our relationship to time. The proliferation of concepts in their works creates a topography one can explore from this new perspective. In this book I explore this perspective with an emphasis on its phenomenological effects on lived experience in order to present its ethical implications as vividly as possible. Pursuing the conception of human subjectivity their work evokes from the embodied locations of actual thinking has practical implications for how we understand ourselves as well as how we approach the dilemmas of living. The Deleuze–Guattarian conceptions of human becoming and an ethics that appeals to immanent criteria of human flourishing that thus emerge can foster and support viable solutions to the ethical and political conundrums with which we are currently faced.

My readings have been truly deepened and enriched by all the commentators who have developed such intriguing and exciting readings of Deleuze and Deleuze and Guattari's work. Their influence has been so rich and varied it would be impossible for me to extricate the precise effects of each of the commentators I have read on my work; many points that puzzled me were clarified through their readings, although of course the misunderstandings with which I am left are my own. Additionally, I have benefited from my immersion in the extremely rich tradition of feminist and continental philosophy as well as cultural theory. Because the range of debt I have to other thinkers is so large, and because tracking such a debt would turn out to complicate the breadth and depth of my references past the point of manageability, I have erred on the side of minimalism by restricting my references, for the most part, to citations. In light of my main goal of providing a path through Deleuze and Guattari's work that is as clear and helpfully suggestive as I could make it for others interested in conceiving innovative ways of promoting ethical living in the 21st century, I have chosen to leave the genealogy of my evolving understanding of their work as well as of the particular feminist problems through which I exemplify my understanding of their work largely unmarked. It is my hope that this book—concerned as it is to do justice to both the richness and nuance of Deleuze and Guattari's work as well as its pragmatic value when it comes to questions about theory (what it is and what it should do for us), subjectivity (who we are and who we could be), and ethics (how we ought to live—especially with one another—and how we can make the world a better place) will encourage my readers to not only delve further into Deleuze and Guattari's work as well as the responses it has inspired, but to instigate new experiments in their own living that move us closer to collective flourishing.

I would like to take this opportunity to thank the anonymous reviewers of this project for helpful comments, Jane Bunker at SUNY Press for her role in bringing this project to fruition, Peter Baumann, Alison Brown, Tim Burke, Tina Chanter, Richard Eldridge, Kelly Oliver, Sunka Simon, and Patricia White for supporting my work in various ways over the years, Swarthmore College for a nurturing environment and crucial leave support, and my students for demanding that philosophy matter, even as the world continues to change.

Acknowledgments

Parts of chapter 2 and 3 were published in a different form as "Feminist Lines of Flight from the Majoritarian Subject," in *"Deleuze and Gender," Deleuze Studies* Volume 2: 2008 (supplement), edited by Claire Colebrook and Jami Weinstein (Edinburgh: Edinburgh University Press, 2008), pp. 60–82.

Abbreviations

AO: Deleuze, Gilles, and Félix Guattari. 1983. *Anti-Oedipus: Capitalism and Schizophrenia*. Translated by Hurley, Robert, Mark Seem, and Helen R. Lane. Minneapolis: University of Minnesota Press.

ATP: Deleuze, Gilles, and Félix Guattari. 1987. *A Thousand Plateaus: Capitalism and Schizophrenia*. Translated by Massumi, Brian. Minneapolis: University of Minnesota Press.

EP: Deleuze, Gilles. 1992. *Expressionism in Philosophy: Spinoza*. Translated by Joughin, Martin. New York: Zone Books.

LS: Deleuze, Gilles. 1990. *The Logic of Sense*. Translated by Lester, Mark. Edited by Boundas, Constantin V. New York: Columbia University Press.

NP: Deleuze, Gilles. 1983. *Nietzsche and Philosophy*. Translated by Tomlinson, Hugh. New York: Columbia University Press.

WP: Deleuze, Gilles, and Félix Guattari. 1994. Translated by Burchell, Graham and Hugh Tomlinson. New York: Columbia University Press.

Chapter 1

Introduction

Gilles Deleuze and Félix Guattari are two theorists (one an academic philosopher, the other an activist and antipsychiatrist as well as theorist) who wrote a remarkable series of books together.[1] Coming out of the same traditions of phenomenology and structuralism as French "poststructuralist" thinkers like Jacques Derrida and Michel Foucault,[2] their work also is informed by the "maverick" philosophies of Benedict Spinoza, Friedrich Nietzsche, and Henri Bergson.[3] Their ontology of self-organizing processes and becoming rather than substance and being entails conceptions of time (as duration rather than chronology), subjectivity (as a dynamic process always in relation rather than an autonomous subject), and ethics (as premised on immanent criteria rather than transcendental ideals) with galvanizing potential for resolving ethical and political questions about who we are and how we should live with human as well as nonhuman others in a world that is rapidly changing.

The reading I give here of Deleuze and Guattari's work suggests that it is through open-ended attunement with the multiple forces of our life that we can unfold, rather than attempt to dictate or control, the responses that will best serve the evolving capacities of the interdependent life-forms of the communities to which we belong. Deleuze and Guattari's conception of an immanent ethics calls on us to attend to the situations of our lives in all their textured specificity and to open ourselves up to responses that go beyond a repertoire of comfortably familiar, automatic reactions and instead access creative solutions to what are always unique problems. My reading of their conception of ethics emphasizes its pragmatic efficacy for resolving the often-painful dissonance we experience as embodied human beings struggling to live good lives. Although progressive thinkers and activists have not yet achieved a world where change is no longer needed (despite some claims to the contrary), our concerns have shifted as the world changes, and theory has attempted—often with great success—to keep pace with these changes. With this book, I hope to contribute to such efforts by rendering a Deleuze–Guattarian approach to life accessible in light of questions about what it means to be human, normative and alternative conceptions of identity

1

and subjectivity, and ethical and political questions about how we can live from day to day as well as work toward making the world a better place.

Deleuze and Guattari's conception of doing theory is that of an intervention that can help one answer the question of "how one might live" rather than a representation of the world (May 2005, 1–25). Philosophy, in their view, is (or should be) an evolving force that affects and is affected by other forces as they play out over time; meaning unfolds and evolves through the differentiated becoming of the multiple forces of life. This perspective prompts a creative approach toward reading and writing theory as well as toward thinking. Arresting the dynamic force of concepts by restricting their meanings to past formulations overlooks how their meanings evolve in response to the shifting configurations of the life problems they address. Far from prompting an anarchic sloppiness, Deleuze and Guattari's approach invites tracking the subtleties of meaning that emerge when one attends to the texture of specific contexts. Concepts cannot mean in abstraction from life; their power can only unfold in relation to other concepts as well as the heterogeneous forces of life as evolution. Unfolding incipient meanings of concepts in ways that will suggest satisfying solutions to the problems life poses requires skillful attunement to the interrelations of words to other words as well as words and the material situations in and through which words mean.

Deleuze and Guattari's conception of an immanent ethics and politics premised on affirming what is as well as unfolding what could become invites creative resolution of the obstacles that prevent us from our individual and collective thriving. Their life-affirming approach attends to what Susan McManus in a recent article terms the "affective register of subjectivity" in ways that prompt resolution of "nihilistic blockages in agency" (McManus 2007, 1–2) and instigates the belief in the earth and the invention of a new people for which Deleuze and Guattari call. Furthermore, their approach to ontology and doing theory suggests a constructive way of "mapping" a variety of projects against the background of a virtual whole that connects all projects promoting progressive change as well as individual and collective projects invested in living "good" (as in ethical) lives. This ability to provide a framework loose enough not to exclude disparate projects, and yet coherent enough to allow us to connect various kinds of progressive projects without assimilating those projects to specific theoretical paradigms, may provide impetus for the kind of joyous hybrid connections Rosi Braidotti calls for in her inspiring book, *Transpositions* (Braidotti 2006). Although it is impossible for any given path to affirm everyone equally, acknowledging the mutual implication of our unfolding projects as well as creatively thinking in terms of the larger wholes connecting us could help us find new solutions to how to live and work toward collective solutions.

The key motif of Deleuze and Guattari's thinking that I pursue as the unifying theme of this book is the provocative instigation to conceive our human living from the perspective of immersion in a durational whole made up of heterogeneous durations that includes nonhuman as well as human processes that are always unfolding toward an unpredictable future. Because my own trajectory is primarily informed by feminism, I draw on feminist issues and examples to illuminate the viability of Deleuze and Guattari's approach for the practical dilemmas of daily life. Although Deleuze and Guattari's work can be applied to a wide range of problems from a variety of social locations and perspectives, using concrete examples to exemplify my reading, I hope, shows how timely and relevant their approach can be for the pragmatic problems we face as human beings struggling to live ethical lives.

Bergson's critique of representational intelligence and his conception of intuition, as well as his critique of the conventional opposition of the possible and the real and his conception of an alternative opposition between the virtual and the actual, are important influences in the work of Deleuze as well as the work of Deleuze and Guattari. According to Bergson, representational intelligence, for practical reasons, conceives time in terms of static states and thus overlooks the durational becoming in which we are immersed.[4] Human beings have the capacity to pull back from conventional representations of life and habitual patterns of living in order to intuit some of the durational becoming of which we are a part. This ability to widen the gap between perception and action (rather than repeating automatic responses to what we perceive) allows us to attune ourselves to the incipient tendencies that are an important aspect of duration. This can in turn allow a creative response to life's problems attuned to the specificity of particular times and places. Such attunement entails attending to not simply reality as it manifests (the actual), but to the intensities insisting in that reality (the virtual) that given certain actions could lead to the unfolding of new ways of living. In the next section, I elaborate on these ideas and the conception of time as becoming that goes with them. In the last section of this chapter, these ideas are explored in the context of the view of philosophical thinking put forth in Deleuze and Guattari's book, *What is Philosophy?* (Deleuze and Guattari 1994, hereafter abbreviated as WP). The latter work suggests that philosophical thinking is an intervention in habitual patterns of thinking and living rather than a representation of the world that is more or less correct. I consider how this perspective affects our conception of, in particular, progressive forms of thinking like that of feminism. This introduction to a different way of thinking about what theory can do for us sets the tone for the remaining chapters of this book; it invites my reader to take the views expressed here not as claims that better express the "truth" about what it means to be a human being or how we should live our lives, but as interventions in my own flow of life, as well as the flows of my reader, that might precipitate revitalizing flows of meaning and action as well as more skillful, joyful composition of the relations of life.

In chapter 2, I consider the question of what it is to be human. The latter topic has been of ongoing importance to feminism in its struggle to claim full humanity for women as well as other marginalized subjects. Considering how Deleuze and Guattari account for who we are and how we got here will suggest new perspectives on who we could become and how we might move forward. I lay out Deleuze and Guattari's characterization of three different social regimes in order to give a sense of how a shifting field of social practices (always in interaction with the other processes—both human and nonhuman—through which humanity becomes) provides the background for variations in human subjectivity and, in particular, to suggest that contemporary forms of subjectivity take a distinctive, oedipal form, that could mutate into forms of subjectivity more receptive to affirming variations in subjectivity in its differing divergence from already lived forms of human existence. Deleuze and Guattari posit a notion of faciality machines that require binary designations of relatively static identities organized with respect to a majoritarian subject. If majoritarian forms of subjectivity require ranking human beings in ways that privilege some by denigrating others, then welcoming and supporting new forms of subjectivity that can affirm variations in human living could, from a perspective informed by an immanent ethics, enable more skillful compositions of humanity and the world.[5]

In chapter 3, I consider some examples of feminist cartographies that converge in suggestive ways with the Deleuze–Guattarian perspective developed in the first and second chapters. Although none of these examples reference Deleuze and Guattari's work, they resonate in illuminating ways with my reading of Deleuze and Guattari's conception of subjectivity in light of the specific problem of marginalized forms of subjectivity. I consider an example of transgender confusion (the case of David Reimer) to illustrate the lived dissonance faciality machines can produce, and I appeal to Linda Alcoff's conception of identity (despite the non-Deleuze–Guattarian cast of her work) as an orientation lived through collective patterns of corporeal and symbolic activity that she derives from her reading of phenomenology in order to elaborate a notion of identity that I argue would be in keeping with Deleuze and Guattari's conception of subjectivity (despite their resistance to more traditional notions of identity). This reconception of identity suggests that it is (or could be) a practice of naming lived orientations that intensifies some incipient meanings and tendencies of one's situation rather than others with important effects on individual and collective becoming. Although Deleuze and Guattari are at times critical of phenomenology, far from denying a phenomenologically inspired notion of lived orientation, their view conceives of such orientations as emergent effects of larger processes and implies that the corporeal and semiotic practices that require positioning oneself and others according to the binary identities of multiple faciality machines are but one aspect of the myriad ways through which we ground our subjectivity.

A conception of lived orientations as emerging from repeating patterns suggests multiple ways in which we as self-organizing subjects-in-process with relative autonomy from the becomings in which we are immersed could intervene in our individual and collective becomings in productive ways. In particular, the Deleuze–Guattarian perspective I develop throughout this book suggests that although we may not have the kind of control in our lives a traditional conception of the subject as an autonomous, rational individual might imply, there are more and less skillful ways of navigating the flows of living. Attending to the nuances of our perceptions, actions, and thoughts, as well as mapping our locations with respect to the global, political, and social flows of our varying durations, allows us to unfold the incipient tendencies of our present toward futures we can affirm. In chapter 4, I address some strategies in gaining and enacting what we might call the embodied knowledge of lived orientations in terms of Deleuze and Guattari's notions of constructing plateaus or bodies without organs, as well as in terms of thought forms like philosophy and art. Deleuze and Guattari's notion of constructing a body without organs suggests pragmatic ways of attuning oneself to the creative potential of the present as well as unfolding forms of subjectivity more adept at navigating the differentiating forces of durational time. I consider some examples of forms of thought like philosophy and art that, in distinctive ways, can contribute support to such experiments, including the concept of becoming-woman that I read as a strategy for evading the binary machines of faciality.

In chapter 5, I elaborate a Deleuzian ethics through readings of Deleuze's interpretations of the naturalist ethics and politics of Spinoza and Nietzsche premised on what bodies can do and become rather than overarching principles; I argue that Deleuze's notion of being "worthy of the event" involves attuning ourselves to the multiple durations of our lives in ways that allow us to skillfully unfold the creative possibilities of the multiple assemblages of which we form a part rather than fixate on our representations of life. I consider Dorothy Allison's novel, *Bastard Out of Carolina*, as an example of how such an ethics might work (Allison 1992). Allison's aesthetic rendering of the complicated situation of Bone, the traumatized girl who is the novel's protagonist, on my reading, manifests how Bone is part of a larger story whose participants co-participate in the unfolding of a collective life, and suggests that an ethical response demands attunement to the actualities and implicit tendencies of the multiple durations making up her life in all their reciprocal give-and-take in order to find the solution to her situation that would best support the flourishing of the assemblages of which she forms a part. I end this chapter by expressing some reservations with Deleuze and

Guattari's perhaps overly romantic emphasis on the revolutionary novelty of the nomadic subject, and advocate a reading of their work that supports fledgling subjects struggling to emerge.

In chapter 6, I start by considering Moira Gatens and Genevieve Lloyd's conception of Spinozist ethology to elaborate Deleuze and Guattari's immanent ethics in the context of a politics. Gatens and Lloyd's reading of Spinoza suggests that embodied knowledge derived through our encounters with others circulates in the narratives communities create; a social imaginary is the open and evolving set of imaginaries in which the identities of a community's members are negotiated and renegotiated. Gatens and Lloyd's conception of ethology suggests that a rational approach to life emerges when the embodied knowledge developed in experimental encounters and circulated in the social imaginary becomes ever more attuned to how shifting compositions of powers of affecting and being affected can be harmonized. Such an ethology amounts to mapping events in terms of the singularities of specific durations rather than with respect to universals and so, I argue, requires subjects able to intuit duration and become with time, as well as cultural practices that encourage embodied forms of knowing. I then elaborate how the shifts in thinking regarding time, the human, subjectivity, and identity explored in earlier chapters, might be summarized in a conception of subjectivity able to support such forms of immanent ethics and politics, and I end by re-examining the role of theory in promoting such forms of subjectivity.

My goal throughout this book is to render the Deleuze–Guattarian perspective as clearly as possible with an eye to the implications such a shift in perspective might have for forms of thought such as feminism that strive to rethink what it means to be human in light of ethical and political concerns. My hope is that some of the excitement I feel as I read Deleuze and Guattari's work will come through to my readers and perhaps inspire some unexpected solutions to current impasses in theory and practice in various locations invested in promoting the flourishing of all of humanity in harmony with the world that sustains us.

Intuition and the Durational Whole

The key difference between Deleuze and Guattari's ontology and a more traditional one can be read as a response to Bergson's claim that traditional ontology spatializes time. To understand a state of affairs in terms of what is spatially present in extended space without taking into account the dynamic unfolding of time insisting in that state of affairs is to miss an important part of our present reality, one that we need to take into account if we are to engage in skillful living. Instead of understanding each state of affairs as a static state from which the next state of affairs can be deduced, we need to understand each state of affairs not only in terms of what is overtly manifest in them, but in terms of implicit tendencies toward unfolding capacities of the bodies involved. These tendencies may or may not actually materialize, but they nevertheless have dynamic impact on what occurs.

Giovanna Borradori, in a helpful commentary, explains that according to Bergson, describing events in terms of properties or causal effects requires extracting them from becoming. Entities are "in" time, but when viewed as becoming "through" time they are "phases of becoming." Describing events in terms of properties or causal effects requires extracting them from becoming. Extracting an event from becoming reduces it to a present state "where the changing character of time is ontologically deactivated. This way, the event is rendered a steady, self-contained presence that allows us to think of it 'as if' it were located in space" (Borradori 2001, 5). Time taken as a durational whole cannot be divided into homogeneous units. In order to measure time, we need "to ontologically deactivate the passing character, or durational feature of time, and spatialize it" (ibid.). Bodies are comprised of tendencies, some of which are expressed in a specific duration. What is expressed depends on how tendencies differ from one another. A tree comprised of tendencies toward bending and falling will finally express falling and crashing to the ground if enough tendencies intensifying those tendencies (saturated ground, strong wind) also are expressed. It is the difference among tendencies (a tendency to absorb water vs. a tendency to become saturated) where certain tendencies manifest rather than others that gives expression, during a specific time, to a specific overt thing we can perceive (by spatializing time) in terms of properties and causes. If we understand phenomena in terms of overt causes with determinable effects and the manifest properties of individual bodies, we miss the interplay of imperceptible tendencies that are a part of the condition of any actual event. For Deleuze and Guattari, a thing "is the expression of a tendency before being the effect of a cause" (Deleuze 1999, 45, quoted in Borradori 2001, 7). This way of looking at things suggests that we interpret phenomena as the "dynamic expression of forces" (Borradori 2001, 10). Thus, on Deleuze and Guattari's view, the world becomes "a multiplicity of virtual tendencies, in a constant state of becoming" rather than a set of static things (14). The virtual is Deleuze and Guattari's term for this real, if imperceptible, aspect of the dynamic flow of time.

On Deleuze and Guattari's (Bergsonian) view, to think time in terms of what unfolds moment by moment in a Newtonian conception of extended space strips it of its dynamic intensity. Time as it is lived is rather a durational whole that shifts qualitatively as it unfolds in specific forms of reality, shifting further tendencies in becoming in the process. If we stabilize out of the flux of time an understanding of space in terms of stable objects and fixed relations, it is because this allows us to live. Instead of living in a constant flow of the continuously new, we perceive the world in terms of our memories of the past; we perceive not this completely new moment of living tree, but a tree that extends past tree-memories. Instead of patterns of becoming, we perceive constant forms that remain the same over time. We then extract from these forms an extended space to which we attach a spatialized time. Thus, although our lives are always unfolding in dynamic temporalities, we take the constant forms that are the effects of relatively "territorialized" routines of life—habitually repeated patterns of inorganic, organic, semiotic, cultural, and social forms of life—to be the reality.

It has been of great practical advantage to abstract things from the flux of becoming in order to reduce them to entities stripped of their virtual intensities about which we can then generalize across contexts. This allows us to communicate as well as apply lessons learned in one situation to other situations. As Bergson points out, this ability to abstract the features of a thing or situation that are of practical interest to us has allowed us to learn and adapt to changing situations with more creativity and flexibility (Bergson 1998, 140–45). Whereas living creatures ruled entirely by instincts automatically respond to stimuli from a limited repertoire of behavior, sentient creatures have varying abilities in opening a gap between perception and action that introduces a range of choices. The more complicated an organism, the more sophisticated its central nervous system, the more networks of synapses of its brain, the more the gap between perception and action can be widened. Linear stimulus–response patterns become complicated by the superposition of past responses and memories. Due to the complicated delay set up by our nervous system as well as cultural systems of meaning, we are not limited to merely instinctual reactions; the way we react is mediated via the neuronal paths of our brains and the networks of meaning of our culture.

According to Bergson, the more instinctual an organism is, the more its responses will be in keeping with repeatable patterns of the past; perception will be selective, taking from a situation what the organism needs to know in order to launch the response from a limited repertoire of responses that seems most appropriate. Intelligent perception entails a selection of sensation in keeping with the needs of the body. Life is a combination of tendencies and states—the implicit forces that could push it to a novel outcome, as well as the states of affairs that are already fully manifest—but we perceive that part of the present that can be compared to representations of the past that allow us to repeat successful patterns established on the basis of past experience. As organisms with complicated nervous systems, we have what Bergson calls sensorimotor systems with the capacity to achieve self-regulation (Ansell Pearson 1999, 49). This allows us to quickly make sense of each new situation and act effectively. Our human ability to access a wide range of representations drawn from the past allows us to access recollections independently of our present perceptions and thus expands our range of possible responses to the present (Ansell Pearson 1999, 54–56). Bergson points out that the price of intelligence is a loss of specificity (as our perceptions and understanding filters out only what is of practical use to us) as well as a spatialized conception of time that strips it of its intensive features (Bergson 1974, 11–29).

Even instinctual creatures that live out their lives in mindless repetition of set patterns of behavior evolve new behaviors over time in the differing flow of life. Human beings, according to the story Bergson tells, were able to complicate their responses by extending what they learned in previous situations to a present conceived as analogous to a representable past. This greatly enhanced our adaptability at the same time as it entailed reducing the future to a reshuffled extension of the past, canceling out an understanding of novelty in the process. The codified space and time of representational thought covers over the dynamic quality of time, rendering its creative unfolding a mystery. According to a spatialized notion of time, everything remains the same until there is some reason for a specific event to occur and what is possible is conceivable only as an inversion of a representable past. The dynamic intensity of durational time is overlooked and what can happen is thought in relation to a past that can only repeat itself in configurations that are analogous, comparable, and similar to what has already been experienced. Sanford Kwinter discusses the cultural impact of the spatialization of time and its relation to capitalism. He argues that the regimented ringing of the bell in Benedictine monasteries in the early Middle Ages was a significant development that contributed "immeasurably to the already staggering discipline and regimentation of monastic life" (Kwinter 2001, 15). This "modern process of reduction and spatialization" was reinforced by the fourteenth-century invention of double-entry bookkeeping practices, the invention of linear perspective, and the rise of quantitative methods in science (22). Clock time "fixes in order to correlate, synchronize, and quantify, renouncing the mobile, fluid, qualitative continuum where time plays a decisive role in transformative morphogenetic processes" (ibid.).[6]

Bergson advocates overcoming the intellectual bias toward a spatialized notion of time—as pragmatically effective as it has been and still is—with a form of intuition able to grasp phenomena in terms of dynamic time or duration. Dynamic time unfolds in terms of difference and divergence, unfolding variations in form as it plays out the actualizing power of its becoming. The present as durational whole carries with it virtual tendencies that intensify toward thresholds of actualization in keeping with its dynamic unfolding. The delay or interval between perception and action that our complicated nervous system allows opens up to us the possibility of intuiting the present in terms of the virtualities implicit in it that speak to the past as well as the future. Bergson proposes a method of intuition that is able to directly experience the world in terms of real time or the durations we live and the durational whole in which we are immersed.[7] Perception that can be expanded past the range of automatic instinctual response as well as the intellectual response of representational thought—as human perception can be through certain forms of memory, art, science, and thought—makes intuition possible. And it is intuition that is able to access the durational whole of time, thus allowing creative responses to life that exceed the reach of representational schemas.

Bergson's notion of intuition resonates with feminist conceptions of ways of knowing beyond the merely cognitive or rational that are more attuned to the concrete and that refuse to abstract people or things from their relational context in deference to overarching laws. Complete immersion in a flux of becoming with no means to reduce the complexity of life to what our sensorimotor systems can process and act on would dissolve us into a chaotic sea of becoming. But we need to, as feminist and Deleuzian philosopher Elizabeth Grosz puts it, "acknowledge the in-between of things, the plural interconnections that cannot be utilized or contained within and by things but which makes them possible" (Grosz 2005b, 141). The interval between perception and action is replete with affections, body-memories (or habit-memory), and pure recollections (duration). "Through their interventions, perception becomes 'enlivened,' and capable of being linked to nascent actions" (100). Allowing the fleeting emotions, sensations, openness to the body, and intuitive access to the past (often associated with women) opens up creative links with the past toward the future.

> We cannot help but view the world in terms of solids, as things. But we leave behind something untapped of the fluidity of the world, the movements, vibrations, transformations that occur below the threshold of perception and calculation and outside the relevance of our practical concerns. . . . Intuition is our nonpragmatic, noneffective, nonexpedient, noninstrumental relation to the world, the capacity we have to live in the world in excess of our needs, and in excess of the self-presentation or immanence of materiality, to collapse ourselves, as things, back into the world. (136)

Each individual, on Deleuze and Guattari's view, is an individuating process that maintains its boundaries through habitual patterns of activity that sustains its processes relative to surrounding processes. A mountain exists at a much slower speed than organisms like human beings. A mosquito exists in a different duration than a human being or an elephant. All have their own durations that combine with other durations to make up a flux of different forms that maintain their shapes at different speeds relative to other organic and inorganic life-forms. These different durations come together in the totality of all events or life that continues to unfold actualized forms as well as shifting virtualities in keeping with differentiating forces that are always releasing new potentials. The durational whole is an open-ended whole that is never defined by one set of virtualities, but whose virtualities, like its actualities, always are altering at each moment of its continual unfolding. This open whole cannot be conceived in terms of a conception of time thought of as a dimension that extends moment by moment, a container of space within which events unfold. Instead, time as durational whole is a multiplicity that changes quality as it unfolds. As new actualized relations shift the virtual potential insisting in reality, that potential, in turn, qualitatively shifts what new forces those actualities could unfold. The movement of life is thus—from the myriad perspectives of the individuals constituted and dissolved in that movement who attempt to think life in its totality—a whole that qualitatively shifts at each moment of its unfolding.

Viewing phenomena in terms of the differentiating forces making them up can have important repercussions for how we live our everyday lives. An understanding of what we perceive as the effects of the processes that produced them—processes that could have gone differently given sometimes very subtle shifts in the arrangement of the forces of which they are made up—challenges us to hearken to the edges of our perceptual and cognitive awareness in order to pursue not yet intelligible resonances that could take on further form and solidity through skillful living. Mapping change in terms of topographies allows us to take into account the specificity of what always are unique situations in relation to other situations. Furthermore, conceiving nature in terms of difference and divergence—creative evolution—in an age that is already going too rapidly for many, challenges us to nurture those stabilities that we would like to continue, as well as work with what is changing toward a future of which we want to be a part.

Deleuze and Guattari's conception of time inspires a way of thinking, an ethics, and a politics that thinks time differently. As Grosz puts it, feminism needs "to look more carefully at the *virtuality* laden within the present, its possibilities for being otherwise, in other words, the unactualized latencies in any situation which could be, may have been, instrumental in the generation of the new or the unforeseen" (2005b, 76–77). With this ontology of the new in mind, instead of figuring the future in terms of a recombination of elements of the past, we could perceive the present not just in terms of women's oppression, but as also containing within it "the virtual conditions of feminism and the openness of a future beyond present constraints" (2005b,

75). In the next section I present Deleuze and Guattari's notions of language speakers as assemblages that are parts of other assemblages, philosophy as the creation of concepts, and the concept as event in order to evoke a pragmatic conception of doing theory that exemplifies this ontology of the new and takes the virtual into account.

Theory

Deleuze and Guattari's *A Thousand Plateaus* (hereafter abbreviated ATP) presents a marvelous vision of life as a complicated and differentiating flow of matter that creates various forms of nonorganic and organic life in a continually diverging unfolding of multiple forms (Deleuze and Guattari 1987). The manifest forms of life actualize its virtual potential, creating further possibilities in manifest form as virtual potentials intensify or relent in keeping with changing configurations of forces. Geological strata, the organic strata of organized life-forms, a proliferation of life-forms in the unfolding of species, as well as the material and discursive practices of human life all participate in the forward flow of time. Human life unfolds out of this flow of life with specific features that we can map, but that are bound to shift and mutate in the incessantly creative unfolding of life.

Deleuze and Guattari suggest a different way of understanding individuals, as well as the interconnection of individuals to one another and their surroundings. Instead of things with essential attributes, or human beings with specific, fixed identities, their vocabulary evokes individuals in the Spinozist terms of what they can do and the assemblages into which they enter. Deleuze and Guattari use the term *assemblage* to emphasize the coming together of forces into relatively stable configurations with particular capacities to affect and be affected that have specific durations. In their view, life is already one interconnected whole with various components that engage with other components in order to make working machines. The question is not how to connect with the world around us; it is rather the kind of connections we want to foster and sustain. When I sit down to eat at the dinner table, I enter into an assemblage of chair, table, plate, fork, hand, mouth, and food. I become a working part of a whole that makes something happen. How I conceive the assemblages of which I am a part depends on my perspective. At the same time that I am part of a dinner assemblage, I also am part of a digestive assemblage, a family assemblage, and a town assemblage. I am a working part at once of multiple assemblages at different levels. My capacities to affect and be affected by my world relate to the relations I form with others—from the relations my body forms with the chair and table, to the relations I have with other members of my family, to the relations I compose with members of the school board or town council or the sidewalk I walk at night or the trash can I drag out to that sidewalk on Thursday mornings.

Deleuze and Guattari distinguish between two kinds of assemblages affecting human existence: collective assemblages of enunciation (roughly analogous to Foucault's notion of discursive practices) and machinic assemblages of desire (roughly analogous to Foucault's notion of nondiscursive practices). Collective assemblages of enunciation comprise the signifying and interpreting activities we engage as we carry out our business; they entail enacted rules and linguistic practices governing a subset of speech acts of the social field. Machinic assemblages of desire comprise specific subsets of the habitual practices and routines our bodies undergo as we get things done. They comprise the physical routines and procedures of a particular location of the social field. Both kinds of assemblages exist at any one location, but the two have a certain autonomy from one another, despite their mutual implication; they are heterogeneous, but in reciprocal presupposition. That is, they are not linearly determined, but like a function in calculus, are mutually implicated in ways that entail specific singularities or limit points that govern their relations. Thus, for example, the cultural ways we have of talking about sex (e.g., that most of us know what is meant when a woman is labeled a "slut" or "whore" or a man is labeled a "womanizer" or "stud") is in some ways autonomous from and yet mutually implicated with ways of behaving with which we may be familiar (sexual activity of a non-monogamous sort). The words make sense in the context of meaningful ways of talking. The actions make sense in the context of familiar behaviors. There are instances of non-monogamous behavior at the limit point of what could be designated as "slutty" behavior (heterosexual men are not typically designated as "slutty," a state of affairs to which we could attribute the meaning of either an affair of the heart or an unwanted act of rape may qualify the use of the designation). The label of "slut" can inform our understanding of an act and vice versa.[8]

The relation between words and behaviors is not one-to-one and words and actions have social significance in the context, respectively, of other words and actions, as well as in mutual implication with a whole context of, respectively, nondiscursive and discursive practices. This renders any specific meaning of a statement or behavior the effect of a convergence of many factors. Every speech-act or action has meaning against a background of possible variations in meaning due to the small differences that can and do emerge in specific instances. Because discursive and nondiscursive social practices are not defined by constants (i.e., are not referred to a standard measure in each case), but rather operate according to background presuppositions and implicit rules that can vary over time without losing their connection to a specific assemblage, any given event of meaning constitutes a kind of selection from a range of continuous variation in possible meaning. For example, as a feminist philosopher with an academic post in the United States, I am aware (whether consciously or not) of the accepted format for presenting my interpretation of a specific philosopher (whether it be through the presentation of a paper at a conference, an article in a journal, or an academic book). There are various implicit or explicit rules governing my presentation to which I may rigidly adhere or which I can freely vary in order to stretch the limits of acceptable practice. Specific speech acts are meaningful with respect to the background presuppositions and immanent rules relevant to them. But because such presuppositions and immanent rules do not necessarily hold for language as a whole, but may be relevant for a small subset of the social field, there is room for variation in terms of what could be meaningfully communicated. Additionally, there is a range of meaning that may deviate from standard usage of any subset of the social field, and thus may approach nonsense and yet still make some sense. The free variations on more accepted productions of meaning give a dynamic quality to collective assemblages of enunciation as well as machinic assemblages of desire. In approaching the limits of acceptable philosophical practice, I may choose to present my paper in a manner approaching that of performance art. Depending on the subset of the philosophical social field I am on (an audience of feminist philosophers might be more receptive to such variation than a more mainstream philosophical audience), my paper will be interpreted as crossing or not crossing the threshold of what can be accepted as "philosophy." Most of the possible variations on any given line of continuous variation are not actualized and yet are "real" in the sense that they inflect manifest reality with dynamic intensity. For example, as my philosophical performance goes beyond the threshold of generally accepted practices in paper-presentation (perhaps I use crude language or burst into song), members of the audience may cringe. A kind of tension may develop that either relents (as I pull back from that limit point and return to a more staid style of content and delivery) or intensify (as my performance crosses any acceptable threshold and the moderator decides to ask me to cease and desist). The lines of continuous variation that insist in the speech acts and actions that actually manifest are specific to particular social fields at given times.[9]

What Deleuze and Guattari call "abstract machines" are diagrams of social fields that suggest certain connections among lines of variation rather than others. Abstract machines are, as Paul Patton puts it, like a software program that can turn "a given assemblage of computer hardware into a certain kind of technical machine" (2006, 31). Although collective assemblages of enunciation and machinic assemblages stabilize certain rules in the working machines of social meaning comprising them, the rules of an abstract machine are optional and each move changes the rules. The social field contains virtual centers orienting signifying practices and ways of being social subjects. An abstract machine constitutes and conjugates the semiotic and physical systems of the social field, distributing the expressions of the collective assemblage of enunciation and the contents of machinic assemblages of bodies. Feminism as an abstract machine accesses aspects of women's bodies and notions of sex, gender, and sexuality that are in continuous variation beneath the thresholds of dominant and socially recognizable ways of understanding and living gender in order to conjugate those elements in new ways. Thus, a feminist abstract machine can inform an assemblage of teaching in order to make it do something different than an assemblage informed by a sexist abstract machine. All the concrete components may be the same (the vocabulary and theoretical content of a given discipline presented in textbooks and lectures, the format for writing acceptable papers and acceptable ways of behaving in class, holding one's books, raising one's hand to be called on, and so forth), but the virtual ideas informing the functioning of those components will govern it differently. The abstract machine of feminism selects certain relations rather than others in the range of relations available. Through the human ability to think that opens the gap between perception and action, feminist thought actualizes virtual relations, thus creating new intensities in specific situations previously unavailable. For example, the idea that male students tend to be called on more frequently in class leads to deliberate attempts to give male and female students equal speaking time. The actualization of specific relations from the virtual relations of sense thus shifts the social field and what is possible for us by shifting intensities and allowing other actualizations that previously would have been unavailable.

From a Deleuze–Guattarian perspective, we could conceive of feminism as an abstract machine that meshes various ways of speaking and acting into an intensification of the tendencies in the social field that could lead to constructive experiments in gendered living, experiments that would liberate lines of flight from dead or deadening ends—places where gender has blocked possible ways of living that could have produced joy and an increased capacity to act in the world. Assemblages of very different kinds could be connected through the feminist abstract machine without having to resemble some model of feminist identity, thought, or action. The question, from this perspective, would not be whether or not the bodies involved fit into the category of being feminist; the question would rather be whether or not the effects the assemblage produced were feminist effects (i.e., effects entailing what are, from a feminist perspective, viable lines of thought and action that were previously unavailable). Or if a given feminist abstract machine is one of "overcoding" and so blocks available lines of flight and replicates or even amplifies "molar" structures (as, e.g., certain feminist perspectives unwittingly centered in a white perspective could be said to do), the question would be how to remove such blockages and create a feminist plane of consistency or abstract machine of mutation that would allow creative resolution of such conflicts.

Lived experience unfolds in keeping with the selections made through the imbrication of the various strata of human existence (in particular, the strata of the organism, signification, and subjectification that I discuss in the next chapter). It is the emergent effect of dynamic processes unfolding beneath the threshold of consciousness that result in the specific configurations of forces we can grasp as representable experiences. We select and organize our experiences in keeping with the machinic assemblages and collective assemblages of enunciation of our social field that allow us to make sense of what we perceive and take action that makes sense. Deleuze and Guattari suggest that lived experience entails correlating qualities "supposedly common to several objects that we perceive" with "an affection supposedly common to several subjects who experience it and who, along with us, grasp that quality" (WP 144). Social practices and ways of speaking or making sense of our experience set up habitual patterns of such correlation. These empirical opinions or clichés of perception and affection that lead to "sensible" actions propose particular relationships between "an external perception as state of a subject and an internal affection as passage from one state to another" (WP 144). The propositions of belief arise this way:

> [I]n a given perceptive-affective lived situation (for example, some cheese is brought to the dinner table), someone extracts a pure quality from it (for example, a foul smell); but, at the same time as he abstracts the quality, he identifies himself with a generic subject experiencing a common affection (the society of those who detest cheese—competing as such with those who love it, usually on the basis of another quality). "Discussion," therefore, bears on the choice of the abstract perceptual quality and on the power of the generic subject affected. (WP 145)

Contemplation (the recognition of a quality in perception), reflection (the recognition of a group in affection), and communication (the recognition of a rival in the possibility of other groups and other qualities), give an orthodoxy to the recognition of truth: "a true opinion will be the one that coincides with that of the group to which one belongs by expressing it" (WP 146). Discussion, according to this view, is more about coming to a consensus about what qualities to extract from perception and their effects on a generic subject than about philosophical thought. What are thus hammered out are the rules of opinion and what will count as true. These opinions resonate and reinforce what has already been actualized rather than move thought onto something new. One may put forward a rule of correspondence about a selected quality and the subject affected by it and find others who agree with that rule and thus are eligible to join the group. But "opinion triumphs" when the group itself determines the rules of correspondence members of the group must follow (WP 146).

In this information age, we are glutted with communication. Communication, in Deleuze and Guattari's view, operates according to an extensional logic that simply extends what we have already grasped and recognized in representational form about the actualized past and attempts to extend this information to the future. We need creation rather than communication. Deleuze and Guattari distinguish philosophy from the contemplation, reflection, and communication of various forms of opinion and discussion that, in their view, amounts to a consolidation of past ways of thinking rather than the creative evolution of thinking that can occur when philosophy involves the creation of concepts. "*We lack resistance to the present. The creation of concepts in itself calls for a future form, for a new earth and people that do not yet exist*" (WP 108). Philosophy is not the only cultural thought-form that can open us to an intuitive understanding of time as duration, but it is the thought-form pursued by, in particular, Deleuze and it has its own distinctive structure. Theory can create concepts that give us new perspectives on living, but on the Deleuze–Guattarian view put forward here, it can and should have a kind of autonomy from practical living and political action. When one is engaged in philosophical thought—be it feminist thought or another form of philosophical thinking—one is engaged in a process of concept creation in which considerations involving personal selves and practical action are put to one side in deference to the principle of consistency that allows new relations among components of meaning to emerge. The pursuit of virtual connections among the meaning of words actualizes some of those connections rather than others, stabilizing new concepts in the process. The "taste" with which those concepts are created relate to a plane of thinking and intuitive insight into time as a durational whole in light of problems of specific times and places. But ultimately conceptual creation defers to pursuing consistent connections among the mental components of thought rather than preconceived political goals. Although Deleuze, and Deleuze and Guattari, are known for de-emphasizing the personal self as the foundation or origin of thought, however, the ability of thought to approach the virtual can only occur through the thinking of embodied individuals.

Just as animals establish territories through the refrains of repeated patterns of activity (e.g., through the songs of birds or scent marking of wolves), so do the empirical thought movements of embodied individuals create concepts through the survey of a set of components of meaning connected by what Deleuze and Guattari call their "zones of indiscernibility."

Out of a range of possible connections among meanings a concept entails the territorialization of a certain set of relations through refrains of thought movements that establish connections among the components of a concept. The concept is a refrain in a state of survey in relation to its components (WP 20–21); it is a stabilization or plateau of a set of virtual relations of meaning with components as limit points with something "undecidable between them"—zones of indiscernibility that determine the internal consistency of the concept. For example, the medical concept of a female human body links the components of XX chromosomes, a preponderance of the "feminine" hormones estrogen and progesterone, "female" genitalia, and secondary sex characteristics like breasts (Stone 2007, 34). These components of meaning are attributed to specific states of affairs, but cannot be exhausted by states of affairs in the sense that there always can be yet another variation in femaleness to which the components can be attributed. The zone of indiscernibility linking all these components is the meaning of "female" ("female" chromosomes, hormones, genitalia, secondary sex characteristics), making one concept of what would otherwise be a set of disparate meanings; the limit points of what counts as female govern the various attributions of the concept actually made in specific thought movements. Concepts are incorporeal, although they are incarnated or effectuated in bodies, but the concept "speaks the event, not the essence or the thing—pure Event, a hecceity, an entity" (WP 21). It is a system or structure of mental components that allows us to approach the chaos of the virtual relations of thought in order to select and stabilize a specific order. It thus allows a way of approaching the chaos of possible relations of thought in an organized way. It is a set of virtual relations that can be actualized through thought movements and ascribed to a thing or state of affairs. A concept is a virtual multiplicity, a system of intensive ordinates that can be actualized in many specific thought movements without exhausting all the different ways that it can be actualized.

A thought movement actualizing a concept is governed by a principle of consistency that organizes the components according to their overlap (or zone of indiscernibility) with other components. Each component is an intensive feature or a pure and simple singularity; the component is a limit point rather than a constant or a variable—"pure and simple *variations* ordered according to their neighborhood" (WP 20). Actual thought movements pursue these variations of the component in different relations to the other components of the concept in keeping with the limit points of the components (the crossing of which would turn the thought movement into the thought or creation of another concept). We may think of the concept of woman as comprising the component elements of "human being," "breasts," "vagina," "nurturing," and "relational" (whether or not others agree). Those elements are incarnated in actual bodies, although it may be that they do not all occur together in one body. As components in the concept of woman, they have no particular coordinates in space and time and they act as virtual conditions in the sense that it is only when all those virtual components are actualized in a specific human being that we can say that the concept itself is ascribable to a specific state of affairs (in our example, a human being with breasts and vagina who is not nurturing would not be a "real" woman). Even then, that state of affairs does not exhaust the concept; many other bodies or states of affairs also could incarnate that concept. And because of the range of continuous variation of each component and the varying ways the zones of indiscernibility of those components could play out in the actualization of a specific set of relations, the concept can be expressed in a durational process of actualization—that is, the woman to whom we wish to attribute the concept of woman may unfold over time variations in states to which we could attribute the concept of woman, but all those states would be within the constraints set by the components as singularities or limit points dictating when a body or state of affairs is no longer the body or state of affairs incarnating a particular concept. The virtual relations implicit in a process of becoming (be it the process of being a woman or the process of thinking a concept) constitute the singularities or limit points that, in keeping with the forces actualized, send a state of affairs over various threshold points into another state of affairs (a woman turns into a man; my thought of a woman turns into my thought of a man; rain turns into sleet instead of snow; walking turns into sliding across the ice). Philosophical thought can access some of the singularities that are not actualized in states of affairs to which we attribute a concept because it organizes itself not with respect to what was actualized in specific states of affairs, but rather with respect to the meanings of words (events of sense) extracted from, but not exhausted by, specific states of affairs. This in turn can lead to new actualizations. For example, disarticulating sex from gender in the concepts of woman and man enables a way of thinking about one's sex and the possibility of a gender identity at odds with one's sex that influenced certain sex change practices. Thus, although propositions have to answer to a specific configuration of material forces, concepts have a kind of independence from the material world. "If one concept is 'better' than an earlier one, it is because it makes us aware of new variations and unknown resonances, it carries out unforeseen cuttings-out, it brings forth an Event that surveys us" (WP 28).

Deleuze and Guattari's ontology suggests that understanding being in terms of static essences reifies phenomena that are the end result of historical processes into categories that are then imposed on the world. The possible is then thought of in terms of an inversion of what has already been the case. From this ontological perspective, the possible forms life can take adhere to categories that derive from life as it already was. Deleuze, by contrast, insists that ontology address the transcendental field of the virtual that conditions what actually occurs. According to Daniel Smith, for Deleuze the essence of a thing "is a multiplicity, which unfolds and becomes within its own spatio-temporal co-ordinates . . . in perpetual relation with other multiplicities." The concept of a thing that answers the question about what it is extracts from the actual thing not an essence that can be thought of in terms of a static form, but rather the virtual conditions of the unfolding of a thing over time. The thing as a multiplicity "necessarily changes dimensions, and enters a becoming, every time it is affected by another multiplicity" (Smith 2006, 52). The various encounters a thing has introduces variations in how that thing affects as well as how it is affected in further encounters it goes on to have. A concept of a thing adequate to its essence must extract from that thing the virtual conditions governing the unfolding of the thing's process of actualization over time rather than the characteristics it has at one moment of time abstracted from its duration.

For Deleuze, and Deleuze and Guattari, concepts entail lines of continuous variation in meaning structured by limit points or virtual singularities that inhere in any thought movement actualizing the concept. Thus, I may think of "woman" as "not-man" in one thought movement and as a "female human being" in another. Both thought movements actualize the concept in different ways in keeping with other forces affecting the unfolding of those thought movements (e.g., flows in my thinking concerning other concepts like "man" or the "body" or sensations like happening to glance at a razor or grazing a hand across my breast). Thought movements are durations that pursue specific ranges in continuous variation of the interconnecting web of meanings that a concept virtually comprises, and the virtual relations of the concept itself changes over time in keeping with how it is actualized in concrete thought movements (thus, the virtual relations of the conventional concept of "woman" has changed over time as women's position in society has changed). Creating a concept entails creating a plateau of meaning by pursuing the zones of indiscernibility of a set of thought components, thus constituting a new singularity on a plane of thinking—a set of virtual relations of meaning that resonate with one another in a way that invites new patterns in thought movements that may result in new perspectives on lived experience as well as new patterns of behavior.

This way of conceiving the concept in terms of temporal becoming manifests a process ontology that Deleuze and Guattari extend to entities in general. A chair is not a static thing with specific properties. It is rather a stable patterning of "unformed matters" that unfolds effects in keeping with how it affects and how it is affected by the ongoing processes that surround and sustain it as this space-time duration of being-chair. The chair, because it is, like everything else, part of the differentiating activity of life, is always a becoming-other. It may do this at a different speed than a mountain or an ice-cream cone, but it is always changing nevertheless. A concept of "woman" attempting to approach the essence of woman as a dynamic force (rather than an entity with a static set of characteristics), must take into account the virtual tendencies insisting in women as well as the forms actually manifested by living women. The state of affairs of being woman instantiates one way of being a woman, but the concept or event of being-woman is a becoming that cannot be pinpointed to any one time or place. Thus, no one actualization or even all "possible" actualizations of that event can ever exhaust the sense of being-woman. Women appear to us in specific forms that are, for Deleuze and Guattari, actualizations replete with virtual tendencies as well as actual components. These virtualities are not representable, but one can think them by extracting concepts—pure events that can be expressed in states of affairs although they can never be fully represented. The pure events that can be extracted from a specific woman (when we think her) express a configuration of virtualities in excess of the actuality of the woman herself. Although resting at a description of the actual woman speaks only to what that woman already has become, the virtualities or pure events that are, for Deleuze and Guattari, part of the reality of that woman, speak to what she could become. And what she could become shifts as the virtualities inhering in the actual women expressing the event of sense of "being-woman" shifts.

If what feminists are trying to do is pursue the consistency of thought components in order to destabilize old identities and perspectives and stabilize more promising identities and perspectives in keeping with the life flows of becoming-other that we are, then feminist theory is more about creating ways of skillfully evolving with life rather than getting a static representation of reality "right." On this view, the meaning of concepts that we can represent and repeat constitutes but a selection from a range of continuous variation in meaning that shifts in keeping with the pragmatic contexts in which they are thought and spoken. This suggests that we should explore and experiment with, for example, the permutations in meaning the concept of "woman" can unfold rather than turning it into an "order-word"—a standardized representation to which the state of being a woman "should" conform.[10]

This way of understanding concepts brings out the generative aspects of thinking and posits thinking as a dynamic movement that always is played out in tension with material reality and alternative paths of thinking. Concepts are not stable entities that can be pinned down with static definitions. They are thought territories created through the refrains of thought movements that give structure to our thinking. Concepts can shift and mutate (just as the concept of sex did) as thought movements survey alternative zones of indiscernibility, thus shifting its configuration. Meaning plays out in the chronological time of actual thought movements in tension with the stratigraphic time of

Aion—the virtual real of the ways components of meaning can be related that inflect any actualization of meaning (see LS 162–68; ATP 261–62). In this view, a theory must respond to a pragmatic context as well as adhere to principles that allow one to move beyond already established perspectives of ordinary life, thus allowing new perspectives on lived experience as well as a shift in the very nature of that lived experience, that can lead to new forms of human living. Theory, in this view, is only meaningful in terms of the intensities it can introduce into life that produce new thresholds in action.

It is a distinctive feature of philosophical thought to evoke, through the creation of concepts, an intuition of the time of Aion, the meanwhile of the event of events, where anything can be related to anything and everything else through the power of thought. Just as, in a different medium, cinema can evoke a durational whole of time by bringing together different slices of time that supersede any one embodied perspective, so can the creation of concepts tap the creative resources of time as a durational whole in order to create new perspectives on lived experience. A concept is an event of sense that can precipitate new avenues in thinking—new connections, new relations, among components of thought. This can, in turn, shift a dynamic situation, tipping it over some threshold point to action, inducing experiments that might not otherwise have been performed. A given set of concepts is on Deleuze and Guattari's view the singularities or limit points that settle actual thought movements into certain grooves that could always go otherwise. Thought, with its special access to the virtual, thus always can offer new ways of understanding the topography of our lives. According to Deleuze and Guattari, concepts are not Platonic ideals that reign for all time over specific states of affairs. They are critical points inhering in actual states of affairs without themselves being actual. They are real virtualities that can shift and change with the unfolding of time. As Grosz puts it, they are " 'haecceities,' which do not form systems but induce intensities, do not cohere to form patterns but function as modes of affection, and as speeds of variation" (Grosz 2005b, 159). That is, they are singular configurations of mental components that affect the landscape of our thinking by leading us to certain thresholds rather than others, thresholds that affect how we experience our world as well as the actions in which we engage. A concept can never be separated from the concrete thought movements that actualize it and yet it allows a livable approach to a chaotic range of thought possibilities. Concepts are inseparable from the concrete thought movements that think them and yet always are in excess of those thought movements. This excess of meaning evokes the virtual that insists in every speech act and intimates the rich resources of time as durational whole and the intensities that inflect each and every present moment whether or not they actually unfold into new forms of life.

The conception of concepts as events of sense has important implications for feminist thinking: Concepts require careful attention to both nuances of meaning and the problems of specific space-times to be effective, they need to be evaluated in terms of life-experiments rather than how well they function within the parameters of already established debates, and they can and should mutate as problems shift. Furthermore, concepts can open up lived experience by rendering implicit relations explicit and by thus attributing meaning in a different way to states of affairs bring out previously imperceptible possibilities in actualization (e.g., recent work in disability studies suggests that "able-bodiedness" is an implicit component of the concept of "woman" with problematic effects [Garland-Thomson 2002]). Thus, feminists can explore and experiment with the possibilities implicit in concepts of sex and gender in light of the problems that interest them.

Thought forms like philosophy allow a livable access to what goes beyond the mundane range of territorialized experience and so gives us access to a future that is new rather than a repetition or inversion of the past. *Conceptual personae* is Deleuze and Guattari's term for a kind of partial perspective beyond the perspective of the personal self of the author that is activated through philosophical thought. They "carry out the movements that describe the author's plane of immanence, and they play a part in the very creation of the author's concepts" (WP 63). When the thinker thus pursues connections among components with imagination (see Massumi 2002, 134) and a "taste" for combining them in terms of their zones of indiscernibility that goes beyond deducing the logical inferences of propositions (which Deleuze and Guattari think of as simply consolidating standardized opinions), she starts thinking from the perspectives of conceptual personae that defy the coherence of her personal self. Concept creation thus allows a deterritorialization from personal identity as well as a deterritorialization of old ways of thinking that can reterritorialize onto new identities and new perspectives on lived experience. Thus, a thinker may have perspectives that exceed or even conflict with the perspective she may have as a consolidated personal self with a recognizable character or set of beliefs. Whereas a personal self may be motivated by beliefs she knows she has or considerations of which she is consciously aware, conceptual personae are thinkers whose "personalized features are closely linked to the diagrammatic features of thought and the intensive features of concepts, intensities that insist apart from an empirical thought-movement. A particular conceptual persona, who perhaps did not exist before us, thinks in us" (WP 69). The role of conceptual personae is "to show thought's territories, its absolute deterritorialization and reterritorializations" because rather than repeat the habitual refrains of conventional thought, they pursue connections available on a given plane of immanence that have not yet been pursued (ibid.). That is, instead of deferring to what "makes sense" or debates and discussions as they have previously been played out, they pursue intensities of thinking by linking the components of thought in new ways.

The process of concept creation is not "rational" in the traditional sense of pursuing logical deductions from propositions. Instead, it operates with "taste," pursuing the overlap of components in all their variations in ways that defy conventional thinking, creating new perspectives on lived experience in the process. The perspectives of conceptual personae are created in the very process of these thought movements. They think in us beyond our conscious control since they are dictated by the topology of the plane of immanence we are exploring rather than by a preexistent self that goes to that plane with a preconceived attitude vis-à-vis what she is thinking about. Thus, in Deleuze and Guattari's view, conceptual creation done to consolidate the personal self of the author will preclude accessing creative possibilities in meaning that are not in the interest of that self's survival. Their notion of writing as a form of becoming-imperceptible both shuns notions of the philosopher as authoritative expert as well as invites a de-selfing similar to those that some feminists invite, for example, in encounters with an other that refuse to assimilate the other to oneself.[11] Additionally, it provides a way of conceiving a practice of such de-selfing. The creation of concepts then becomes one way through which one could allow a self to dissolve without losing meaning or succumbing to overwhelming confusion in the process. Writing—or thinking—as a form of becoming-imperceptible allows one to rework the self again and again by enabling one to release one's hold on a stable conception of self long enough to allow new connections to form and a new, perhaps more provisional, self to form in the process.

This notion of the concept allows us to see the specific meanings of concepts in terms of a dynamic field of meanings that is always in excess of and yet dynamically informs the meanings actually played out in conscious awareness. It thus allows us to see how the meanings of a concept actualized in the specific thought movements of embodied individuals always entails a process of selection from a range of continuous variation in meaning, much of which may never become overtly manifest. It is this range of continuous variation that is cancelled out in discussions and debates that emphasize repetitions of past meanings rather than pursue the permutations of meaning that arise in the pragmatic contexts where concepts are put into play.

Judith Butler's reconceptualization of "sex" is an example of concept creation. Butler, in a sense, created a new concept of sex by making unprecedented connections among the components of "effect" and "apparent cause" (thus displacing the component of "biological given"). Her argument that sex, rather than the "natural" basis for variations in gender, was as much an effect of social processes as gender (and thus only appeared to be the cause of binary sexual difference), instigated cascades of effects in our understandings of gender and sex that at the time of publication of *Gender Trouble* had important resonance throughout at least some portions of the social field (Butler 1990). A new way of thinking about what it meant to say "I am female" or "I am male" as a discursive effect of normative social processes set off other deterritorializations that shifted in incremental ways those territorializing forces toward thresholds of change. One could say that Butler, through the practice of concept creation, approached what would have been the chaos of a social field deterritorializing from old ways of thinking about sex as a biological given that had previously anchored concepts of identity, through the careful pursuit of zones of indiscernibility of components of thought that had not previously been pursued. The stabilization of a new concept of sex prompted unprecedented thought movements regarding sexual difference and new perspectives on experiments in sexed identity.

Butler's plane of immanence entailed certain nonphilosophical presuppositions, including the value of psychoanalysis in characterizing contemporary forms of subjectivity. She thus made bridges among Freudian, Lacanian, and Foucauldian concepts in order to create a Butler abstract machine that emphasized certain virtual relations rather than others insisting in the contemporary social field. Articulating the specific problem to which her concepts were a solution would entail reducing her thought to fit a preconceived format instead of following her thought out to the new places to which it could lead. However, we could say that her problem was one that insisted in the perceptions, affections, and actions of lived experience as well as the planes of philosophical thought she brought together in her own plane of thought. One could say that Butler thus constructed a plateau of meaning that resonated the intensities of virtualities extracted from her situation with actualized reality in a way that interrupted habitual patterns of thinking and living and allowed lines of flight to unfold for many of her readers as well as, presumably, herself. In this kind of view, it is not that Butler got the concept of sex more or less right. Rather, the intensities selected through her concept creation have a creative fecundity suitable for our place and time that can combine with present capacities in sexual being in productive ways.

A philosopher lives a life, has sensations, emotions, perceptions that she acts on, needs she must take care of if she is to survive. Creating concepts entails extracting virtualities from lived experience rather than representing it. The philosopher is not trying to say what life is like, but rather to experiment with virtual relations not yet actualized. This means that she needs to be attuned to becomings and intensities rather than remain fixated on history or the representation of what has already been actualized. Such attunement entails paying attention to nuances of meaning even if this means violating ways of organizing sensation, perception, and thought grounding a socially recognizable self. Concepts are attributable to states of affairs even if they are not exhausted by them. It is by "counter-effectuating" the events of sense we ascribe to states of affairs in order to explore new permutations in meaning that one gets at becomings in excess of what has happened. Approaching the chaos of thinking all that is as the event of all events (a thinking that Deleuze associates with Nietzsche's notion of the eternal return) entails laying out a plane or image of thought. Laying out this plane entails the invention of perspectives from which concepts can be created. All perspectives are included in the chaos of all becoming (with no God's eye view transcendent to the becoming to order it). A plane is laid out through the orientations of the philosopher as a becoming-other in excess of any stable perspective of a personal self. The strange personae this entails are perspectives that relate to the philosopher's becomings rather than a past that can be represented.

Various forms of feminist theory—say care ethics, feminist philosophy of science, or poststructuralist feminism—could be said to be laying out their own planes of immanence in keeping with the nonphilosophical presuppositions shaping the taste with which individual philosophers combine component elements of concepts. Each of these forms of feminist thinking could be said to make an abstract machine in its own right: a transcendental field constituted of virtual multiplicities. Conceptual creation is not about representing past patterns of lived experience, but rather is about extracting the virtual potential of lived experience in order to explore alternative connections among the meanings ascribed to its differential elements in an organized way that would allow new perspectives on it. This creative process needs not simply rational reflection, but also intuitive insight and the style and taste to be able to make the kind of connections that could incite joyous alternatives to past representations of what it means to be female or male, feminine or masculine, a woman or a man, transgender or intersexual. The various abstract machines of feminist thought have engaged in precisely this kind of process with these kinds of joyous results in many occasions. It has provided new perspectives on impossible situations that have elicited the joyous creation of new selves and futures.

Feminist theory always has had an open-ended structure that encouraged and elicited from its participants narratives of the lived experience of "minoritarian" subjects as well as imaginative outlooks based as much on passionate and imaginative response to the world as logical deduction. A Deleuze–Guattarian ontology shows how a spatialized time and a set of consolidated opinions as the basis for action can be successful and practically expedient, as well as how they can lose touch with our most precious resource for skillful living: the continuous variations of life itself. It thus provides a perspective on what feminists (as well as many others) have known all along: There is more to life than a realism that would make the future an inversion of the past; to evolve with an unimaginable future, we need creativity and imagination. On a Deleuze–Guattarian view, it is not the "realism" of a dogmatic adherence to past patterns of thought that we need in our philosophical reflection; intuitive insight and creative flexibility is actually more in keeping with a realism that would respond to the dynamic tendencies existing in our present—tendencies that although real are always in excess of the manifest forms of actuality susceptible to representation.

A Deleuze–Guattarian outlook suggests a different way of reading as well as doing theory. Feminist theory is a toolbox of concepts with which to experiment in order to solve life's problems. The point is not to come to a consensus about which inferences can be deduced from a philosopher's set of propositions, but rather to reactivate the concepts of a philosopher on one's own plane of immanence in light of problems pertinent to that plane. Deleuze and Guattari vary their concepts as the problems they are addressing shift, exploring the range of continuous variation of each concept in its relations to other concepts, unfolding the full force of the concepts by actualizing them in varying lines of thought. Feminist concepts, as well, can be read with an eye to how they can be varied in shifting contexts. Specific configurations of the concepts will be actualized in specific thought movements and states of affairs, emphasizing certain convergences of the unfolding force of the concept's components as well as of that concept with other concepts and the material forces that actualize in specific situations. The virtual force of concepts as tools always unfolds in conjunction with the actualization of material bodies and states of affairs as well as specific thought movements. For Deleuze and Guattari, language and meaning never operates independently of material bodies and states of affairs. Collective assemblages of enunciation and machinic assemblages of bodies always are in reciprocal presupposition in mixtures of words and things that can never be pulled apart. Feminist theory may approach the infinite speed of connecting virtual singularities of thought in ways that allow new perspectives on lived experience, but those singularities always are in keeping with actualizations of thought and matter that relate to the present problems of living.

Feminist theory always has had a strong commitment to lived experience; it always has been a theory created in the service of human life rather than in the service of an intellectual ideal that is more important than life itself. Deleuze and Guattari's conception of theory, with its emphasis on pragmatic context and the ability of theory to inflect situations in a way that emphasizes the intensities most conducive to productive change, honors this feminist emphasis. It is a conception that refuses the mechanical deduction of inferences in favor of attentiveness to pragmatic living, as well as insists on a principle of consistency that is pursued in defiance of "commonsense" understanding. The former allows theory to speak to the needs of living human beings; the latter allows theory to move beyond already established perspectives and suggest new perspectives in keeping with the unfolding of life. Additionally, the distinction between the actual and the virtual with its concomitant notion of intensities that are not representable, but insist in the actual in dynamic tension with the virtual, speak to the feminist concern to theorize from the heart as well as the intellect. Intensities are not representable because they speak to shifts in energy on physical, conceptual, and affective levels that are related to what could next unfold out of what has been. Because what could happen next is not, in Deleuze and Guattari's view, constrained to what can be deduced from a representation of what has been (because reality entails the virtual push of what could have happened as well as what did), the "irrational" arena of fleeting half-thoughts, feelings, and inarticulate intuitions turn out to play an important role in indicating what direction a revitalizing thought might take us. Theory, on the Bergsonian view put forward by Deleuze and Guattari, is a thought-form that allows us to move beyond the automatic living of habitual stimulus–response patterns and tap the full creative potential of a nervous system able to enlarge the gap between stimulus and response and explore alternative possibilities in living. It is but one component in an art of skillful living that entails coming into attunement with the world around us in ways that unfold our capacities for joyful living rather than engage us in deadening repetitions of what worked for us in the past.

Feminism as a form of life can become fully what it is only by diverging from what it has been in order to exhaust its own potentials. Each form that feminism has taken has provided a solution of the problematic field of intensities from which it has emerged, making perceptible various tendencies implicit in lived reality that allowed new ways of thinking and living to actualize. For feminism as well as other practices promoting human flourishing to be effective—that is, for such practices to produce the kind of changes in ameliorating our lives that we would like it to—we need more than one form of theory or practice. And we want such practices to creatively evolve and proliferate in the various situations to which they are solutions. We also must expect that they should mutate and transform as they shift contexts or as problems shift in keeping with what unfolds. Mapping various forms such practices take with respect to one another allows new connections to be fostered so that we can see how other projects that might seem fundamentally different from our own may exploit a set of potentials that we are also exploring in ways that may converge with our own lines of flight. Concepts that foster enlivening connections at one point may not be suitable to the intensities of another set of problems, but other concepts may be useful if we can allow them to mutate in keeping with shifting intensities. Mapping theories vis-à-vis one another rather than comparing them, can allow a topographical approach where we see various theories as suited to different terrains rather than assuming we need a one-size-fits-all theory that can provide a foundational framework for all progressive projects. Mapping can foster solidarity by allowing us to root our commonalities in the genetic processes that have created our situation rather than in the settled forms that have emerged from those processes. Progressive theory and projects can then be seen as experiments with the virtualities we extract from our surroundings rather than true or false depictions of our reality. The question of which tendencies to intensify would then depend on what would joyfully enliven the individuals of that specific social field. It would be a matter of what would work, rather than what was correct. Choosing one approach over another would thus be a matter of the heart as well as of the mind.

An important theme in feminist thought has been that women in the Western tradition have been aligned with the body and nature at the expense of their position as active participants in cultural production. Relegating women to the "nature" side of the culture–nature divide entails excluding women from their role in cultural production; rescuing women from this position by both showing their active participation in cultural production as well as working toward their greater inclusion in ongoing practices of cultural production, has been important to feminist work. Theorizing women in this way, however, entails assuming a fairly unproblematic understanding of the culture–nature divide, one that feminists have been concerned to contest. Recent work such as that of Elizabeth Grosz challenges the notion of nature as somehow unaffected by culture and shows that we cannot take this dichotomy for granted (Grosz 2004, 2005b). In the next chapter, I look at Deleuze and Guattari's conceptualization of human beings as emerging from the ongoing process of life in a way that challenges old dichotomies of culture–nature, human–inhuman, and even organic–inorganic. In their view, human beings not only emerge from the ongoing processes of life that include inorganic as well as organic processes, but they also distinguish and stabilize themselves as specific life-forms from the ongoing processes of life through mechanisms that are repeated over time. With the understanding that theory is an intervention designed to intensify certain relations at the expense of others rather than a "true" representation of what is, we can read their narrative of human becoming as an experiment in activating incipient tendencies in human becoming whose unfolding they (and perhaps we as well) can affirm.

Chapter 2

A Genealogy of (In)human Existence

The question of what it is to be human has special relevance from a feminist perspective because the answer has implications for who women are, the possibility we have for measuring up to our ideals of the human, and the direction and form our efforts to promote social change can and should take. Feminists have challenged claims of women's inferiority or properly subordinate status vis-à-vis men by either accepting the normative view of the human put forward and arguing that women can meet those norms as well as men can (perhaps after receiving the same opportunities in education or employment) or challenging the norm itself. Deleuze and Guattari's ontology posits human norms as fleeting idealizations of particular flows of life that are inextricably intertwined with other flows. Like Hegel, Marx, Nietzsche, and Foucault (among others), they present a human rationality, consciousness, and productivity that are related to the historical and cultural contexts from which they emerge. In Deleuze and Guattari's view there is no telos to human becoming, thus there is no ontological form of the human we can or should instantiate (despite the norms prevalent in any given time and place), and thus no human ideal against which we should measure women—or any other group—in order to find them wanting. This does not mean, however, that Deleuze and Guattari think that we could not live better lives. Rather than find certain human beings wanting for failing to live up to a transcendent ideal of the human, they suggest that we affirm the reality of being human—in its virtual tendencies as well as its actualized forms—and they appeal to a Spinozist notion of composing bodies in joyful ways to suggest that we could enhance the collective unfoldings of humanity in its imbrications with impersonal as well as nonhuman flows.

In this chapter I give a Deleuze–Guattarian narrative, drawn from *Anti-Oedipus* and *A Thousand Plateaus*, of the emergence of human subjectivity and its development in the Western social formations of primitive tribalism and despotic imperialism to its modern, oedipal form in late capitalism (Deleuze and Guattari 1983, 1987). In developing their descriptions of these social formations, Deleuze and Guattari appeal to contemporary anthropological

31

research of the 1960s and 1970s—Meyer Fortes, E.E. Evans-Pritchard, Edmund Leach (1971), Claude Lévi-Strauss (1971), and Robert Lowie, among others. Christopher Miller notes the "extraordinary liberties" Deleuze and Guattari take in making use of this research, and warns that "if our dream of smooth space, flow, and negotiated assemblage remains based on fantasies of the non-Western world as a realm beyond representation and division (the 'Orient of rhizomes and immanence' that Deleuze and Guattari continue to invest in), then it will inevitably replicate primitivism, as I believe Deleuze and Guattari do" (Miller 1993, 33). The quick sketch I give in this chapter is not meant to suggest that their account is beyond such criticisms. According to the Deleuze–Guattarian view of philosophical thought I take here, however, Deleuze and Guattari create concepts in keeping with anthropological thinking that give us new perspectives on life's problems, but the problems to which we respond will vary with the topographies of our situations. For example, contemporary readings of Deleuze and Guattari will be inflected by three decades of cultural and postcolonial theory that suggest ways of pursuing their concepts that would be otherwise unavailable. Whether Deleuze and Guattari should have been aware of the authoritarian overtones of some of their appropriations matters less than whether or not the lines of flight we can now unfold through reading them can be productive ones. Although I am wary of their sometimes overly glib characterizations of specific cultures, the distinctions they make among three social formations are provocative. The main points I take from their narrative are the notions that humanity evolves within and from the myriad forces of life, that different forms of subjectivity can emerge from different social formations, and that how we understand ourselves affects the forms our evolution takes. It is the experimentation that can come from these notions and what they suggest about one way (among others that one could explore from the perspective of other problems) we might understand the contemporary normative subject (i.e., the oedipalized or majoritarian subject) that interests me.

Any narrative of human subjectivity is bound to be extremely schematic in any case, and I here present a condensation of Deleuze and Guattari's story from my own perspective with no attempt to capture all the nuances of their account. By giving a quick rendering of a sweeping narrative of the human, I bring out their view of the human as a diverging and creative force played out and through the other life forces from which it emerges. This perspective on the human brings out our commonality with the rest of life, the contingency of sexed and gendered identity, and strategies for mapping the present in ways that will enhance our future. Rather than putting us in the position of subject vis-à-vis a world that is the object of our knowledge and mastery, Deleuze and Guattari emphasize the ways in which we merge with and emerge from surrounding forces of which we are always an integral part.

This undermines human–inhuman, culture–nature, subject–object, self–other, and mind–body dichotomies and evokes ways of working with rather than in opposition to nonhuman as well as human others and the environment as a whole. Additionally, their narrative presents a dynamic and always evolving understanding of the human that renders masculine–feminine, man–woman dichotomies problematic and invites a notion of the human as always unfolding new capacities in the ability to affect and be affected. The strategies they present for mapping the human in its social, cultural, and natural context allow us to better articulate the imbrication of various aspects of human life with respect to the semiotic and corporeal practices that condition specific formations of human subjects and brings out the virtual past-in-the-present in ways that invite intensifying creative possibilities in our present that we might otherwise overlook.

Deleuze and Guattari's narrative resituates the human, loosens up what we think of as possible for humanity, and posits idealized notions of the human as well as of the personal self as constraints on human becoming. They provide suggestive maps of economic flows of production and consumption along with flows of meaning and subjectification as well as strategies in mapping and reading maps that theorists interested in promoting social change can appropriate in their own work. Their approach suggests that mapping critical points concerning issues of material, corporeal, and psychic health could show us where and how we could unblock the flows that might allow all human beings to claim their humanity as fully participating members of the human collective. Just as the creation of concepts can intensify the virtual relations of meaning into new configurations, skillful intuiting of key points of converging forces and the heightening of intensity can allow us to push over threshold limits the kind of changes we would like to foster. On Deleuze and Guattari's ontology, change is inevitable, but with the help of mapping and a greater emphasis on thought-forms and intuitions less constrained by rigid paradigms of what can count as "true" or "realistic," we can become more adept at bringing about the kind of changes we can affirm.

(In)human Genealogy

As seen in chapter 1, Deleuze and Guattari's ontology suggests that what we perceive is only a selection of the becoming unfolding within and around us. We tap the temporal whole of becoming through rules of perception and living that can sustain us in relatively stable forms. Inorganic objects as well as other organisms more like ourselves live at different speeds, speeds that are slower or faster with respect to the various speeds of human existence, through the creation of patterns of movement that sustain the enduring forms of life.

What we perceive of this ongoing flow of differing and diverging creation is what allows us to survive as the forms we are. As seen in chapter 1, everything unfolds in terms of the tendencies or intensities that inform the forces making them up in interaction with other forces. What we experience of becoming, however, is given to our intelligence with its spatialized conception of time in the form of extension. Because the intensity of matter is cancelled out in such descriptions of lived experience, philosophical and scientific common sense tends to, as Constantin Boundas puts it, "conclude that intensity cannot be the sufficient reason for what is actually given, because the actual tends to eliminate intensity. But the truth is that intensity, despite its self-concealing nature, is what constitutes the diversity of the sensible" (1996, 90). What we perceive in terms of extension and quantity comes about due to the differentiating activity of becoming. The virtual conditions of actualized reality always are differing from themselves in the sense that, as things and states of affairs are actualized, the virtualities informing further actualization shifts. Processes of actualization unfold because the tendencies insisting within matter become implicated with other tendencies in ways that block certain lines of becoming and extend or transform others. Virtual tendencies or intensities are further intensified or relaxed in keeping with what actualizes and are thus always implicated with the extended forms of actualized reality. What Deleuze in *Difference & Repetition*, calls the transcendental field of the virtual (i.e., the virtual relations that condition manifest reality) can thus not be taken to be a static realm of Platonic forms because that field shifts in keeping with processes of actualization. "It is as if virtualities exist in such a way that they actualize themselves in splitting up and being divided" (Boundas 1996, 91).

     If to be a realist means to understand reality as the manifestation of extended matter that endures in a spatialized time, then Deleuze could not be called a realist. If, however, you take into account a Deleuzian ontology that conceives time as dynamic, then the reality of matter consists not only of its actualized forms, but of the tendencies insisting in it that given specific interactions with other actualized forms and their insisting dynamic tendencies, will unfold new actualizations of matter. Because such a conception of reality includes virtualities that insist in the actual whether or not they unfold into actualized forms, reality and our access to it turns out to exceed any one way we might have of grasping it either in perception or conception. The view that emerges from *A Thousand Plateaus* as well as other works by Deleuze and Guattari, and Deleuze, challenges us to think the world not in terms of static entities arrested in one moment of their duration, but as an ongoing flow of interconnected things that are in process and from which emerge the outlines of that which we identify and categorize as stable things. Deleuze and Guattari present an ontology of becoming where individual bodies are conceived as being what they are in terms of their duration relative to other durations (rather than in terms of unchanging forms they instantiate). Life is one flow of creative evolution that continually transforms and invents new ways of being. What is real are not merely the forms that actually emerge, but the tendencies and potentials that could unfold in many more ways than actually occur. This perspective does not explain change in terms of mechanical causes or teleological ends, but rather views things in terms of, as Keith Ansell Pearson puts it, "the vital movements of a virtual and actual process of creative evolution" (Ansell Pearson 1999, 33). Change does not have to be explained, for the universe is inventive change itself, an ongoing movement of self-differentiation that continues to unfold.

For patterns of movement to be able to sustain themselves as specific forms rather than simply dissolve back into the larger flux, they must also sustain the movements that allow them to keep those forms. The territorializations of life are not confined to human life, but serve inorganic as well as organic life, creating boundaries and the means to negotiate the different speeds of surrounding fluxes of becoming that sustain their existence. Deleuze and Guattari's perspective displaces human beings from the center of the cosmos and perceives them instead as one form among many others emerging from the creative production of life as a whole. The same processes that produce human beings and social existence also produce rocks, mountains, forests, and animals. Rocks may unfold at a slower speed than trees or human beings, but like human life, they are only what they are due to the differential relations of the forces of which they are composed. Human life, as a form of life diverging from other forms, is, like all life-forms, always engaged in a process of creative differing. Social and cultural forms of territorialization have led to the territorialization of human perception of the divergence of life in its human forms onto various norms or ideals for what it is to be human against which human life in its diverging forms can be measured, but in the account given by Deleuze and Guattari, such ideals always are bound to be out of step with the ongoing becoming of life. Life is only incessantly creative, proliferating difference, trying new things, and creating new forms, in keeping with tendencies that insist without being overtly manifest to human perception, but that have their effects in concert with actualized life.

The earth from which human life emerges can be viewed as a plateau of intensities, a specific form actualized in time at the edge of unfolding in one way rather than another, but replete with the virtualities or singularities that are the limit points governing its endless possibilities in actualization. In the unfolding of time, various strata form at inorganic and organic levels. Patterns of energy evolve that repeat in habitual patterns, but always in continual variation from patterns already actualized, and always with the possibility of forming unprecedented patterns given the accumulation of molecular flows pushing a system over the threshold point (a previously unexpressed singularity) that qualitatively changes the system from one form to another.[1] Thus, organisms form and species evolve in ever diverging patterns that actualize new forms. The states of being that are produced by these patterns qualitatively shift over time in keeping with the singularities structuring the actualization of specific configurations of bodies with their specific capacities and powers to affect and be affected. All bodies, be they atoms, rocks, mountains, or words, have the power to be affected and the power to affect that comes from being an actualizing force of energy among other forces. Organisms are open systems undergoing continual flux rather than closed systems subject to external forces.[2] They achieve a relative independence from surrounding processes that allow them to sustain relatively stable forms. They are self-perpetuating flows of becoming that have achieved enough deterritorialization from surrounding fluxes to slow down their becoming-other relative to other flows and achieve the ability to reproduce themselves (ATP 60).[3]

In the third plateau of *A Thousand Plateaus*, "10,000BC: The Geology of Morals," Deleuze and Guattari lay out a characterization of specifically human life in terms of three strata: the organic stratum, the stratum of signification, and the stratum of subjectification. Physicochemical processes are territorialized onto the self-organizing activities of organic life. Some of these processes "deterritorialize" from their initial patterns and "reterritorialize" into new patterns of organization. Organic forms of life (that have stabilized the patterns of being of an evolving species through sustainable forms of self-organizing activity) further detach from the surrounding environment through the deterritorialization of the hand (from locomotion) and of the mouth (from eating) and unfold new patterns of activity. Human beings are the emergent effects of the patterns of semiotic and productive activity of organisms with capacities for using and interpreting symbols as well as transforming their surroundings through the use of tools. Technology and language, tools and symbols are, according to Deleuze and Guattari, properties of a new distribution of life rather than the properties of individual human beings (ATP 60).

An individual human subject with conscious and self-conscious awareness emerges from the juncture of the three strata of human existence. Deleuze and Guattari's use of the term *assemblage* emphasizes the coming together of forces into relatively stable configurations with particular capacities to affect and be affected that have specific durations. As discussed in chapter 1, machinic assemblages of desire include the heterogeneous processes of material practices through which we engage in projects and handle tools. Any such assemblage is drawn from the stratum of the organism (insofar as we are embodied), as well as the stratum of significance (the system of explicit and implicit rules and statements of semiotic systems that provide part of the background for meaningful action) and the stratum of subjectification (the processes through which we take up and come to identify ourselves as having a specific place and role in patterns of behavior). Collective assemblages of enunciation are the heterogeneous processes of signifying practices that constitute us as language speakers. Any such assemblage is drawn from the stratum of the organism (insofar as we are embodied creatures), as well as the stratum of significance (the system of explicit and implicit rules and statements that are the condition of any given speech act) and the stratum of subjectification (the processes through which we take up and come to identify ourselves as having a place as specific speakers and actors with concrete solutions to the negotiations of social systems of meaning). To elaborate on the characterization of reciprocal presupposition between the two kinds of assemblages given in chapter 1 (in a somewhat different context), consider a wedding where everything is proceeding smoothly. The bride and groom are dressed appropriately, the church ceremony has been performed, and the guests have been congratulatory. Then the bride's brother stands up at the reception and begins making accusatory remarks toward his sister, thus drawing close to breaking an implicit rule of the collective assemblage of wedding enunciations that prohibits revelation of family tensions in public. The energy in the room intensifies as the guests wonder if a point will be reached where the "perfect wedding" becomes a "family disaster." Someone makes a joke, the brother sits down before going too far, the tension breaks— the threshold where one kind of wedding would turn into another kind is not reached. The wedding as a machinic assemblage of desire comprising the couple to be married, their families and guests, the church, the procession down the aisle, the reception hall, the food and flowers, the eating, the ritual of standing up with a microphone in hand, and so forth, in an unfolding process of productive parts making something happen comes together in complicated ways with the ways we have of talking about weddings, talking at weddings, the vows pronounced, the congratulations given, the small talk engaged in, and the toasts made, that are the speech acts making up a collective assemblage of wedding enunciations. Although one can distinguish between the two kinds of assemblages, they can never, in Deleuze and Guattari's view, be separated, and their relationships are never one of linear causality or a one-to-one correspondence. Instead, moments of intensification are determined by the singularities or limit points of the line of variation in the relation between two elements; specific intensities increase or decrease as what actualizes draws closer or moves further away from the limit points where something different will happen.

Deleuze and Guattari's ontology suggests that human life is in continuity with other forms of life—inorganic as well as organic. There are distinctive features of human existence—the strata of significance and subjectification may be unique to human beings (although the processes of territorialization and deterritorialization are not)—but that is not to say that other life-forms could not develop similar strata, depending on the virtualities and actualized forces composing them and their environments. Semiotic practices, although not unique to human beings, have taken a distinctively human form. Signification refers to the strata of meaning prevalent in the human social field. There are some signs, symbols, and words that have meaning and others that do not. There are specific rules governing how meaning is formed, and nonsense that is distinct from what makes sense. The events of sense, like the singularities of physical happenings, are singularities governing the actualization of specific speech acts: I may insist that wearing high heels is a feminist act and may get you to agree, but when I also insist on laughing at blatantly misogynist jokes, you may draw the line and say I have crossed the threshold to what you would call nonfeminist behavior. These possibilities in meaning are governed by nonactual and yet real virtual relations of meaning that insist in any given speech act. Subjectification refers to social practices that render me a recognizable subject. One such practice is that of being a speaker of language who knows how and when to say "I." Another is to know what seat to take when entering a classroom, or how to hold one's fork when at the dinner table. Some behaviors "make sense" and others are ruled deviant or abnormal: I can wear heels and make-up if I am a woman, but if I am a man I better have a good reason for it (and what counts as a good reason depends on one's location in the social field).

Deleuze and Guattari's narrative of the emergence of human life and its development through varying configurations of the strata of the organism, significance, and subjectification, as partial (in both senses of the word) as it is, brings out a notion of humanity as an always evolving force of life that is always diverging from its manifest forms and whose capacities are always changing. In particular, their narrative suggests that the structure of human subjectivity has shifted over time, and that these shifts have affected how human beings experience their embodiment as well as their sex. Their account, although based in anthropological evidence, is neither scientific or disprovable (like the narrative of human becoming Nietzsche gives in the *Genealogy of Morals* that clearly influences Deleuze and Guattari's version [1967]), and yet it suggests that the relationship of things and words, bodies and significance, lived experience and psychic identity, mutates over time in keeping with forces larger than any given human individual and uncontainable by essentialist notions of what it means to be a woman or a man. The deterritorializations resulting in tools, speech, and the intelligence to contemplate various options in action before choosing one, as well as the sense of self (and the ability to make promises) necessary for extending human life in its social and cultural forms, were all developments crucial to humanity as it currently actualizes.

Like everything else, the three strata of the organism, signification, and subjectification are made up of processes that evolve and change over time in flows of diverging and differentiating activity. Strata are processes that due to the self-reinforcing and resonating nature of their patterns of activity remain fairly stable over time, but even strata are continually deterritorializing from habitual patterns and spinning off in new directions.[4] Societies must manage the flows that diverge from the relatively stable social patterns composing their three strata if they are to be self-sustaining. How this is done varies with different times and places. In *Anti-Oedipus* and *A Thousand Plateaus* Deleuze and Guattari characterize primitive, despotic, and capitalist social formations where the three strata come together in different ways. In *Anti-Oedipus* they characterize the differences among the social formations they describe in terms of the varying degrees of repression exerted by the social machines on the desiring machines that would transform them (AO 262). In *A Thousand Plateaus* they characterize different semiotic regimes or "regimes of signs" and their relationship to managing mutant lines of flight.[5] In both books they emphasize the flows of larger patterns of collective assemblages of enunciation and machinic assemblages of desire—that is, patterns of signifying and corporeal activity—from which individual subjects with their intentions and ability to act emerge. In both books, they also emphasize the *"desiring machines"* (their preferred term in *Anti-Oedipus*) or *"molecular"* flows (their preferred term in *A Thousand Plateaus*) that connect or break with other flows at levels below the "molar" levels of entities such as social wholes, individual subjects, or personal selves in ways that could precipitate changes in habitual patterns.

Anti-Oedipus presents a genealogy of the human subject as it emerges in primitive and despotic social formations and culminates in the modern, oedipal subject of late capitalism. Eugene Holland suggests that Deleuze and Guattari are giving "a genealogy of the Oedipus" in *Anti-Oedipus* that foregrounds "the *differences* between Oedipal reproduction and other forms of social reproduction" (1999, 58). Thus, the Oedipus complex in Deleuze and Guattari's view is not universal but rather is shown to be "cobbled together out of elements from previous social formations, in which they had different roles to play" (ibid.). Deleuze and Guattari's genealogy depicts human subjectivity as evolving with and through the social and natural flows of which it is a part. What remains the "same" is not a human essence that exists throughout human history, but only the patterns of living and experience that continue to replicate what our representational intelligence can recognize as human forms of living. By showing the genealogical origins of the oedipal subject in earlier social formations they not only undermine the notion that human subjectivity has one universal form, but invite the creative evolution of contemporary forms of subjectivity.

Human beings, in their own differing becoming, are the products of converging forces that are affecting and being affected by their surroundings in ways that make things happen, but as self-sustaining processes with relative autonomy from surrounding flows, they also have their own capacities to affect and be affected. Desiring machines constitute the productive activity of life itself in its creative evolution. They do not express or mean anything; they are assemblages—the coming together of forces that unfold in keeping with the virtual intensities that condition their actual manifestations. They operate according to immanent principles of unfolding activity, and are thus always ready to mutate from established patterns of activity in order to unfold new capacities in doing. Social machines are desiring machines whose patterns of activity are regulated in keeping with "molar" patterns of resonating activity. That is, they are desiring machines that have come to desire their own repetition rather than mutation and metamorphosis down lines of flight that continually escape any repeating pattern that might stabilize them into enduring entities (be they institutions, communities, families, or selves). Mutant desiring machines or molecular flows are the flows of life's production that answer only to the need to continually unfold the latent tendencies of stabilized patterns of activity.

If mutant desiring machines continually actualized a large proportion of the tendencies implicit in a living collective, that collective would be in a state of constant transformation that would soon disperse in diverging flows. The self-sustaining repetition of any enduring form of life—be it a social collective, a subculture, or a human individual—requires suspension of the lines of becoming that would entail its demise. The production of desiring machines that might unfold capacities incompatible with the repetitions of social activity that sustain the collective must be regulated if the community is to survive. To establish and repeat the social relations of alliance necessary for sustaining the collective, the "intense, mute filiative memory" of desiring production associated with biological lines of filiation must be repressed. That memory is the representative of the noncoded flows of desire capable of submerging everything (AO 185). "Man must constitute himself through the repression of the intense germinal influx, the great biocosmic memory that threatens to deluge every attempt at collectivity" (AO 190). Habitual patterns of activity securing relations that extend beyond those required for meeting basic survival needs are required.

In primitive social formations, collectives emerge with respect to tribes occupying territories and clans with traceable lineages (ATP 209). Tribal and clan identifications are literally marked on the body in order to establish it as part of a group. As Claire Colebrook puts it, "some specific difference is *selected* as a way of assembling or gathering bodies together to form a territory. The primitive body was, Deleuze and Guattari note, literally marked by tattooing, scarring or painting in order to gather one assemblage of different bodies and establish it as the same" (Colebrook 2004, 182). The filiations of primitive or territorial social formations go from one generation to the next and alliances are made through relations of credit and debt that indicate the standing and status of various members of the community, their roles and positions. Local authorities indicate what marriage alliances can be made on the basis of various political and economic investments of the social field; kinship and lines of descent take different forms in different societies and may shift over time. "A kinship system is not a structure but a practice, a praxis, a method, and even a strategy" (AO 146). Restrictions on desiring production are relatively fluid, changing in keeping with the changing filiations and alliances involved. These restrictions are located in taboo social relations; not all assemblages that could be made are socially acceptable, and the desire to make such assemblages is figured in terms of relations to concrete others that are prohibited. Holland points out that the emphasis in primitive social formations is on requiring the circulation of resources rather than the prohibition of certain relationships (Holland 1999, 71). What matters is that the process of satisfying immediate needs is deferred long enough to foster social production and reproduction.

Kinship systems are not, on this reading, simply relations organized around "natural" family formations. According to Deleuze and Guattari, those with whom one has intensive ties (due to the assemblages formed with them in day-to-day life) become discernible as persons with whom one has specific forms of kinship through the alliances that are decreed to be acceptable or forbidden. Early forms of the incest taboo that prefigure the oedipal complex of modern subjectivity are manifest in territorial social formations, but primitive identifications take the form of "group identifications that are always partial, following the compact, agglutinated series of ancestors, and the fragmented series of companions and cousins" (AO 143). Flows of desire are still fluid and polyvocal; forbidden behavior emerges in the context of concrete filiations and alliances rather than being dictated in advance through fixed categories indicating one's social identity or position. Social segments—the differences between being the member of one tribe rather than another, being a daughter, or honoring one's debt—are always in process. The differences between being on one segment rather than another are worked out in ongoing negotiations.

In the despotic social formation, signifying activity becomes that of a properly signifying regime of signs. The local relations of filiation and alliance that were "coded" in the context of concrete interactions among the community's members are now "overcoded" through the despot. Local relations of filiation and alliance still hold, but now they are resonated in a system with the despot at the center. A mute voice is detached from the signifying chain and set up as the ultimate source of meaning. It is only now that the question "what does it mean" emerges and laws are instituted (AO 206). Imperial inscription makes alliances and filiations converge into the direct filiation of the despot with his god and the new alliance of the despot with the people. Concrete debts to specific others become a debt of existence to the despot and his god (AO 197). Social segments are less supple because they all center on the despot who overcodes them so that they reinforce one another. Social positions unfold in terms of concrete interactions and the body is still able to encounter the world in terms of polyvocal desires, but laws are instituted that apply to subjects abstracted from their concrete contexts and incest taboos become more regulated. Signifiers are abstract (the body is no longer a sign in its own right) and their meaning are all referred to a central source of meaning that can never manifest, rendering signifying chains endless as one attempts to interpret them in light of true belief in their source. In *A Thousand Plateaus*, Deleuze and Guattari illustrate the difference between the presignifying regime (associated with primitive social formations) and the signifying regime (associated with despotic social formations) with the different reactions of Crow and Hopi men to a similar situation: "(the Crow are nomadic hunters [i.e., members of a "primitive" social formation] and the Hopi sedentaries with an imperial [i.e., despotic] tradition): 'A Crow Indian whose wife has cheated on him slashes her face, whereas the Hopi who has fallen victim to the same misfortune, without losing his calm, withdraws and prays for drought and famine to descend on the village' " (ATP 113). The Crow Indian marks the body of his cheating wife, thus indicating a shift in their alliance that will have repercussions that will be negotiated among the various filiations and alliances of the community. The Hopi's reaction to a similar situation is mediated through an appeal to a central authority that relates to the community as a whole.

In the capitalist social formation, despotic overcoding and territorial coding are decoded in favor of abstract flows of labor and capital. With private property, wealth, commodities, and classes comes the breakdown of codes (AO 218). Social production and reproduction in modern society no longer takes place through the articulation of political and economic associations in kinship structures and collective identifications (whether overcoded or not) and instead unfolds through the circulation of capital. There is a complete reorganization of social repression and psychic repression (AO 217). Debt to concrete others or the despot becomes the infinite debt to a mysterious source (the father as source of paternal law) and is internalized. The reproductive activity of family life becomes separated from the social field; relations lived out with respect to sustaining the bodies, minds, and hearts of human beings as well as sexual reproduction and the raising of children becomes privatized.

This separation of a private realm of the family from the public realm enables the full emergence of oedipal subjectivity.

A rigidified form of the incest taboo is interiorized through the family that designates persons with fixed positions (father and mother) as objects of desire (incestuous desire for the mother, desire to be the father) and all desire is reduced to desire for what one as a totalized self with a personal ego lacks (the phallus one either wants and cannot have if one is female, or wants to inherit if one is male). The phallus, originally a partial object among others, is detached and becomes a complete object. Whereas polyvocal desiring production machines partial objects and flows ("doing this makes this happen"), now a total unity (an autonomous self) is posited as that which partial objects and the subject of desire "lack" ("if I could only have x, I could be the subject I want to be") (AO 72). If you are female, you lack what you need to be fully human. If you are male, you have to continually prove "you're a man" and have what it takes to be fully human (and therefore inherit the phallus). All the political, social, and economic fluxes of the social field are translated and reduced to desire attached to the positions of the oedipal triangle and the differentiating activity of desiring production is reduced to finding the objects that might make the subject whole. The unconscious is subjected to the requirements of representation; rather than a productive unconscious it becomes an unconscious that knows how to express itself and its desiring production becomes that of a particular person with particular objects of desire. According to Deleuze and Guattari, this reduces desiring production to the production of fantasies designed to fill in the lacking subject. Libido is reduced to producing what concerns the ego, as if it had no interest in experimenting with the political, social, and historical fluxes within which it is immersed (AO 54–57).

The investments of the family are determined by the family's investments in the social field (AO 276). Modern subjects tend to experience such investments through a personal story about familial positioning (daddy–mommy–child). These investments can oscillate between paranoid investments in authority or schizoid investment in lines of flight:

> [T]he nature of the familial investments depends on the breaks and the flows of the social field as they are invested in one type or another, at one pole or the other. And the child does not wait until he is an adult before grasping—underneath father–mother—the economic, financial, social, and cultural problems that cross through a family: his belonging or his desire to belong to a superior or an inferior "race," the reactionary or the revolutionary tenor of a familial group with which he is already preparing his ruptures and his conformities. (AO 278)

Oedipal subjectivity entails experiencing one's identity as that of an individual in relation to various permutations of an oedipal triangle rather than the collective identities articulated through the various alliances and filiations of primitive and despotic social formations.

In capitalism the subject positions laid out through debtor–creditor alliances and kinship filiations diminish in importance. Abstract flows of labor and capital now take precedence over the relations formed through concrete interactions. Meaning as it plays out in social and cultural practices of signification and interpretation take precedence over the flux of sensory experience, the way it does in a despotic social formation, but the despot in direct relation to god no longer secures a believable source of meaning for the signifiers that circulate. Revelations from the source are no longer believable and meaning-making becomes groundless, if incessant. Oedipus-the-despot becomes oedipuses-the-subjects as the source of meaning once located in the despot and the royal family are now interiorized into each oedipalized individual. With the diminished importance of subject positions related to the relations of alliances and filiations—relations that organized and channeled desiring production and the molecular flows of individuals in ways that allowed social life to carry on in relatively stable form—comes an emphasis on the personal. Whereas in another social formation a subject's identifications as a member of a given tribe or a given location in a kinship system, whether that was further subjected to the organization of the despot's law or not, may have constituted defining features of her subjective significance, now a personal self takes on unprecedented importance; her identifications come to be organized around two subject positions—that of either having or not having the phallus—and her personal ego revolves around her particular resolution of the familial romance. The specific forms a predominantly oedipal subject's desires take will depend on how she solves the problem of filling in the hole opened up by a psychic structure that demands renunciation of immanently satisfying desiring production. Through the personalization of desire, oedipal subjects become able to take up positions in social practices that demand relatively interchangeable subjects that can be satisfied by equally interchangeable objects of desire in the form of consumer goods.

On Deleuze and Guattari's view, capitalism deterritorializes the coding of earlier societies because it is axiomatic. Capitalism has precipitated an unraveling of cultures, reducing all cultural difference to a set of variables that can be inserted into a globalizing axiomatic that welcomes difference without being affected by it. Whereas in societies rooted in a foundational culture, beliefs and practices were rooted in a way of life that was taken for granted and provided the backdrop for the vicissitudes of life, capitalism tends to replace such belief systems with the ongoing change needed to produce and market commodities.[6] All social formations need to manage the deterritorializing fluxes of mutant production. Just as organisms have ways of handling the mutant production of cancerous cells (or suffer the consequences), so do social formations need to manage the mutant flows that would otherwise destroy them. According to Deleuze and Guattari, capitalism entails such a high degree of deterritorialization from the overcoding of despotic social formations as well as the territorial coding of primitive social formations, that it requires an especially paranoid form of desire management at the level of individual human beings. Although sexual difference is important to primitive and despotic social formations, it is not personalized in the form of sexed and gendered identity and sexual preference until the social formation of capitalism brings about the repression of such mutant flows by oedipalizing the desiring production of human subjects through its delegate, the family.[7]

In Deleuze and Guattari's reading, the incest taboo is a way of organizing and representing the need to manage uncodable, noncoded, and decoded flows that would threaten the existence of a particular social formation by dissolving or transforming it (AO 164). The forbidden object of desire that is sexually differentiated according to the Oedipal story is thus, on their account, "the lure or fake image, born of repression, that comes to conceal desire" (AO 162). The key difference between the subjectivity of primitive cultures and that of capitalist society is that the primitive subject's desire was directly invested in the social field, whereas the oedipal subject's desire is directly invested in objects designated in terms of sexual difference. "Oedipus is the baited image with which desire allows itself to be caught (*That*'s what you wanted! The decoded flows were incest!). Then a long story begins, the story of oedipalization" (AO 166).

In primitive families, the father, mother, and sister always also function as something other than father, mother, and sister; families are coextensive with the social field.[8] Deleuze and Guattari present Victor Turner's case of a shamanistic cure in "An Ndembu Doctor in Practice" (Turner 1964) as an example of a primitive cure that, unlike psychoanalysis, works through a wide range of social investments rather than remaining fixated on a personal story about familial positioning.[9] When Kamahasanyi, a resident of a small village of the Ndembu tribe in northern Rhodesia studied by Turner in the 1950s, became ill (rapid palpitations of the heart, severe pains in the back, limbs, and chest, and fatigue after short spells of work [Turner 1964, 255]), Ihembi, a "ritual specialist" was called in to rid Kamahasanyi of the ancestral "shades" that his illness indicated were afflicting him. Turner emphasizes Ihembi's skill in studying the various networks of relationships affecting Kamahasanyi, diagnosing "the incidence and pattern of tensions" (Turner 242) in those relations, and reducing them by presiding over collective rituals in which a general atmosphere maximizing sympathy for the patient is generated through drumming, singing, prayers, and the airing of grievances (259). Some of the tensions in the various networks of relations arose, according to Turner's description of Ihembi's diagnosis, from colonial relations between whites and blacks (the chieftainship that entitled the village to certain resources from the British had been abolished, creating various resentments due to resulting shifts in power), power struggles between two branches of the lineage of chieftainship (affected by the colonial situation), relations among the villagers that threatened to divide the village, and Kamahasanyi's life's history (which included shirking duties toward his matrilineal kin [Turner 1964, 253]). As Turner explains,

> the Ndembu "doctor" sees his task less as curing an individual patient than as remedying the ills of a corporate group. . . . The patient will not get better until all the tensions and aggressions in the group's interrelations have been brought to light and exposed to ritual treatment. . . . The doctor's task is to tap the various streams of affect associated with these conflicts and with the social and interpersonal disputes in which they are manifested—and to channel them in a socially positive direction. (262)

Deleuze and Guattari point out that Ihembi's analysis is never oedipal, but rather directly plugs into social organization and disorganization. Through the intense affect created in hours of drumming, the patient's rhythmic shuddering as the afflicting shades are exorcised, rituals various participants are asked to perform, and induced confessions testifying to hidden resentments, social synergy is revitalized. Ihembi creates "a veritable group analysis centering on the sick individual" that discovers

> the preconscious investments of a social field by interests, but— more profoundly—its unconscious investments by desire, such as they pass by way of the sick person's marriages, his position in the village, and all the positions of a chief lived in intensity within the group. (AO 168)

It is never a question for Ihembi of determining Kamahasanyi's desires and position in an oedipal triangle considered independently of his position in multiple social networks, but rather of directly accessing those social networks through rituals that tap into various flows of the social field in order to address blockages and thus allow the various members of those networks to successfully perform their allotted social roles.[10] Deleuze and Guattari add that the Ndembu analysis only becomes oedipal "under the effect of colonization": "The colonizer says: your father is your father and nothing else, or your maternal grandfather—don't mistake them for chiefs . . . your family is your family and nothing else" (AO 168–69). Ihembi's purpose, contrary to a psychoanalytic analysis, is to reveal the hidden tensions and unconscious investments of the social field as they converge on the specific location of the affected individual. It follows that the cure also must address the social field itself rather than the psychic structure of an individual subject considered in isolation from the assemblages of which that individual forms a part.

Sexual difference is integral to the markings of the primitive body and permissible marriage alliances, but equally important are the political and economic alliances of chiefs, lineages, and clans that enable the production and distribution of goods and prestige. In primitive social formations, bodies are marked, authoritative voices decree what filiations can be extended through acceptable alliances, and eyes take pleasure in the punishments inflicted on those not yet marked deeply enough to abide by social law, but it is only in capitalism that polyvocal desire is reduced to oedipal forms making dominant forms of desire the pursuit of the personal happiness of a self primarily identified in terms of her or his sex, gender, and sexuality. The oedipal subject of capitalism is much less identified with her position in multiple and conflicting networks of concrete relations with specific others that unfold in ongoing and open-ended negotiations. Instead, her social positioning is determined through the abstract calculations of the market while her personal identifications insure that she will comply with that positioning.

A genealogy of (in)human existence provides an account of humanity that foregrounds the inherent creativity of all life and our emergence and participation in the creative process of that life in its ongoing movement. We emerged from the flux of inorganic life and evolved as a distinct species that then unfolded semiotic and corporeal patterns of meaningful activity that played out variations in signifying and interpreting processes in combination with processes of subjectification. Such a story emphasizes our continuity with the life around us instead of setting us against it and demonstrates resources for creative living much broader and deeper than we might have thought. It suggests that any story about what it means to be human will need to start with the social field as a whole rather than individual human beings and specify the particular social fields of a given time and space with its concrete economic, social, cultural, and political investments, rather than give a universal description. Thus, like a Foucauldian perspective from which one can give genealogies of the discursive and nondiscursive practices from which emerge particular configurations of subjects, one also can, from this Deleuze–Guattarian perspective, give genealogies of the social field that take into account social flows of semiotic as well as material activity. Because for Deleuze and Guattari any (relatively) autonomous life flow is a self-organizing flow that stabilizes into repeating or territorialized patterns with its own speed relative to surrounding flows, as well as mutating or deterritorializing patterns, individual human subjects, as well as social collectives, are always agents that make things happen as well as respond to impinging forces. The dynamic force of time is always unfolding and the nature of that unfolding depends as much on the interaction of the actual with the intensities insisting in it as it does on other already actualized forces.

Faciality and the Majoritarian Subject

According to the story Deleuze and Guattari tell in *Anti-Oedipus*, oedipalization as a psychic structure of human subjectivity arose in the wake of capitalism's deterritorialization from the social systems of meaning and patterns of activity of previous cultures. *Anti-Oedipus* is in large part a critique of psychoanalysis for further entrenching oedipal subjectivity rather than (as Deleuze and Guattari propose) moving us beyond it, but it is important to remember that Deleuze and Guattari "have never dreamed of saying that psychoanalysis invented Oedipus. Everything points in the opposite direction: the subjects of psychoanalysis arrive already oedipalized, they demand it, they want more" (AO 121). Although they think that psychoanalysis gets the unconscious wrong and has fallen for the ruse oedipal subjectivity entails—that what the subject wants but cannot have is an incestuous relationship with his mother (rather than, as they see it, to engage in forms of desiring production that might unravel or revolutionize the social status quo)—the oedipal subject characterized by psychoanalysis is an ideal type of a transient form of modern subjectivity. This type may be actually manifest in a relatively small number of instances given the deterritorializing flows that undermine it as well as the vagaries of family life, but it is a form of subjectivity whose further unraveling they hope to promote. If the oedipal subject is the retrenchment of a more traditional form of subjectivity precipitated by the frantic deterritorialization of capitalism, the schizo subject is a new form of subjectivity also precipitated by the deterritorialization of capitalism—and it is the latter subject that Deleuze and Guattari prefer to support.

On Deleuze and Guattari's view, oedipal subjectivity obscures not only the larger social investments determining familial investments, but also the joyous lines of flight desiring production could unfold. If one understands who one is as primarily a question about personal identity rather than one's standing in multiple relational networks of the social field, if questions about one's motivations and goals are primarily understood as questions about desires understood in terms of a personal story related to one's family rather than collective stories related to group identifications and various investments of the social field, and if failures in reaching one's goals and obtaining what one desires tends to be understood in terms of one's personal failure to live up to an ego ideal rather than the need to map lines of flight from where one is, then one's becoming is likely to be blocked. Since one's sex, gender, and sexual preference tend to be crucial to personal stories about identity, life goals, and the success (or failure) of one's life, Deleuze and Guattari's de-emphasis of personal identity in favor of experimenting with the molecular flows from which molar identities like that of sex, gender, and sexual preference emerge has special importance for feminism.

Identity as a designation applied to one by others or oneself refers to, in Deleuze–Guattarian terms, one's placement on the molar segments produced by social machines. Racial segments, gender segments, biological sex segments, and so forth, all are laid out by the social machines that consolidate and codify physiological, economic, political, social, and cultural differences through concrete assemblages of desire and collective assemblages of enunciation (one is either on the black segment of race or another racial segment, one is either on the feminine segment of gender or another gender segment). From the moment a child is born, she is immersed in flows of signification and subjectification, and she enacts, through her perceptions, thoughts, actions, and emotions, the habitual patterns and orientations of her location on the social field with its particular configurations of human and nonhuman flows. The subject emerges from myriad routines and habitual patterns of living in which she understands herself and what she says and does through meanings made available by the practices engaged in at home, at school, at work, at places of worship, at the doctor's office, at court, and so forth, as well as by multiple forms of cultural production ranging from network news and printed materials to video games and cinema. The biology and physiology of a specific human subject unfolds and evolves in differentiating life processes in imbrication with ways of talking and semiotic processes that make sense in a specific part of the social field and with specific practices concerning how subjects play out their social roles and ways of being as human subjects. In living out variations in organic body processes with the variations in the ways words signify over time that are in reciprocal presupposition with the practices a subject engages as, say, a daughter, a mother, or a worker in day-to-day activities, various threshold points will be reached (one is at home or at work, one lives with one's parents or lives alone, one is childless or has a child). These threshold points can be labeled by oneself or others ("now I am a wife," "now I am a manager"; "now I am a daughter," "now I am a single woman"; "now I am a wife," "now I am a mother") and that identity can be consolidated and codified ("it means this to be a mother, not that"). Such identifications—whether made by oneself or others—will have further effects as they become intertwined with the ongoing processes of social living.

The oedipal subject of modern life is flexible enough to adapt to a wide range of situations without feeling a loss of self or purpose, despite unmooring from traditional patterns of living with their settled cultural significance, because her purpose is interiorized. What the oedipalized subject lacks will always relate to the familial romance that funnels all desiring production into the desire for a body part—the phallus—that is detached from the continuous unfolding of making different things happen and presented to the child as what she wants but cannot have or what he has but may lose if he breaks with paternal law. This oedipal subject maintains self-sameness through the repetition of habitual patterns of meaning and behavior. Barred from the self-overcoming transformation of productive connection with the world, this subject stays the same with respect to interchangeable objects of desire. Her desiring production is restricted to fantasizing the objects that once acquired will give her the satisfaction she seeks. She is thus diverted from engaging in the immanently satisfying production of machines that would connect her in various ways to the flows around her (that would extend her capacities and engage her in the kind of ongoing metamorphosis that makes subjects hard to pin down).

Holland explains that capitalism entails the isolation of the nuclear family from society: The market dominates the public realm and the belief systems that sustain personal identity and communal relations are confined to the home. This "drastically reduces to only two the range of subject-positions generated within it" (1999, 40). A personal self is consolidated through identifications organized around the sexually differentiated positions of prohibited object of desire (the mother) and agent of prohibition (the father). In this reading, sexual difference is crucial to personal identity. In Deleuze and Guattari's view, what one encounters, feels, and tries to make happen, is always from the start implicated with the political, social, and historical flows of one's social field. Flows implicated with race, religions, collectives of various forms, the history of one's group, and so forth, always, for them, come before the reduction of these different flows to the gendered flows of the family story. Oedipalization obscures these other differences and emphasizes the personal stories of oedipal subjects. The nuclear family cuts individuals off from "all the non-personal flows traversing society at large" in order "to focus desire exclusively and precisely on those whom the prohibition constitutes as global persons" (Holland 1999, 52). Human subjectivity as processes of individuation unfolding productive connections with the world of multiple and heterogeneous kinds become sexed and gendered subjects with personal stories to tell about what will satisfy their hearts' desire.

In *A Thousand Plateaus*, Deleuze and Guattari's characterization of the modern subject de-emphasizes the role of the family in narrowing desiring production to that of the oedipalized subject and elaborates the larger social flows that resonate and affirm the constricted desires of a subject premised on lack. Their notion of the faciality machine suggests that the triangulation of identity with respect to sexual difference in the family is replicated and affirmed with respect to multiple flows of the social field in a way that fixes the subject on a "white wall" of signification where she can always be categorizable and plunges her into a "black hole" of subjectification where her psychic habits of self devolve into sterile patterns.[11] Machinic assemblages of desire and collective assemblages of enunciation actualize in day-to-day living. Molar segmentarity precludes subtle differentiations, reducing identity to yes–no categories rather than allowing molecular mutations of these roles. My role as daughter reinforces my role as worker, sergeant, and parishioner, setting up redundancies that further reinforce segmentarity rather than pursuing the mutant flows that always eludes segments. If there is to be a resonating and self-reinforcing web of subjectivities, there has to be a central eye, "a black hole capturing everything that would exceed or transform either the assigned affects or the dominant significations" (ATP 179). It is the faciality machine that "carries out the prior gridding that makes it possible for the signifying elements to become discernible, and for the subjective choices to be implemented" (ATP 180).

Everyone must submit to the dualism machines of subjectification, either identifying their subjective experience with one of two opposing categories in a series of opposing categories or being subjected to such identification by others. A recognizable subject with a specific position vis-à-vis the majoritarian subject is thereby produced "depending on which faciality trait is retained: male–(female), adult–(child), white–(black, yellow, or red); rational–(animal)" (ATP 292). The faciality function shows us the form on which the majoritarian subject is based: "white, male, adult, 'rational,' etc., in short, the average European" (ATP 292). "Man constitutes himself as a gigantic memory, through the position of the central point, its frequency (insofar as it is necessarily reproduced by each dominant point), and its resonance (insofar as all of the points tie in with it)" (ATP 293). A subject finds herself on specific molar segments (now I am a daughter; now I am a student; once I commit a crime, I am a criminal). These segments all are organized around the central point of the majoritarian subject. All the points defining the molar segments are amplified through a resonating repetition of the patterns established in keeping with the majoritarian subject, canceling out variations in individuality that could lead to ways of being beyond the patterns of dominant memory (now that I am identified and identify myself as a criminal, I am the bad daughter and student as well). Insofar as one's identity is regulated with respect to the majoritarian subject, the oedipal subject positions of the family are affirmed and amplified rather than unraveled or undermined through competing lines of identification.

In primitive societies circular segmentarity establishes ever-larger circles through which people are segmented ("my affairs, my neighborhood's affairs, my city's, my country's, the world's" [ATP 209]). But these circles do not necessarily have the same center and thus do not resonate segments in such a way that they converge in the same black hole (ATP 211). In modern society, "all centers resonate in, and all black holes fall on, a single point of accumulation that is like a point of intersection somewhere behind the eyes" (ibid.). The face of the father, teacher, colonel, and boss resonate and reinforce one another, thus rigidifying segmentarity. A concrete face is a specific configuration of elemental faces. These faces are then brought into resonance through molar segmentation. I am at home or work, at my job or on vacation, in the army or at church. I have the face of a mother or daughter, a worker or boss, a worker or tourist, a sergeant or colonel, a priest or parishioner. The abstract machine of overcoding (the State) sets up points of resonance between social identities that are the elemental faces of the faciality machine. The abstract machine of faciality constitutes an arborescent set of elementary faces that are in biunivocal relation with one another—man *or* woman, rich *or* poor, adult *or* child, leader *or* subject. These faces then can be linked together "two by two" (ATP 177). Labels like man or woman, white or black, are laid out on the white wall of signification and then accepted or rejected in the choices computed by the black hole of subjectification. Faces that seem suspicious are rejected, but "the white wall is always expanding, and the black hole functions repeatedly"; successive divergence types from the elementary faces are produced that establish binary choices between types of deviance: "A ha! It's not a man and it's not a woman, so it must be a transvestite" (ibid.). Thus, all faces are inscribed into the overall grid of the abstract machine and everyone will be recognized (ibid.).

The State "substitutes fixed or ideal essences for supple morphological formations, properties for affects, predetermined segments for segmentations-in-progress" (ATP 212). As a woman, mother, professor, citizen, I may experience various configurations of my body as it mutates in keeping with the experiences related to these various roles. But these mutations are cancelled out in deference to the ideal essence of each of my roles as established by social and state institutions and as redundantly affirmed and resonated through the convergence of all those roles in one "personal" identity. Whatever the mutant flows that affect my concrete individuation, these flows are not taken up into the ways of speaking, interpreting, and behaving, that are available to me as socially meaningful, unless I engage in some form of minoritarian resistance to dominant norms. Although I may access potential lines of force, these potentials are reduced to properties I manifest; I am a sexy woman rather than a process of individuation becoming-other in an encounter with a specific person, I am a nurturing mother rather than engaged in a process of becoming-other with my child. Rather than being a work-in-progress, always moving from segment to segment, I exist in either one segment or another with no variation. Once I "become a woman," I am sexy (or not) until I am "off the market" (i.e., married); once I give birth, I am a mother for life. Segments are overcoded on a uniform grid so that they enter into redundant resonance.

Faces are produced "only when the head ceases to be a part of the body, when it ceases to be coded by the body, when it ceases to have a multidimensional, polyvocal corporeal code" (ATP 170). The complexity of embodied existence is reduced to what can be captured and coded through the faces that are socially recognizable (faces that show up on society's white wall as readable) and psychically convincing (faces that can be internalized as one's personal identity). Faces thus entail a reduction of the lived experience of another in all her specificity to the selected perception of another in terms of relatively fixed social categories of identity and a psychic identity that comes to, in a sense, stand in for the continuous variation in corporeal living. They also entail a personal psychic identity that comes to, in a sense, stand in for the unrepresentable subtlety, variation, and ambiguity in the lived experience of one's own corporeality. The abstract machine of faciality brings together aspects of signification and subjectification in different combinations through the assemblages enacting it and thus produces what currently counts as recognizable faces and coherent psychic identities (ATP 168). Mutant fluxes and flows of the body, for example, various forms of becoming-animal, are no longer elements that are taken up into the socially sanctioned organization of human individuals. "Bodies are disciplined, corporeality dismantled, becomings-animal hounded out" (ATP 181). Instead, the lived experience of one's body is brought together with the extant significations of possible faces spread on the white wall that are then chosen in the computation of the black hole that decides on the right combination of elementary faces.

At the level of the lived orientation of embodied subjectivity, each subject, whether oedipalized or not, lives out her life as a unique configuration of the concrete flows of physiological, corporeal, and semiotic processes that inform her day-to-day life. How well this orientation fits with the categories through which she is designated and interpellated by the various practices she engages depends on her specific situation. No subject in contemporary society can escape dealing with sex and gender categories in one form or another. Whether one lives out these designations and interpellations in comfortable conformity or painful dissonance depends on whether the multiple forces converging in the durations one lives resonate with dominant memory (i.e., the representational memories and history sanctioned by the mainstream) or induce varying tendencies toward counter-memories and minoritarian resistance. Furthermore, binary sexual difference turns out to entail a form of subjectivity structured in terms of bifurcating categories that valorize some subjects by marginalizing others. Identification with one or the other of two sexually differentiated positions (despite the molecular connections subverting or complicating that identification) is paradigmatic for other selections made from the faces of the faciality machines. The active–passive dichotomies of sexual difference are replicated in other social binaries with one identification of two possibilities being always better or worse (i.e., either closer to or further from the majoritarian subject).

According to the story given in the last section, oedipalization as a psychic structure becomes increasingly important as other codes deterritorialize in the wake of capitalism's axiomatization. Although sexed and gendered identity may appear to be primary aspects of personal identity (checking off one's race or religion may or may not be required, but checking off one's sex usually is), on Deleuze and Guattari's view, oedipal subjectivity obscures the multiple social flows implicated in family life. Markers of difference that have stable social significance in the territorial and despotic social formations Deleuze and Guattari describe lose their credibility in a capitalist social formation. Deference to abstract calculations of the market such as the need for workers who can migrate from one workplace to the next in keeping with the skills needed to produce the products that will sell the best take precedence over the significance of concrete relations with others in a variety of relatively stable social networks.[12] Cultural and institutional support for various identities is weakened by the commodification of ethnic and cultural differences. The flows affecting a subject's life are organized around sexed and gendered identities produced through a process of oedipalization that requires constituting oneself as a lacking subject and taking up a position on either side of a sexual divide. Sexual difference becomes a crucial structural feature in the psychic structure of a personal self able to negotiate the speeds of capitalism without unraveling, but the flows affecting us as subjects are social, economic, political, cultural, racial, pedagogical, and religious, as much as sexed or gendered (AO 274). Internalization of paternal law suppresses pursuit of the mutant lines of deterritorialization that emerge from the swiftly changing circumstances induced by the incessant drive for profit, allowing relative stability of the oedipal subject (if of a paranoid sort) despite the breakdown in both traditional codes in living as well as the habitual patterns of life that actualize such codes.

Sexed and gendered identities are crucial to the stabilizing identifications required by the faciality machines; taking up a definitive stance with respect to a transcendent representation of desire separated from the differentiating flux of life—the phallus as signifier of whatever one might desire (with its implications of the passive or active relation of the sexed subject vis-à-vis the likelihood of achieving satisfaction)—excludes pursuit of the lines of becoming connecting one to the world and thus totalizes a self that can be ranked with respect to the majoritarian subject. Forming a central identity as a woman or a man with a specific gender identity thus entails a conception of self in relative autonomy from the world who takes a passive or active desiring stance with respect to that world. This division of humanity into two sexually differentiated groups obscures a wide range of social investments of the contemporary social field stratified into various configurations of power by highlighting sexed identity as key to determining who one is and how to live one's life. A variegated range of differences among human subjects is thus reduced in significance when compared to identification with one of two categories, woman or man. This binary configuration allows resonating patterns of binary identifications that situate subjects with respect to the majoritarian subject in ways that clearly delineate one's position according to a relatively static social hierarchy.

Deleuze and Guattari suggest that the face of the majoritarian subject is Christ, "in other words, your average ordinary White Man," making the first divergence types racial (ATP 178). According to Deleuze and Guattari, it is primitive society that designates the stranger as an "other." The European faciality machine designating racial differences is less concerned with excluding certain groups than it is with determining degrees of deviance from the majoritarian subject. Thus,

> European racism . . . operates by the determination of degrees of deviance in relation to the White-Man face, which endeavors to integrate nonconforming traits into increasingly eccentric and backward waves, sometimes tolerating them at given places under given conditions, in a given ghetto, sometimes erasing them from the wall, which never abides alterity. (ibid.)

If a variegated range of social flows (from physiological and cultural flows related to one's race and able-bodiedness to economic and political flows related to one's class and political affiliation) become subsumed under one's sexed and gendered identity with respect to a familial story about sexual difference (one is a black woman or disabled woman rather than a black or differently-abled variation in being-human; one is black *or* white, disabled *or* abled, just as one is a woman *or* a man), then the latter will loom large in one's attempts to live a meaningful life, despite the crucial importance, as Deleuze and Guattari see it, of other ways of marking deviance from the majoritarian subject. Deleuze and Guattari's suggestion that "all becomings begin with and pass through becoming-woman. It is the key to all the other becomings" suggest that even in *A Thousand Plateaus*, where oedipalization is de-emphasized, sex and gender still play a crucial role in modern subjectivity (ATP 277).[13] In the context of the faciality machines, their suggestion would seem to indicate that taking up a position with respect to the sexual divide is a move that is replicated and resonated throughout the binaries of the faciality machines.

In chapter 3 I consider Deleuze and Guattari's conception of the modern, oedipal subject and its concomitant alternatives in light of some examples of feminist investigations of subjectivity. Feminist mappings reveal the complicated imbrications of gender, sex, and sexuality with the varied range of flows—organic, economic, cultural, social, and political (to name a few)—that mark contemporary forms of being-human.

Chapter 3

Feminist Cartographies and Minoritarian Subjectivity

Feminist Cartographies

In view of the Deleuze–Guattarian conception of subjectivity presented in chapter 2, troubling the waters of contemporary forms of binary sexed and gendered identities by revealing the complexities subverting them as well as their imbrications with other aspects of identity would appear to be especially threatening to forms of subjectivity organized with respect to the majoritarian subject (i.e., forms of subjectivity whose distance from the white, male, heterosexual, propertied, able-bodied norm is marked in terms of assignation to one or the other of a series of binary categories). If this is the case, the feminist imperative to map sex and gender in relation to other social designations could be read from a Deleuze–Guattarian perspective as a project of mapping forms of subjectivity structured in terms of their divergence from a normative subject in order to explore and experiment with the possibilities implicit in our present of a subjectivity that could welcome differences without ranking them. In this chapter I present some examples read from this perspective. Although my examples are drawn from feminists who are not advocating a Deleuze–Guattarian perspective (and so may even disagree with such an approach), by reading these examples in relation to the Deleuze–Guattarian concepts I have thus far developed, I hope to both show dynamic convergences of thinking that can inflect our reading of Deleuze and Guattari as well as of the examples I consider in ways that incite further experiments in productively mapping minoritarian forms of subjectivity. Mapping subjectivity in terms of sex and gender in this way respects the importance they play in orienting lived experience in its contemporary formations at the same time as it fosters lines of flight that could lead to forms of subjectivity that do not require marginalizing others with respect to a majoritarian norm.

Subjecting a range of evidence to abstract social categories like race and gender tends to obscure the imbrications of social flows as well as the intensities insisting in them. Understanding identity categories such as those designating one's gender, race, (dis)ability, or sexuality in terms of the concrete situations in which they are used reveals the varying flows that converge in the pragmatic contexts in which embodied subjects are submitted to and/or identify with specific categories. Mapping these flows with respect to one another allows one to see how various flows of meaning produce identity categories inflected by the specific forms social flows take in a given time and place.

My first example of a feminist cartography of minoritarian subjectivity is Abby Wilkerson's mapping of erotophobia. In an essay using disability and queer perspectives to explore continuities in the effect of erotophobia on oppressed groups, Wilkerson shows how social flows can be coded in divergent and yet mutually reinforcing ways (Wilkerson 2002). She argues that a paraplegic may be coded as asexual, a black as hypersexual, and a lesbian as perverted, but in all cases, the effect is to render the lived experience of one's sexuality less comfortable, thus *blocking* (to use Deleuze–Guattarian terminology) one's power in the world to a greater or lesser extent. She presents some examples of how erotophobic judgments of the sexual behaviors or "natures" of members of various groups suggests that

> [c]ultural erotophobia is not merely a general taboo against open discussions of sexuality, and displays of sexual behavior, but a very effective means of creating and maintaining social hierarchies, not only those of sexuality but those of gender, race, class, age, and physical and mental ability. (41)

Medical literature that presents moralizing restrictions on the sexuality of the physically or cognitively disabled, hypersexualized images of black and Latino men, legal obstacles to the sexual agency of lesbian, gay, bisexual, and transgendered people, the shame and alienation connected to the sexuality of heterosexual women that Sandra Bartky discusses in her book, *Femininity and Domination* (42–45): These are some of the effects of social practices that designate certain bodies as deviant. From a Deleuze–Guattarian perspective, we could say that it is through such practices that bodies and their desires are delineated in terms of their distance from the majoritarian subject acting as an orienting reference point (in more or less overt forms) in those practices. Such delineation, through more or less subtle approbation (a doctor who neglects to discuss birth control with a disabled patient) or outright exclusion (laws against sodomy) renders certain lines of becoming uncomfortable, dissonant, or impossible, diminishing the power of those groups and their individual members to affect and be affected in the process.

My second example is Rosemarie Garland-Thomson's consideration of how concepts like disability and gender pervade society's "structuring institutions, social identities, cultural practices, political positions, historical communities, and the shared human experience of embodiment" (Garland-Thomson 2002, 4). Garland-Thomson contends that disparate cultural and social systems form an aggregate of systems that operate together to support "an imaginary norm and structure the relations that grant power, privilege, and status to that norm" (4). In her view, disability is "a culturally fabricated narrative of the body" that "stigmatizes certain kinds of bodily variation" (5). The disability system interprets and disciplines bodily variations "that call into question our cultural fantasy of the body as a neutral, compliant instrument of some transcendent will" (ibid.). The unmodified bodies of the disabled are depicted as unnatural and abnormal, whereas bodies surgically altered through plastic surgery are portrayed as normal and natural (12). "The ideology of cure directed at disabled people focuses on changing bodies imagined as abnormal and dysfunctional rather than on changing exclusionary attitudinal, environmental, and economic barriers" (14). From a Deleuze–Guattarian perspective, we could say that the faciality machines computing various permutations of identities designating one's distance from the "normal" body of the majoritarian subject (if I wear my prosthetics I can "pass" in these situations, whereas my inability to climb stairs forces me to identify as "handicapped" in other situations) carry implicit value judgments about one's entitlement to exercise the capacities one does have, the kind of assemblages one can enter into, and one's worth as a human being.

My third example of a feminist cartography is Ladelle McWhorter's Foucauldian argument that the modern concepts of race and sex share a common genealogy (McWhorter 2004, 39). Feminists inspired by the Foucauldian notion of genealogy have mapped various aspects of the social field to investigate how identity designations have evolved over time, leaving legacies in the present that might not be immediately obvious. Feminist genealogies of race can demonstrate not only a telling resonance with Deleuze and Guattari's notions of the abstract machine of faciality and the majoritarian subject, but also reveal how designations of the Eurocentric faciality machines are implicated with capitalist and colonialist investments of the social field, and how sex and gender designations intertwine with race designations according to the configurations of forces of specific times and places.

According to McWhorter's argument, bodies came to be thought of as organisms with functions ("temporal processes that developed over time"), rather than machines ("collections of parts that interacted in space") in the latter quarter of the eighteenth century (McWhorter 2004, 44). This, along with the development of the science of statistics, made it possible to study large groups and describe "normal" processes. "People came to be identified in all sorts of ways with reference to their place on developmental curves, with reference to norms" (45). McWhorter contends that the "modern Western idea of sexuality is unthinkable without this idea of developmental normalization" (ibid.). For example, the designation of the "homosexual" described by Foucault as an invention of late nineteenth-century medicine is predicated on a normative understanding of sexuality; people labeled "homosexual" were supposedly sexually immature. Because sexuality was thought to be fundamental to human identity, it was thought that such "immaturity" extended into all areas of life (46).[1] McWhorter refers to Foucault's account of the emergence of sexuality, sexual identities, and the concept of sex in the nineteenth century to make the argument that race was constructed in a similar fashion in the same period of time (47). The notion of "biology" as "the study of life," was not introduced until 1802. It was biology as the study of living beings viewed as organic systems engaged in temporal processes that allowed a notion of race as a morphological type of human being at a particular stage of development. From a nineteenth-century Eurocentric perspective, the "hierarchy of stages seemed pretty obvious" (51). Study was directed at the "lower races," in order to rank them and "figure out what flaw in each of them had slowed or stopped their group's progress toward civilized perfection" (ibid.).

According to McWhorter:

> [race] functions in social institutions—both officially, as a means for distributing goods and determining representation, as in affirmative action law and the U.S. census, and unofficially as a means of identification, discrimination, and affiliation. It does not so much *mean* (i.e., direct our attention to a given object) as *operate* (i.e., create divisions that enable systems of control to maintain themselves). And, again, in this respect race is very much like sex. (McWhorter 2004, 52–53)

Thus, in McWhorter's view, both sex and race are concepts that emerge in the power-knowledge and biopower networks that arose in the early nineteenth and mid-twentieth centuries as control over large populations arose and intensified (54). McWhorter points to this shared history and function to argue that race and sex operate in the ways we speak and act in institutional and daily life "primarily at points where people think in terms of normality and abnormality or deviance, where people have major managerial goals for large populations, and where there is strong desire to control human development" (ibid.).

McWhorter's (partial) genealogy of sex and race presents a map of converging forces that emerged and shifted over time to form categories still very much with us today, with effects that we may have naturalized or take for granted without realizing the social investments and power struggles relevant to their formation and evolution. Although Deleuze and Guattari prefer to talk about desire rather than power, the Foucauldian notion that subjectivity is produced through discursive and nondiscursive patterns of activity through which subjects are informed, both through the ways they are corporeally and semiotically designated, as well as the positions they assume as speaking and acting subjects, resonates with Deleuze and Guattari's notion that social practices entail designating and assuming identities with respect to a majoritarian norm.[2]

My fourth example is that of Georgia Warnke's genealogy of race in which she explores how the institution of slavery affected racial designations in the nineteenth century (Warnke 2005). Warnke points to the different racial constructions of the Irish American and African American. Whereas in the 1840s, "American Anglo-Saxons defined the 'race' of new Irish immigrants in terms of their dark skin, big hands and feet, broad teeth, and pug noses," with a "genetic propensity to violence and ignorance," such differences became a matter of health and environment with the implication that over time, Irish immigrants could be restored to health (100–01). This was in contrast with those of African descent. "Because slavery had to be shown to be legitimate, other racial differences had to be distinguished from the African racial difference" (101). Thus, being Irish became what Warnke calls a "recreational" identity for a group of people considered to be fundamentally white in a way that reverberates in our present understanding of being Irish. "The case of blacks remains more monolithic: one cannot be recreationally African because one remains fundamentally black. One still cannot be either recreationally white or recreationally black" (ibid.).[3]

Other feminist genealogies show that sex and gender are not only intertwined with race, but with other perhaps less obvious (at least if you are closer to the majoritarian norm) designations of cognitive and physical ability. Thus, my fifth example of a feminist cartography of minoritarian subjectivity is Anna Stubblefield's argument that the concept of feeblemindedness became linked with "off-white' ethnicity, poverty, and gendered conceptions of a lack of moral character" (Stubblefield 2007, 162) in the eugenics movement of the first three decades of the twentieth century in the United States. The eugenics movement was widespread and according to Stubblefield its impact still influences scientific research and public policy. In her investigation of how, in particular, "feeble-minded" white women became subject to coercive sterilization, Stubblefield examines distinctions white elites drew between the white race and other races; (untainted) whites (supposedly) have a superior intellectual capacity to produce "civilization" (169). Stubblefield cites research by scientists such as Paul Broca, Robert Chambers, and J. Langdon Down, in the mid-nineteenth century that investigated how to measure intelligence by first assuming that white people were more intelligent than black people, and then, on the basis of that assumption, construing differences between white and black people as reasons for why white people were further along an evolutionary path of ethnic types than black people. When Henry Hubert Goddard, writing in the early twentieth century, described intelligence (understood in terms of this model of ethnic evolution) as hereditary and impervious to environmental influence, the stage was set for designating "heritable" forms of white impurity (172).

In 1908, Goddard adapted Alfred Binet's intelligence test for use in the United States by adding the category of "moron" (designating people with a mental age of eight to twelve) to the original scale that included the "idiot" (designating people with a mental age of two or younger) and "imbecile" (designating people with a mental age of three to seven years). The notion that extreme poverty was hereditary and linked to the moral defect "of a supposedly shameless willingness to live on public charity" (Stubblefield 2007, 173) was a widespread belief that became increasingly linked to the concept of the moron in family studies done in the early twentieth century. Feeblemindedness became linked with "white poverty, off-whiteness, and lack of civilization-building skills" and the "category of the moron—the feebleminded person who appears normal but who is prone to immorality, incapable of being a contributing citizen in a democratic society, and who will pass feeblemindedness on to his or her offspring" became "a powerful device for drawing a distinction between tainted and pure white people" (176). Additionally, white women who demonstrated their failure to understand their role in the advancement of civilization by engaging in unchaste behavior manifested, like impoverished white women and off-white women, a "lack" of intellect that tainted their whiteness. Thus, intertwined constructions of race, class, gender, and cognitive dis/ability came together in a conception of feeblemindedness that "became gendered in a way that led to women bearing the brunt of eugenic sterilization" (178–79).

"Disabled" subjects may be divergent enough from the majoritarian norm that their disability becomes a salient feature of their designated identity. Even in such cases, however, their sexed and gendered identity will be central to how that identity is interpreted and lived. Stubblefield's mapping reveals specific physiological, economic, colonizing, and cultural flows in the use of the term *feeble-minded* that manifest the imbrications of gender, race, cognitive (dis)ability, and economic status in that designation in a way that belies the primacy given to sex and gender in organizing and understanding the converging flows of concrete individuals. From a Deleuze–Guattarian perspective we could say that a wide range of practices resonates with familial positioning in order to reinforce and naturalize distance from the majoritarian subject. Maps like Wilkerson's reveal the social investments and configurations of power that such positioning conceals.

In addition to revealing the multiple forces that come together in one designation of social identity, feminist maps reveal critical points in the present where intensification of various sorts could result in significant change. Thus, Wilkerson's and Stubblefield's genealogies reveal relations of flows of which we may not have been aware that condition our understanding of disability. Intensifying these connections in new ways of understanding designations of disability and racial designations, as well as the social practices related to them, could in turn lead to action from within the relevant practices that shift them (to a larger or lesser extent) into divergent forms of those practices or directly challenge them (through discursive critique or some other form of resistance). These genealogies, incomplete as they are, show how important it is to understand how identity designations—be they those of sex, gender, sexuality, race, or otherwise—emerge and are interpreted in keeping with specific investments of the social field best understood in terms of the confluence of multiple forces of particular durations. The bifurcating sorting of personal identity into yes–no categories obscures the shifting vagaries of their evolution as they are put into effect in a multitude of day-to-day situations. Although an emphasis on the personal identity of an autonomous subject and the demand for clearly defined identity designations tend to suggest that a given identity is a property of persons, in Deleuze and Guattari's view, identity is produced, reproduced, sustained, and transformed through the unfolding of social life over specific periods of time in particular places.

A designation of gender, race, or disability can never, from Deleuze and Guattari's perspective, be a static category. Its meanings inevitably shift along with the faciality machines (as they are actualized in specific patterns of meaning and activity) that enact it as well as the molecular flows of lived orientations and identifications that resist those machines. Such shifts are in response to the convergent forces affecting the relevant assemblages and will resonate with patterns organized around the majoritarian subject or proliferate lines of flight. Words such as "disabled" or "feeble-minded" and the racial, gendered, and economic connotations associated with them, leave traces in the present of which we may be unaware, even if those specific words are no longer used. Ways of speaking and doing become habitual patterns that self-replicate even if in doing so they continually diverge from past repetitions. Mapping an association among variations in cognitive style, skin color, financial income, and cultural practices of the duration connecting us to an earlier time renders some of the relations now only implicit explicit, making us more aware of the habitual patterns informing our naturalized reality, and thus provide insight into how to shift those patterns in ways we can support.

These genealogies track social practices that constitute subject positions informing the categories through which people are designated as well as identify themselves. These practices, from Deleuze and Guattari's perspective, are corporeal and semiotic assemblages that tend to replicate and extend themselves, thus settling into stratified configurations of power. Individual human beings with their personal identities and desires emerge as individual solutions to the problem of subjectivity from processes they collectively share in various ways with others. Although sexed and gendered identity is a crucial feature of dominant forms of subjectivity, these genealogies show how other investments of the social field are equally, if not more, crucial. Even when one's personal identity is still experienced in terms of one's sex, gender, and sexuality (e.g., one's primary identification is as a woman), these genealogies show the myriad social investments that coalesce around that identity (it turns out a woman who primarily identifies as a woman may be more likely to be relatively closer to the majoritarian norm and so has not been confronted with other ways that she differs from that norm—that is, she is a physically and cognitively "normal," white, heterosexual, middle-class woman).

The deterritorializing of cultural codes precipitated by capitalism opens human existence to an unprecedented amount of creative evolution by releasing old constraints on proliferating change. Thus, capitalism actually enacts more of the differing and diverging becoming of life than some earlier social formations and so, according to Deleuze and Guattari, on the one hand, puts us in a better situation to become more aware of life as process, but on the other hand, has produced a reterritorialization onto oedipal or majoritarian subjectivity, the reduction of productive desire to desire premised on lack, and the incessant pressure to produce and consume in keeping with the axioms of capitalism. The former tendency they align with their notion of schizophrenia and a nomadic subject able to creatively evolve and the latter tendencies they associate with paranoia and absolute systems of belief where all meaning is, as Holland helpfully puts it, "permanently fixed and exhaustively defined by a supreme authority, figure-head, or god" (Holland 1999, 3). Thus, along with the high speeds of contemporary life with its frantic pace of technological change and globalization goes paranoid reterritorialization onto consumerism as well as fundamentalist religion and fascist politics.

Faciality machines are not universal to human life; subjectivity in modern capitalism requires excluding more of the corporeal fluxes running through any line of human becoming than the other two social formations Deleuze and Guattari describe (although this, in itself, does not guarantee the kind of desiring production Deleuze and Guattari would like to promote). Rather than explore possible connections among micropercepts and affects that could lead to aggregates of perception and feeling that violate current opinion and consensus representations of reality, faciality machines interpret sensation as the meaningful experience of a recognizable subject. Rather than pursue the physiological, social, and cultural permutations that inevitably result from hybrid forces converging in particular locations, faciality machines interpret anomalies as exceptions that do not affect the norm or as exceptions that require new categories that resonate with the system as a whole. This entails canceling out subtleties in individual and collective experience and blocking exploration of alternative connections.

From Deleuze and Guattari's perspective, modern subjectivity, insofar as it is oriented with respect to the majoritarian subject, entails organizing multiple flows and investments of the social field in terms of sexual difference. This structuring plays out through the oedipalizing function of the family and the faciality machines that confirm and elaborate the binary structure of oedipalization. Oedipalization and the faciality machines that produce the personal identity of modern subjectivity thus operate not only to render the continuous variation in human becoming that might extend into new forms of subjectivity nonproductive, but also to turn collective stories about power investments into personal stories about achieving meaningful lives. Although Deleuze and Guattari do not themselves pursue this point, this makes feminism an intervention that targets sex, gender, and sexuality as a crucial fault line in modern forms of subjectivity that is just the starting point for unraveling multiple configurations of power detrimental to our collective unfolding.

A subject is a highly variegated multiplicity of forces converging in a singular line of individuation. In order to be designated by the speaking and signifying practices of social life (so that I can be enrolled in school, get proper medical attention, be protected by the law, and so forth), in order to identify with those designations (I am a student, I am a patient, I am a citizen), and in order to engage in meaningful action (I walk to school, I sit patiently in the doctor's office, I walk into little booths and press some buttons or pull some knobs in order to vote), my highly differentiated process of becoming must be assimilated into a social hierarchy of faces. But there is always something that eludes the binary organization of molar segments. Oedipal patterns of subjectivity, like any of the habitual patterns of being-human, open onto an always changing social field of which they are a part and so can never remain constant (AO 96).[4] The oedipal triangle of father, mother, and self, in the best of circumstances, never can fully represent the unconscious. Oedipal figures directly are coupled to elements of the political and historical situation that constantly break all triangulations. Families are filled with gaps and breaks that are not familial. Molecular assemblages combine at a level beneath the molar organization of rigid segments, making finer distinctions than those of the binary social machines. The more rigid the segments of society, the more it induces a molecularization of its elements

(ATP 215). There always is something that escapes binary organization, the resonances set off among the segments so organized, and the overcoding that further fixes those resonances (ATP 216). And the mutant flows that escape the binary social machines can connect with other flows. One's beliefs and desires, for example, may not adhere to the fixed essences ascribed by molar segmentarity to specific segments and may connect with surrounding flows in ways that do not resonate with the black hole of subjectification constrained to the yes-or-no choices that define recognizable forms of personal identity.

We cannot escape the white wall of the signifier or the black hole of subjectivity. We are who we are through them. But on Deleuze and Guattari's view we can invent new uses for faciality machines. We can run lines of asignificance across the wall of the signifier that "void all memory, all return, all possible signification and interpretation" (ATP 189). We could set faciality traits "free like birds" and invent combinations with other traits freed from their respective codes (ibid.). We can explore minoritarian forms of subjectivity already with us. There are always myriad movements of decoding and deterritorialization operating at different speeds on the social field (ATP 220). Flows are connected when decoded and deterritorialized flows "boost one another, accelerate their shared escape, and augment or stoke their quanta" (ibid.). Flows are conjugated when they are brought under the dominance of a single flow capable of overcoding them, bringing about in the process a relative stoppage or point of accumulation that plugs the lines of flight and performs a general reterritorialization. When flows are connected with other flows, they can accelerate a shared escape, and effect new reterritorializations that allow new forms of living. In the next section, we will begin to explore the notion of a lived orientation that can initiate a line of flight from the faciality machines.

Minoritarian Subjectivity and the Question of Identity

According to Deleuze and Guattari's story, the way that the desires of the body enter into assemblages with the surrounding world in order to extend previously unexercised capacities as well as newly emerging capacities is affected by the differing ways human subjectivity has been structured in different social formations. Whereas the body enters more freely into unregulated desiring production in primitive and despotic social formations, it is facialized in capitalism. Facialization entails an embodied orientation organized in terms of a personal identity. That is, all desires of the body are of *one* body with a psychic self that is (more or less) unified with a coherent history that can be represented and collated with the narratives of other members of the community. Sexed and gendered identity form important fault lines of this self because it is through familial positioning with respect to sexual difference that the multiplicity of social flows affecting subjectivity are organized in a way that is assimilable to the faciality machines of capitalism.

Personal identity, especially as it is regulated by the faciality machines that percolate throughout the semiotic and corporeal practices that insist on clearly delineated subjects with identities that fit into already laid-out parameters (to register for public school, I need to designate age, sex, and residence; to walk into a restroom I need to know to which sex my body conforms), becomes the organizing reference point for lived experience. If a lived experience cannot be referred to such reference points, it may be unrepresentable and excluded from having an impact (the knowledge I gain independently of a recognized school may not gain me entry to the conference I want to attend), or it can render lived experience either dissonant or unlivable (ambiguous sexed or gendered identity can make life painfully confusing). But on Deleuze and Guattari's view, personal identity is not necessary for nonpsychotic subjectivity. Habitual refrains and some sort of constriction on desiring production are necessary for relatively stable forms of human subjects to be sustainable. But subjectivity is a self-organizing system of becoming with relative autonomy from surrounding flows grounded in a wide range of territorialized processes that allow emotions, perceptions, and day-to-day life to stabilize into habitual patterns. In a social formation premised on a lacking subject threatened with a loss of humanity insofar as she or he breaks the rules (where the majoritarian subject is the norm for what it is to be human and any deviation from that norm is carefully observed and marked), unregulated refrains in living are not allowed extension into new patterns. Productive desire must be reduced to the lacking desire of a self still waiting to be completed (the child's desire to swirl water into dirt to make mud must give way to the desire *to be* a chef or a scientist rather than simply to make connections), and identity must be computed from the bifurcating patterns of social recognition that select constants from a wide range of continuous variation in order to plug those constants into already delineated rules of living (a woman who is disabled must no longer be interested in sex since she no longer fits the subject positions designated in countless narratives and scenarios emerging in multiple social practices about "what happens when one is sexual," a mother who does not feel the kind of "maternal" love for all her children depicted in various forms of cultural production as well as assumed in social practices connected to childcare, pedagogy, and citizenship must be an inhuman monster).

Deleuze and Guattari's proposed solution is what they call (in opposition to psychoanalysis) *schizoanalysis*. In their view, deterritorialization from the oedipal subject is just what we need to get beyond the impasse of capitalism and move on to a more joyful and life-affirming humanity. The unconscious, rather than expressing secrets concerning incestuous desire for the mother and the desire to replace the father, is a factory wanting to make things happen. De-oedipalization would destroy the notion of the unconscious as a theater always expressing the futile yearning to fill in its insatiable lack and release a nonlacking desire able to make new connections with the world. They posit the nomadic or schizo subject as a subject able to maintain a relatively stable form of human subjectivity without oedipal constraints on desiring production or the molecular flows that lead to transformation of the social field and they proffer schizoanalysis as a strategy for fostering such subjects.

From a psychoanalytic perspective, immersion in a world of partial objects where corporeal fluxes connect (or do not connect) in immanently unfolding flows with surrounding flows where neither self or other, subject or object, are points of reference is a psychotic nightmare. Deleuze and Guattari present us with the provocative possibility that desire does not have to be about what a personal self wants, but could be about connecting with the world, making things happen, and experiencing what happens in ways that defy subject–object and self–other dichotomies. Self–other dichotomies obscure the physiological, social, and cultural flows I share with others; I live at the same speed as other organisms constituted by configurations of processes similar to my own (as I discover in the assemblages I make with others) and the enunciative and machinic assemblages that condition my individual speech and actions are often the same as theirs. On Deleuze and Guattari's view, a personal self or identity as a totalized point of origin to which to refer all desire operates as a kind of stranglehold on the body and the capacities it could unfold as well as the assemblages into which it could enter. By referring my desires to a sexed self with a gender and a sexuality computed according to the faciality machines, I block off intensification of other tendencies insisting in me—tendencies concerning sense experience and perception as well as emotions and beliefs—that could be extended into new ways of living my subjectivity and new ways of connecting with my world including the other subjects within it.

The famous case of John/Joan (who I henceforth call by his real name when living as the sex he ultimately chose, David) is a sad example of how difficult it can be to live one's humanity in a social formation that demands a recognizable identity sorted through the faciality machines.[5] When a botched circumcision led to an anomaly in organic sex (David's penis was damaged beyond repair), a choice was made to try and repress the anomalous range of continuous variation in human organisms he manifested by surgically altering him, designating him as female, and concealing from him his initial status as male. Judith Butler's rendition of his story brings out the violence to which the people trying to deal with his situation subjected him (Butler 2004). Although as he grew older he refused to comply, he was submitted to practices designed to remake him organically so that he would fit certain categories (surgery and hormone therapy), as well as subjectively so that he would identify in particular ways (socialization that encouraged him to engage in "feminine" behavior such as cooking and playing with dolls and interviews that encouraged him to have "feminine" desires).[6]

From a Deleuze–Guattarian perspective, there was no true self attached to either David's "real" sex (his clearly male body as it existed before the accident) or his gender identity as it had been promoted through subjectification procedures designed to create a female gender identity (being identified and treated as a girl, being subjected to interviews designed to elicit "female" desires, etc.). David's flow of individuation involved a convergence of physiological, semiotic, and subjectifying forces to which he—as a self-organizing process of subjectivity needing to navigate the practices of his social location—had to respond in order to solve the problem of living a life. Although David did achieve his desire to marry and have a family, his life was, by all accounts, difficult, and he committed suicide at the age of thirty-eight. It is impossible to know why he made the choice to end his life, but one can imagine how painful dissonance between one's lived experience in all the molecular complexity of one's lived orientation and the molar subject positions designating one's identity in a way that demands the erasure of such complexity can become. His situation was anomalous in a way that could not be easily cancelled out; he simply was neither male or female in the same way as his peers, given physiological anomalies as well as anomalies in his socialization.

Susan Stryker, a male-to-female transsexual who refuses assimilating explanations of her actions (such as the explanation that she was "really" a woman who simply needed to change her body to fit her true identity) is a happier example of how anomalous gender identity can play out in that she is able to intensify and extend her capacities to affect and be affected by the world in ways that challenge the binaries of the faciality machines. She speaks out publicly about her situation and she is a respected member of a transgender community that challenges binary designations of sexed and gendered identity. She thus defies erasure of the range of continuous variation manifest in her particular actualization of humanity despite her deviance from the norm. She gives a provocative challenge to those who would denounce her and her choices (in a performance piece presented in, as she puts it, "genderfuck drag" at an interdisciplinary, academic conference)[7]:

> I find no shame . . . in acknowledging my egalitarian relationship with nonhuman material Being; everything emerges from the same matrix of possibilities. . . . [T]he Nature you bedevil me with is a lie. Do not trust it to protect you from what I represent, for

it is a fabrication that cloaks the groundlessness of the privilege
you seek to maintain for yourself at my expense. You are as
constructed as me; the same anarchic Womb has birthed us both.
(Stryker 1994, 240–41)

In different ways, David and Stryker both resist the faciality machines
that would recuperate their inassimilable differences to binary categories of
designation and interpellation. If David had difficulties identifying with the
categories assigned him (when he was forced to identify as a girl despite his
lived dissonance with that designation) as well as the categories he finally
chose (by choosing to identify as male on discovering some of what had been
hidden from him about the story of his life), it was not because he wanted
to challenge traditional notions of sex and gender. What he wanted was to
live a meaningful life. What his story shows, perhaps, is how important a
sense of self that coheres with one's lived orientations is to making one's
life meaningful and therefore livable. We want to connect with the world,
affect and be affected, in ways that resonate with a self-understanding and
life narrative that makes sense to us, whether or not that sense of self is
conventional or dissonant. In Deleuze and Guattari's terms, we might say
that subjects need to extend not only their embodied capacities to make
things happen, but also their psychic, cognitive, and emotional capacities
to make sense of how they fit into larger wholes. David's lived experience
was too dissonant for a number of reasons (anatomical, hormonal, cultural,
familial) to easily fit into social patterns of making sense—ways of speaking,
interpreting, and behaving available to him through collective practices of
the social field dictating intelligible behavior and interpretations—making it
difficult for him to feel worthy as a human being.

Linda Alcoff, in an insightful essay on identity, argues that we need to
conceive identity as more than a category. Identity entails an interpretative
horizon that "should be understood not simply as a set of beliefs but as
a complex (meaning internally heterogeneous) set of presuppositions and
perceptual orientations, some of which are manifest as a kind of tacit
presence in the body" (Alcoff 2006b, 113). She cites George Lakoff and
Mark Johnson's work demonstrating that the concepts we use in everyday
life emerge from "largely unconscious embodied conceptual systems" (ibid.).
And she draws from the phenomenological descriptions of Maurice Merleau-
Ponty, Simone de Beauvoir, Sandra Bartky, and Iris Young to indicate how
a lived orientation of the body in the world constitutes a kind of implicit
knowledge. In Alcoff's account, identity is an orientation to the world lived
in the gestures, movements, and actions of the body at a nonconscious level
as well as in the presuppositions, assumptions, and beliefs of a linguistic
orientation. Both together comprise an interpretative horizon that grounds a

subject in a perspective that is lived as her own. Social identity is not simply the categories into which one fits, but an interpretative horizon shared with certain others that affects what and how one perceives. These identities are experienced in terms of the imbrications of social flows that converge in the various assemblages through which day-to-day life is lived rather than the abstract categories of identity to which people are often reduced. Identity is thus not necessarily something that is inflicted on one by others; it is an orientation experienced as one's own that emerges through participation in collective patterns of corporeal and symbolic activity. This is why claiming an identity through a rewriting of dominant history can be so important. In articulating and asserting such an identity, a perspective grounded in patterns of collective living experienced by a minoritarian group is brought into conscious awareness and made the basis for an alternative epistemological claim to that of the dominant culture about the nature of social reality. "Real" identity is thus, according to Alcoff, experienced as an orientation grounded in often nonconscious patterns of body, mind, and speech so habitual that they can appear (if they appear at all) to be inevitable or natural.

Although Alcoff does not advocate a Deleuze–Guattarian approach to identity, her conception of identity as an orientation derived through patterns of living shared with others resonates with Deleuze and Guattari's conception of subjectivity in ways that suggest more flexible understandings of both the productive as well as the constraining effects of claiming specific identities. What Alcoff calls "real" identity is, from a Deleuze–Guattarian perspective, the perceptual, cognitive, affective, and embodied orientations of a subject sustained through the habitual patterns of physiological, social, and cultural processes that constitute one as an embodied human subject. Orientations constituted and sustained through organic processes experienced in imbrication with the semiotic and corporeal signifying and subjectifying processes of human living inform how one experiences the world. If one's corporeal and/or psychic anomalies are such that one cannot take up positions with which one can identify without dissonance, then one will experience a sense of discomfort, a sense of not being at home in the world. This discomfort will deepen if dissonance results in derogatory descriptions or exclusion. Subjects marked in terms of their divergence from the majoritarian norm are designated as somehow less entitled to other forms of social power. Unless one can find alternatives, practices available to others as an extension of their capacities into action in the world (of a more or less powerful sort) will block one's lines of becoming and decrease one's power. Individual and collective orientations suffer damaging marginalization and uncomfortable dissonance when they are subjected to faciality machines in ways that mark their divergence from the majoritarian norm and block potential capacities for affecting and being affected from unfolding.

When the lived orientations Alcoff describes as "real" identity are extended and elaborated in the minoritarian form of, for example, a feminist identity or an antiracist identity, identity becomes a form of self-naming that extends some of the lines of flight always insisting in any subject in its divergence from the majoritarian subject. The faciality machines that designate either/or identity positions through prevalent ways of speaking and patterns of activity that resonate with the majoritarian subject attempt to cancel out the corporeal and conceptual fluxes that would lead human subjects in their becoming to resist the dominant patterns of signification and subjectification: You are a man *or* a woman, you are black *or* white. Resistant identities are identities in process—they create new identities rooted in fluxes of living that continually vary from the dominant norm, refusing to let those variations be assimilated to binary categories or their implicit tendencies blocked from unfolding new ways of living.

Phenomenological descriptions of lived experience have the great benefit of bringing some of these habits into conscious awareness, rendering the grounding of some of our assumptions and beliefs more visible, and opening up alternative orientations (whether or not we choose to pursue them) in the process. When the experiences thus described are those of dissonant subjects like David or Stryker, they have the additional benefit of showing us some of the continuous range of variation in human living already in existence in defiance of the binary faciality machines organized around a majoritarian norm. For example, Sarah Ahmed presents a phenomenological account of the lived experience of being queer that vividly illustrates how identity as orientation is lived not simply at the discursive or cognitive level, but at the level of orientations of the body and perceptual and corporeal practices of which we are mostly unaware. She describes sitting at her habitual seat at the kitchen table of her childhood home each morning and evening as a family ritual where "inhabiting the family is about taking up a place already given" (Ahmed 2006, 559). The very act of sitting at the table thus implies acquiescence to an embodied orientation that may never be brought into conscious awareness. A fondue set stands on the sideboard in the dining room (a "cold and dark" room used for more formal occasions). "I do not ever remember using that set. But it is an object that matters, somehow. It was a wedding gift" (ibid.). Of the photographs covering the walls the "wedding photograph has the prime position" (ibid.).

> Everywhere I turn, even in the failure of memory, reminds
> me how the family home puts objects on display that measure
> sociality in terms of the heterosexual gift. That these objects are
> on display, that they make visible a fantasy of a good life, depends
> on returning such a direction with a "yes," or even with gestures

of love, or witnessing these objects as one's own field of preferred intimacy. Such objects do not simply record or transmit a life; they demand a return. (ibid.)

Ahmed argues that a queer orientation entails shifting the very way one's body extends the space of the social. A conventional family home provides a background of objects that directs one's gaze toward the heterosexual couple as a point along a family line. "There is pressure to inherit this line, a pressure that can speak the language of love, happiness, and care, which pushes the child along specific paths" (560). A shift in sexual orientation precipitates not simply a shift in the sex of one's object choice, but a shift in one's orientations toward everyday objects that entails a "reinhabiting" of one's body.

> [I]t affects what we can do, where we can go, how we are perceived, and so on. These differences in how one directs desire, as well as how one is faced by others, can move us and hence affect even the most deeply ingrained patterns of relating to others. (563)

Identity entails territorialization of perception and feeling. But, as we know, territorialization is necessary to live. Without the refrains of habitual patterns of living, we could not create the houses that protect us from dissolution in chaotic flux. Just as mutant flows of matter settled into the refrains that allowed our organic existence, so do refrains of behavior and social meaning allow our psychic survival as conscious selves. Despite Deleuze and Guattari's emphasis on a schizo or nomadic subject who can de-oedipalize, we do not want to abandon the refrains that result in psychic identity. What Alcoff and Ahmed's characterizations of identity as lived orientation show us is that identity designations may be more or less dissonant with the physiological, affective, and cognitive perspectives emerging from our concrete locations, and that reworking those designations can have profound effects on our embodied orientations as well as our propositional beliefs.[8] What a Deleuze–Guattarian perspective can allow is a different way of thinking about identity. In their view, the identity designations of faciality machines reinforce a form of subjectivity conducive to captialism's proliferation, while the subject is an assemblage of organic, signifying, and subjectifying forces replete with molecular fluxes that escape dominant patterns as well as virtual tendencies that could be intensified into lines of flight. If we consider minoritarian identity designations as representations of a specific duration of being-a-self where that state of being was in relative equilibrium, then we could say that the assertion of such representations could constitute plateaus from which new ways of being could emerge; naming the lived orientation of a given duration actualizes some nuances of meaning rather than others, thus shifting the content of words and bodies in ways that could proliferate productive lines of flight. The problem comes not in attributing particular words to a moment in being-human, but rather in reducing a dynamic unfolding of individuation to static representations, stripping the creative resources of intensive becoming in the process.

For Deleuze and Guattari, it would be a tragedy for the present opportunity in human-becoming to be reduced to the homogenizing effects of a process of globalization that reterritorializes onto the oedipal subject of lack whose insatiable hunger can only be fed through consumerism. From their perspective, the oedipal subject is a retrenchment of the vestiges of a culturally informed self. Capitalism is going to destabilize identity in any event. The dualism machines that sort people into binary categories of either this sex or that, this race or that, this religious affiliation or that, and so forth, arrived on the scene relatively recently (ATP 210). Furthermore, the notion of a personal identity that resonates all one's social identities in a unified self with one overarching desire is also relatively recent. The notion that to be a social subject at all we have to have a personal self who is totalized in keeping with the one desire that will satisfy her (i.e., her desiring production will cohere around the central focus of wanting to fill in her lack) is a notion attached to an inherently deterritorializing social formation that relies on individual subjects to set the brakes on social change. Although we may think that we are presented with the choice between either the oedipalized subject who identifies with one of two sexes or the psychosis of a subject dissolved in the molecular flows of incoherent desiring, Deleuze and Guattari insist that there are other forms subjectivity can take already here with us. From a feminist perspective, their story presents an interesting perspective on the role and place of binary sexual difference (already opened up within feminism in the lived experiments and theoretical accounts challenging traditional ways of understanding binary conceptions of sex and gender) as well as its imbrications with other aspects of personal identity and social positioning. Additionally, it opens up the question of the role and place of personal identity itself.

Although feminism rightly has been concerned with supporting rather than undermining personal identity because the latter can be so empowering when it comes to claiming one's humanity, identity politics also has created conundrums for feminism that have yet to be fully resolved. The assertion of personal identity has been an important strategy in the toolbox of feminism as well as other movements invested in progressive social change; identity politics can be personally empowering as well as politically galvanizing. Deleuze and Guattari can be read as advocating a post-identarian form of politics. That is one of the appeals of their work for those frustrated by the stultifying and even annihilating effects identity politics can have when it engages the binary logic of its own form of the faciality machines by excluding those who fail to conform to the identity it represents. But despite Deleuze and Guattari's wariness of and even distaste for personal identity, they are also quite clear that destratification must be engaged with caution and at one's own risk. That is, shifting from contemporary corporeal and semiotic patterns of being-human must be done slowly enough to insure the maintenance of viable and ongoing forms of self-organizing becoming. Despite, then, their reluctance to embrace personal identity, my reading of their work alongside feminist work on identity (as well as other work being done along these lines) suggests a way of rethinking identity as a practice of thinking, reading, and proclaiming an orientation shared with specific others that intensifies empowering tendencies of the concrete situations in which we find ourselves rather than as the labeling of a static self.

Deleuze and Guattari's characterization of subjectivity posits a subject who emerges from collective physiological and social processes as an individual process in its own right by sustaining habitual patterns distinguishing it as an individual from other processes around it. As a specific formation of physiological, social, and linguistic matter with actualized capacities—replete with hidden potential and tendencies structured by virtualities that are part of the wider nonhuman as well as human field conditioning its becoming—the subject is able to affect as well as be affected by what is around it. But its separation is always provisional, its form always on the verge of differentiating into something else, and the actualization of its capacities always dependent on the actualities and intensities that it is and with which it comes into contact. Naming one's identity at a particular time and place is one form that the actualization of specific capacities can take.

Nomadic subjects emerge from collective patterns of living with the configuration of social and nonhuman forces unique to the becoming of specific processes of individuation. The individuation of such subjects cannot be represented. It emerges as a lived orientation constituting one's perceptions, thoughts, emotions, and perspectives through the territorializations of unique individuations and communities grounded in the material reality of shared patterns of living. Some orientation with respect to the identity designations of mainstream social practices is necessary for subjectivity. One's "personal" identity can be thought in terms of the "molar" designations of the faciality machines that enable negotiation of dominant social systems of meaning or in terms of lived orientations too subtle to be captured through such designations, but which one could choose to assert by naming them. Heightened awareness of converging flows and the habitual patterns that orient one along with a sense of one's own location and places to intervene in order to affect individual and collective forms of self-production could allow resolution of the dissonance often arising between the two forms of identity as well as enable collective compositions that enhance mutually joyful becoming.

Nomadic subjectivity as an alternative to oedipal subjectivity invites us to engage in a dynamic process of self-naming rather than reduce ourselves to static self-representations. Identity designations are representations that do not capture the nuances of lived orientations and can block lines of flight by putting people in opposition with one another despite the orientations they share. Drifting from the identity designations of faciality machines in order to experiment with joyful connections entails relinquishing some of the control derived through representational intelligence with its penchant for categorization in order to trust the affective guidance of intuitive insight into processes of becoming. Becoming more aware of how one's subjectivity is produced allows one to participate more actively in one's self-production, develop skillful ways to synchronize becoming with others, and deterritorialize from identity designations in order to unfold new solutions to the problems life poses. Naming lived orientations in defiance of the identity designations of faciality machines is one way among others of putting alternative meanings into play. Flexible living entails individual deterritorialization from personal identity as well as collective deterritorializations from majoritarian subjectivity. A politics influenced by Deleuze and Guattari would investigate different durations, the mutually reinforcing reference points of the faciality machines among those durations, and the places where intensification of virtual tendencies might unfold new answers to how to live together.

Deleuze and Guattari's conception of human subjectivity emphasizes its continuity with the inhuman force of creative life. This emphasis fosters working with rather than against the differentiating forces of life of which we are a part. This ontology conceives individual human beings as singular individuals who more or less diverge from the flows of life currently sustaining themselves in the recognizably human forms with which we are familiar. The question of one's humanity thus shifts from that of measuring up to an essential form of humanity (with respect to which many are found wanting) to the question of what diverging flows of humanity we want to foster in the inevitably diverging and differentiating flux of human life. Shifting the question in this way has practical impact on identity questions key to feminist thought. Women, as well as others who are "other" to the paradigmatic subject of contemporary culture, have been denigrated for somehow failing to measure up to an ideal norm of what it means to be human. But such a norm assumes an ontology where the form one's humanity takes may well count as a deviation. One strategy of feminism, understandably enough, has been to contest what that essence is in order to make room for women. Shifting to an ontology of becoming suggests a different kind of strategy. If what it means to be human is not fixed, if human becoming entails creative evolution—if what it means to be human consists in the specific forms humanity actually takes and could unfold rather than a human essence that is then instantiated more or less well—then what feminists need to do is map where we are in order to find the best places to intervene and foster the human forms we would most like to support. The question then becomes not who we have always been and always will be, but how to intervene in the processes resulting in subjects and identities in order to foster our own becomings. Maps can help us to see how identity designations are mutually reinforcing and the critical points from which lines of flight could be productively unfolded. An identity politics that takes itself to be stabilizing the productive effects of naming shared orientations, rather than staking out territory it must defend at all costs, is one way such a line of flight could emerge.

Given the crucial structural role of sexual difference in oedipalization and given the importance of oedipalization to orienting personal identity in terms of the faciality machines supporting the majoritarian subject, experimentation with the molecular flows of gender identity entails a critical point for intensifying tendencies that might deterritorialize us from other forms of binary identifications that privilege the majoritarian subject at the expense of minoritarian becoming. Deleuze and Guattari's genealogy of subjectivity suggests that subjects of territorial and despotic social formations understood who they were through networks of relations negotiated in concrete interactions that were directly plugged into the varied flows of specific durations. Deleuze and Guattari claim that the images through which we experience ourselves are relentlessly oedipal and familial despite the social investments that familial investments conceal. Being a woman or a man, in such a situation, carries more weight and of a more mysterious kind than in a situation like that of, for example, Kamahasanyi whose cure for what ailed him was premised on directly reworking a wide range of social investments in a collective setting (see chapter 2). Furthermore, facialization, by reinforcing oedipalized desiring production, alienates subjects from their lived orientations by refusing the inchoate intensities and affects of embodied living uptake in more creative forms of desiring production.

Looking at subjectivity in this way allows us to see how a subject can be individuated and sustained without needing to be set into opposition with what surrounds it. The modern subject is, according to this account, a momentary result of a continual unfolding that has no telos and will never reach some final end. We can give a genealogical account of this subject as it emerges from the becoming of life, but of course, because all perspectives entail some sort of selection, this account will be as inflected by the selections we make in keeping with present needs as well as creative insights, as any other selection. From a Deleuze–Nietzschean standpoint, the selections of an active (as opposed to reactive) will to power are those that extend the forces involved to their limit rather than separating them from what they can do. From a Deleuze–Spinozist perspective, an active joy premised on knowledge of how to best compose myself with my world requires experimentation attuned to collective becomings.[9] On this view, the kind of narrative we want to give of humanity is not one that fosters territorialization onto the human beings we have already become, but rather one that will bring out implicit tendencies and connections not yet made or unfolded in order to see what we could yet become. By giving a narrative of human existence that emphasizes its continuity with the nonhuman force of creative life, Deleuze and Guattari bring out aspects of life that we have not yet explored in the context of a viewpoint that fosters working with rather than against the differentiating forces that entail human and self transformation as well as transformations of life itself.

On my reading of Deleuze and Guattari, identifications cannot be determined in advance to be good or bad, repressive or liberating. What matters is how those identifications come together with other forces. From the viewpoint of a specific human subject struggling to sustain herself in human living, forces can come together in a way that provides joyous enhancement and unfolding of the capacities of one's current body, or in ways that shut down and block off that unfolding. Thus, identifications can be either joyous or misery inducing. The danger of identity politics from this perspective is not that it is automatically bad or detrimental for a specific subject (be it individual or collective) to make the identifications for which a given identity politics calls, although it could be, but that molar politics can so easily become fascist in nature. This is why mapping is so important. What matters is attunement to the intensities of the present and a willingness to unfold toward the new. Given the risks involved in nomadic living, identity as an act of self-naming may provide a stabilizing point of reference for further lines of flight, but whether it is the latter rather than a descent into a black hole that blocks one's exits or separates others from what they can do, can only be evaluated through specific experiments in living. Even in those cases where naming a lived orientation intensifies tendencies in ways that actualize the power to affect and be affected in productive ways, such naming can only unfold as one force among others. Thus, if and when proclaiming particular identities can have productive effects could only be determined through attunement to the actualities and incipient tendencies of given durations; naming one's identity is a practice that like any other needs to be skillfully engaged in order to foster one's own flourishing as well as the flourishing of the assemblages of which one forms a part.

Deleuze and Guattari's narrative suggests that the binary categorizations of the abstract machine of faciality recognizes and resonates only a small range of the variegated differences among subjects. It furthermore suggests that those differences support a structuring of subjectivity where those falling into one of two binary categories is considered farther from the majoritarian subject, and therefore less human or less adequate than those falling into the other category. Subjects deemed closer to the normative majoritarian subject are given more freedom to engage in exercising their birthright as living creatures to unfold their capacities. Deleuze and Guattari's advocacy of schizoanalysis as a practice designed to extend the unraveling of subjectivity precipitated and then reterritorialized by capitalism onto the paranoid subjects of modernity, is a practice designed to unravel the binaries of sex and gender along with other binaries. This could move us to new, less oppressive forms of subjectivity.

Feminism, as feminists know, is in an odd position with respect to sex and gender. At the same time that it wants to move society past oppressive sex and gender binaries, its existence is premised on those binaries. Dissolving or moving beyond sex and gender binaries would dissolve feminism's object of analysis and thereby dissolve feminism itself. While we may at some point need to deal with the loss of our demise as feminists (as Wendy Brown points out [Brown 2005, 98–115]), we are by no means at that point. Sex and gender are still fully operative as categories of designation and interpellation in just about every social practice one can imagine, as well as in the orientations lived by embodied subjects. Although we need to exercise some caution if we are not to simply reinforce such categories, they are still critical points of intervention in our contemporary and increasingly globalizing cultures. Capitalism fosters deterritorialization with individual subjects acting as the limit point; as long as subjects stay interchangeably the same (as far as the axioms of capitalism are concerned), capitalism can continue to transform the world and yet maintain itself in the process. Gender identity is a crucial fault-line in oedipalization and oedipalization is a structuring of subjectivity that discourages creative solutions to contemporary problems that entail collective becoming-other. Naming the meanings this fault-line generates in various locations—as long as we do not turn those names into labels that thwart further unfoldings—is one way (among others) of moving beyond the constricting binaries of the faciality machines.

Feminism, as a theoretical and pragmatic process, can intuit ways of living our sex and gender that are more affirming of the continuous range of variation in being sexed and gendered becoming-human entails. By mapping where we are and finding lines of flight from majoritarian subjectivity that can extend our capacities in ways that synchronize with others, feminists, along with other forms of minoritarian and schizo becoming, can promote a joyfully collective and open-ended process of becoming-human.

Chapter 4

Bodies, Time, and Intuition

In Deleuze and Guattari's view, one's existence as a subject with an embodied orientation and unique perspective is constituted through the habitual refrains that sustain one's embodied and psychic existence. Like any self-sustaining system, subjectivity maintains its duration through the extension of its own patterns of being. Shifts in these patterns will not plunge the subject into the anarchic chaos of psychosis or complete nihilism unless the shifts are so radical that the ability to self-sustain is damaged. The designated identities of faciality machines are too general to capture nuances in orientation. To be the subject defined through the faciality machines of multiple practices of social living (the subject who can walk into the "right" restroom and has the physical capacities to make use of the facilities, the subject who has the right kind of address and phone number to list on an application), a range of continuous variations in human living (along with the lines of flight they could precipitate) must be cancelled out. Feminism is one of many abstract machines that pursue lines of continuous variation diverging from the majoritarian subject. The multiple and heterogeneous experiments in minoritarian subjectivity it fosters, along with other abstract machines (constituted by various forms of identity politics, as well as aesthetic, social, and political experiments of other kinds), often push toward the threshold limit of another kind of subjectivity—one not organized via oppositional categories of identity with respect to a "nonlacking" majoritarian subject but rather in terms of differences that exceed the binary identities of the faciality machines. Any form of dissonance among one's identities and lived orientations can lead to friction with faciality machines. Pursuing gender as a fault line of oppositional, either/or identities is one line of flight from orienting one's own identity with respect to a subject vis-à-vis with which one is always lacking.

In Deleuze and Guattari's view, we cannot open up new ways of being human except by extending new potentials and tendencies already insisting within the actualized forms we currently are within the situations in which we currently exist. Deterritorializing from where we are can take as many forms as there are potentials in actual bodies and situations waiting to be further developed and extended. The process of deterritorialization Deleuze and Guattari advocate in *Anti-Oedipus* and *A Thousand Plateaus* is one of reconceiving desire as productive rather than lacking, and deterritorializing from modern forms of subjectivity oriented around the majoritarian subject. This means, ultimately, thwarting the binary social machines that organize identity in terms of either/or categories and experimenting with productive forms of desire. The subject who anticipates action based on a representable image of who she is—an ego ideal she can project—is acting on the basis of an identity she would like to personify as her own. Deleuze and Guattari advocate abandoning identity-based desire in order to pursue making connections that are immanent to the life unfolding around and through one. This requires intuitive insight into the collective machinic and enunciative assemblages that produce shared and conflicting orientations and identities in the specific configurations they take for particular groups and individuals. Such insight can reveal critical points where intensification of previously unactualized tendencies could lead to empowering extensions of one's capacities compatible with the joyous living of others. Intuitive insight involves attunement with fleeting intensities and affects in sensation and thought, as well as attention to the multiple durations with which one is connected and a suspension of automatic reactions that can allow a creative response more in keeping with the specificity of the present to emerge. This entails unpredictable transformations in one's subjectivity, rendering static notions of personal identity problematic.

A nomadic alternative to the oedipal subject pursues corporeal and semiotic vitality. Rather than fantasizing objects that once acquired would resolve the dissonance she experiences, she pursues the connections she could make to foster revitalized circulations of desire. Rather than comparing herself to an internalized ideal ego who transcends her present circumstances, she seeks moments of equilibrium that allow her free-flowing circulation of sensation and meaning in open attunement to her surroundings. Such moments constitute plateaus where the habitual patterns distinguishing one's process of individuation are suspended, creating a kind of oneness of self and surroundings in open attunement to the intensities inflecting a uniquely configured present. It is such a moment that can provide the revitalizing impetus for the new lines of flight that can solve present problems. Rather than a static self who pursues an object that fits her current fantasy of what she lacks, such a nomadic subject's lines of flight would entail the mutual becoming of self and world with new solutions to extending one's power to affect and be affected in synchrony with the durations of which she is a part. For a feminist, the various projects actualizing an abstract machine of feminism entail the invention of "skewed" perspectives that reach beyond the perspective of one's personal—and even human—self, prompting new ways of being feminist and being human.

Deleuze and Guattari's ontology and approach evoke a rich array of resources that we often have overlooked. Constraining our theory and practice to the "realistic" parameters of the already done is from their view to stay stuck in a treadmill of our own making. To follow the dictates of a scientific way of thinking in our theorizing or to expect our theorizing to be able to predict results is from their view to deny ourselves a way of approaching the chaos of the virtual that could open new vistas in experimentation. To relegate art to the realm of the fantastical or unreal is equally shortsighted. To contain our experiments in living to arbitrarily designated restraints is to overlook the full range of options available to us and enclose us in depressive boxes where change seems impossible. Seeing our change as part of the ongoing creation of life—a creative becoming that is inevitable and of which we are always a part—opens up our thinking and our practice to a variegated range of connections not yet made that are waiting to be made, and invites our joyful participation in that creation. Bringing out the full range of human creativity by perceiving our experiments as responses to problems of the various topographies of the social field and then finding the links among those experiments that will induce further lines of flight will enhance the circulation of creative energy in mutual encounters of becoming.

Intensive Plateaus

As seen in previous chapters, the organism is a repeating pattern of matter that has achieved a distinctive speed relative to the flows from which it emerges that gives it a certain degree of autonomy. Deleuze and Guattari say that the stratum of the organism is a stratum on what they call the body without organs (abbreviated in *A Thousand Plateaus* as the BwO; ATP 159). "The organism is . . . a phenomenon of accumulation, coagulation, and sedimentation that, in order to extract useful labor from the BwO, imposes upon it forms, functions, bonds, dominant and hierarchized organizations, organized transcendences" (ibid.). Although there can be many different kinds of bodies without organs, with respect to the perspective I take here of an individual human being, it is stratified into the organism, significance, and subjectification of human subjectivity. It swings between the actual forms it manifests in keeping with the organizing forces of the physicochemical and social fields and the alternate paths of actualization to which the subject could open. It thus evokes the transcendental field of the virtual that is the condition of the body and mind of which one is consciously aware at any given moment. Although one may (and probably will) unfold habitual patterns in perceiving, speaking, interpreting, and behaving, insisting in every perception, thought, and action are virtual tendencies that could unfold into perceptions, actions, and thoughts completely out of keeping with the habitual patterns of a human subject with a personal identity organized with respect to the majoritarian subject. The body without organs constitutes a moment of suspension in which new patterns, actualizing previously implicit tendencies, can unfold.

Deleuze and Guattari's ontology suggests a dynamic conception of the body that challenges not only fixed idealizations of a "normal" human body, but fixed parameters for what can or should count as the lived experience of embodied human beings. Representations of those bodies reduce them to specific slices of the actual, thus stripping them of the dynamic intensities that always accompany what actualizes in the present. Deleuze and Guattari develop a vocabulary that attempts to think bodies in movement. Terms like *territorialization, deterritorialization, becoming, intensities,* and *affects,* evoke actual bodies and consciousness as the effects of always differentiating forces. Their notion of constructing a body without organs promotes a way of thinking the body more present to the virtual unfoldings through which the body and its experiences actualize. This, in turn, opens an interval from which new responses can emerge between what affects the body and reactive responses to stimuli. For feminists interested in attending to as well as alleviating the suffering caused by sexism and other forms of oppression, this strategy entails not only attending to the lived experience of marginalized subjects, but also opening up, through this attention, new possibilities in living. For those interested in mapping the social, political, and economic flows of multiple durations in order to work toward a global community that is more just in a variety of ways, grounding such mapping in an awareness of the open-ended nature of our embodied perspectives can help us be more creative in our collective solutions.

What Deleuze and Guattari call constructing a body without organs entails "deterritorialization" from the habitual patterns that make a process of individuation (such as a human subject) an entity of a specific kind. A human subject of modern capitalist society living at the juncture of three strata including the organic stratum (with the repeated patterns of activity that sustain the organism), the stratum of signification (with the repeated refrains of socially viable systems of meaning), and the stratum of subjectification (with the habitual refrains through which subjects become subjects) makes sense of her lived experience as the lived experience of a particular subject with a body and a particular location on a social field of subject positions. This entails having meaningful perceptions and emotions—ones that "make sense" for the kind of subject she is. Deleuze and Guattari's emphasis on the territorialized nature of perception and emotion allows them to conceive a deterritorialized perception and emotion (the percepts and affects artists are able to compose as well as the deterritorialized experiences of the nomadic subject). In their view, perceptions, habitual gestures, bodily orientations in space, and emotional responses are all as much the effects of repeating patterns of activity as the physiological, organic, and social processes that inform a specific subject's process of individuation.

Instead of playing out our familiar habits and routines with the opinions and familiar thoughts and perceptions with which they are connected, we can attend to aspects of our experience that are there if we only pay attention to them, but that defy our expectations. Attending to the nuances of our perceptions, actions, and thoughts, can allow us to extract virtual tendencies implicit in even the most mundane of experiences in order to make new connections that break with routine and open up new perceptions, new thoughts, and new ways of behaving. Mapping our location with respect to the global, political, and social flows of varying durations allows us to attend more closely to the intensities informing our present. When we experiment with such tendencies we can create lines of flight that allow us to unblock flows trapped in patterns that have become mutually reinforcing to the point of rigidity, and come up with new, more flexible, solutions to the problems of living.

A philosophical perspective like phenomenology that invokes lived experience often has been a point of departure in feminist theory from which to contest accepted assumptions about who women are. From the 1970s slogan that "the personal is the political" to feminist standpoint epistemology and care ethics, feminists have appealed to the practical knowledge of day-to-day living to critique mainstream representations of women, rationality, and what it means to be human. Deleuze and Guattari, however, object to maintaining our conception of the possibilities of life within the constraints of lived experience and want to challenge making representable aspects of the present the basis for how we conceive the future. Although phenomenological descriptions of lived experience can have a liberating effect insofar as it reveals the nonconscious habits that inform subjectivity, especially when that experience is not the "normal" experience of mainstream subjects, it also can have a limiting effect by posing possibilities in terms of what has already been experienced rather than in terms of the intensive force of an actualized present always pushing toward further unfolding. Sense perception itself, on this view, can be constrained within the limits of conceivable perceptions—perceptual clichés—or opened up to the imperceptible. Since consciousness, for Deleuze and Guattari, is the emergent effect of syntheses and patterns of organization beneath the threshold of conscious awareness, consciousness could emerge otherwise; a different set of selections, a different organization, a different set of actualized relations from among the virtual tendencies implicit in a specific state of affairs, could have emerged in the consciousness of a given situation. To reduce what could be, then, to the patterns of lived experience as it has already actualized, is to reduce an open-ended future to what has already occurred.

Our patterns of subjectivity tend to self-replicate—our perceptions, thinking, speech, and action tend to settle into the familiar grooves that allow us to recognize ourselves and feel at home in our world. But precisely because feminists have often been minoritarian subjects who for one reason or another feel less than at home in the world, we are sensitive to challenges to whatever form our specific patterns of being-feminist may take. If I am faced with a transsexual's rage at my resistance to including her under the designation of "woman," do I simply dismiss it by labeling her a freak and exclude the flows of emotion, thought, and perception with which her presence confronts me—flows that intensify virtual tendencies already insisting in my own unfolding in a way that make me uncomfortable? Or do I allow her presence to produce a moment of shock where my habitual patterns of thought, emotional response, and perception are suspended, leaving me, at least for that moment of shock, capable of completely novel responses and actions? When I am confronted by another feminist, in the course of mapping larger social or global flows, with the unintentionally racist or parochial cast of my feminist theorizing, do I dismiss such challenges as irrelevant or attempt to assimilate them into already delineated paths of thinking? Or do I allow my flows of thought to suspend their habitual patterns in disoriented confusion before they form new, unexpected patterns in response to their imbrication with another's way of thinking? Deleuze and Guattari's notion of constructing a body without organs entails opening up to the singularities of a given duration rather than reverting to automatic responses.

Constructing a body without organs entails a notion of the body that fosters an open-ended, intuitive awareness of the durational whole. This opens up the "commonsense" representational perception of spatialized time to an intuitive perception more sensitive to durational or intensive time, and thus widens the interval between perception and action. Constructing a body without organs thus amounts to a way of making perceptions, emotions, and thought less reactive and more active. Insofar as our perceptions are those that "make sense" for a particular kind of subject, they are reduced to perceptual clichés that limit our ability to creatively explore our options in the present. Repeating patterns of response that have been successful in the past allows us to efficiently take care of our needs. Intuiting the intensities of the present entails looking beyond perceptual and conceptual clichés in order to experiment with tendencies we might have otherwise overlooked. This allows us to creatively respond to situations in all their complexity rather than assimilating them to past situations.

Deleuze and Guattari invite the reader to activate the concept of constructing a body without organs in her own thinking in a way that widens the gap between perception and action beyond both instinctual and intelligent living to the more intuitive living of the nomadic subject. The nomadic subject is a subject challenged by capitalism to deterritorialize from majoritarian forms of subjectivity and make the transition to a form of subjectivity more attuned to durational time. When one pursues a line of flight from conventional patterns of signification, interpretation, and subjectification where subject positions are designated by the identities of the binary faciality machines, one can individuate as a haecceity rather than a subject.[1] This entails a process of depersonalization in which one opens up to the assemblages connecting one to the world. A line of flight from conventional forms of subjectivity entails the individuation of a life (ATP 261). Such a life is "the plane of consistency or of composition of haecceities, which knows only speeds and affects" (rather than the "altogether different plane of forms, substances, and subjects") and is in the indefinite time of the event (rather than "the time of measure that situates things and persons, develops a form, and determines a subject") (ATP 262). Unlike a substance defined through its essential properties, a haecceity is an interrelationship of forces with specific tendencies in responding and functioning that stabilizes a duration with a specific speed relative to other durations. It is determined by the specific configuration of forces that constitutes it rather than the materials of which it is composed or the static form those materials take (if only for a moment in spatialized time). "You are longitude and latitude, a set of speeds and slownesses between unformed particles, a set of nonsubjectified affects. You have the individuality of a day, a season, a year, *a life* (regardless of its duration)—a climate, a wind, a fog, a swarm, a pack (regardless of its regularity). Or at least you can have it, you can reach it" (ibid.).

Conventional subjectivity is defined in terms of identities organized with respect to a "nonlacking" subject who transcends its situation and to which it is constantly compared and found lacking. Individuating as a haecceity entails being a working part of the assemblages one enters into, defining oneself not through what is a relatively static ego, but rather through the connections plugging one into the working machines of life. Such a subject is who she is through the assemblages she shares with human as well as nonhuman others. The recognizable subject defined through the faciality machines is a representable subject, whose unfolding line of becoming has been arrested (at least insofar as it is recognizable), stripping its imbrications with other durations in the forward rush of time. But this is to deny the virtual relations always insisting in the present as well as the impinging forces affecting one and the effects one exerts in return that make any boundary between self and the rest of the world no more than an illusion. " 'The thin dog is running in the road, this dog is the road,' cries Virginia Woolf. That is how we need to feel. Spatiotemporal relations, determinations, are not predicates of the thing but dimensions of multiplicities. The street is as much a part of the omnibus-horse assemblage as the Hans assemblage the becoming-horse of which it initiates. . . . The plane of consistency contains only haecceities, along intersecting lines. Forms and subjects are not of that world" (ATP 263). In the floating, nonpulsed time of the pure event, relative speeds and slownesses are articulated independently of the "chronological values that time assumes in the other modes" (ibid.). The event of the dog running down the road cannot be reduced to a series of homogeneous units of time: Its duration eludes such units and is inflected by multiple and heterogeneous durations (the dog's muscle memories of other runs, the pressure on the street's surface of vehicles and pedestrians, the passage of water through various meteorological cycles that leads to rain-falling-on-dog-running-on-the-street).

The subject attuned to the totality of time while aware of the pragmatic value of representational thought would be able to locate the latter as the contingent effect of the always differentiating force of time. The nomadic subject is thus less bound by the "human-all-too-human" *ressentiment* Nietzsche describes (Nietzsche 1966b) and more adept at locating herself in the "intensive time" of the durational whole; rather than experiencing her past in terms of moments that have irretrievably passed down a line of time, she experiences the past as inflecting the present with possibilities of affecting and being affected that could right now be unfolded. The past insists in her present becoming in the form of intensities that can be actualized in pragmatically effective ways.

A conscious notion of the body, oneself as a subject, or one's sense of self as a process replete with the unrepresentable potential of the virtual can be reduced by selective awareness to representations of that process that either regulate and confirm our expectations or open up new perceptions and forms of self-understanding. Representations can be crucial to our survival. Awareness of their contingent nature and the durational whole from which they emerge, however, can allow us to open up our awareness and our way of thinking to what troubles all representations as well as provide "realistic" grounding for creative solutions in living. Sanford Kwinter presents some vivid examples of activities that require orienting oneself in a specific duration in terms of how one's embodied existence comes together with a specific time and place rather than in terms of the stable perspective of a unified body and self in chronological time. He describes a form of rock climbing where the climber uses no tools and is thus required to live her body as "a veritable multiplicity of quasi-autonomous flows" (Kwinter 2001, 30). To maneuver the mountain face, one must attend to the concrete detail of cracks and fissures located on disparate sections of the rock in relation to various parts of one's body; while one hand negotiates a crevice, a foot must negotiate its own terms for gaining enough leverage to push the body upwards. Part of the appeal of this kind of activity may be that it demands a perceptual openness to time as duration—an experience of time in terms of the tendencies insisting within it, the tendencies within and through which one's own line of becoming can unfold. As Kwinter puts it:

> the climber's task is less to "master" in the macho, form-imposing sense than to forge a morphogenetic figure *in time*, to insert himself into a seamless, streaming space and to subsist in it by tapping or tracking the flows—indeed to stream and to become soft and fluid himself, which means momentarily to recover real time, and to engage the universe's wild and free unfolding through the morphogenetic capacities of the singularity. (31)

Although extreme sports like surfing, rock climbing without tools, or free skiing down undomesticated mountains may subvert habitual subject–object, self–other orientations in ways some find exhilarating, experiences of intensive time can take other (perhaps less stereotypically masculine) forms. Roe Sybylla, in a reading of Nietzsche's notion of Dionysian time (the time of "thus I willed it"), suggests that Babette, the protagonist of Isak Dinesen's short story, "Babette's Feast," when she spends her lottery winnings on one grand feast, despite her impoverished circumstances, is an example of someone who lives in such time (Sybylla 2004, 313). In Deleuze–Guattarian terms we could say that Babette's insistence on honoring her gift for cooking despite her come down from famous chef to war refugee is a choice to extend her becoming in terms of a durational whole rather than remain blocked off in a dispiriting present where she is separated from who she used to be (Dinesen 1993). Although she is no longer serving nobility in Paris, she still manages to create an incandescent dinner event. Experiencing the intensive time of specific durations (the duration lived on a mountain face or the duration of cooking the best meal one can given one's circumstances) fosters intuitive awareness of the creative possibilities unique to those durations with their specific convergence of unfolding forces. The notion of constructing a body without organs entails opening our awareness to the intensive qualities of the specific durations in which we are located in order to experiment with such possibilities.

The durations of which we are a part are multiple and heterogeneous. Just as the rock climber's body on the mountain face breaks up into the heterogeneous durations of a hand searching for a grip in a crevice and a foot balancing on a small ledge, theorists also can enter into heterogeneous durations with multiple perspectives and orientations. In *A Thousand Plateaus*,

Deleuze and Guattari call different durations "blocks of becoming" (ATP 294). Experiencing the present in terms of the spatialized time of representational consciousness entails reducing the present to its manifest forms and thus blocking the extension of implicit intensities into new forms of life. Blocks of becoming entail opening awareness to the intensities insisting in the present in a way that renders those intensities actualizable. Constructing a body without organs suspends habitual patterns of embodied subjectivity and fosters the kind of attentiveness to the present that can unfold new lines of becoming. Such becoming will be specific to specific durations; blocks of becoming can consist of the heterogeneous durations of various assemblages—the duration of multiple heterogeneous durations of a rock climber on the mountainside (the durations of different body parts negotiating their own assemblages as well as the superpositions of tendencies in thought and movement intensified through past experiences in rock climbing) or a surfer on a wave, or the duration of multiple heterogeneous durations of a Parisian chef enacting her art in a small town in Norway or a feminist attempting to map the global flow of a transnational subjectivity (durations of chopping food or combining flavors superpose tendencies in Babette's present that can be unfolded in keeping with other tendencies converging in that moment, just as durations of various thought-movements precipitated through reading-assemblages and conversation-assemblages and other blocks of becoming can converge and unfold in a feminist's [relative] solution to a theoretical question about transnationality).

Just as a rock climber must start from where she is in order to open perceptual awareness to the intensities that will allow for creative solutions to the problem of getting up the mountain, so must a theorist start from her own location. The embodied awareness of lived experience has always been a crucial starting point for a feminist orientation. But it is part of the human situation that we can extend our intuitive awareness of various and varying durations through technologically enhanced perceptions (from the probing of space and atoms to the information communicated in various forms from all over the globe) and culturally complicated forms of thought (from the superimpositions of theoretical thought to the perceptions of time made possible by cinema). Thus, although any theorist must start from the lived experience of their own situations, we have the means to intuit the larger durations that encompass us in ways that allow for collective solutions to the multiple durations of an increasingly global community.

Brian Massumi presents astute characterizations of Deleuzian (and Deleuze–Guattarian) accounts of perception and intensity that help to bring out the lived experience of constructing a body without organs, and how such construction can open new ways of being. According to Massumi, even though we are not, strictly speaking, conscious of the intensities inflecting our present, the latter are implicit in our lived experience in terms of what is "too small" to enter perception and relations that are "too large" to fit into perception (Massumi 2002, 16).[2] Although conscious experience always is reactive in the sense that it entails a working over of immediate perception through the regulated categories of social existence (anything from the categories of perceptual clichés premised on habitual patterns that serve basic bodily needs to the linguistic categories that serve a familiar notion of self), immediate experience is already a selection and presentiment of a quality of existence that exceeds conscious experience and yet can be extended into conscious experience through the role thought can play in sensation and perception. The capacity or power of the body to affect or be affected varies with each transition the body undergoes. "Each transition is accompanied by a variation in capacity: a change in which powers to affect and be affected are addressable by a next event and how readily addressable they are—or to what degree they are present as futurities. That 'degree' is a bodily intensity, and its present futurity a tendency" (Massumi 2002 15). Despite the regularities of familiar forms of embodied experience, there are always intensities in one's experience that could unfold new powers to affect and be affected. Forces impinge on the body at thresholds beneath conscious awareness. They are not consciously registered by the subject and yet traces of past actions, "including a trace of their contexts" are "conserved in the brain and in the flesh" rather than the mind or body taken in a more traditional sense (30). Intensity is an action or expression that has not quite taken place and yet is on the verge of taking place. It is the beginning of a selection: "the incipience of mutually exclusive pathways of action and expression, all but one of which will be inhibited, prevented from actualizing themselves completely" (ibid.). Attunement to those intensities, for example, by the redirection of attention thinking can bring about, can disrupt habitual patterns and allow new pathways of action and expression to unfold.

Something is on the verge of happening, but has not yet happened. Once it has, some pathways of action and expression will be shut off, whereas others will become available. Possibilities in actualization will shift in terms of their tendencies toward completion, some becoming more likely and others becoming less likely to actually happen. I may feel completely comfortable when I first sit down, happily opening my book. If I were to reflect on it, I might think to myself that I could sit here forever with the green grass around me, the movement of air through the trees. But with each microperception, most of which I am not consciously aware, there is a qualitative shift that speaks to a shift in how ready I am to take action of a particular kind even though no action has thus far been taken. If I am sitting outside without shade or sunglasses and the sun comes out from behind the clouds and I am becoming bored with an expository passage in the novel I am reading, I may start to get uncomfortable; at some point a limit is reached and I become uncomfortable enough to move into the shade or throw my book down in disgust. If a mosquito buzzes at my ear when I am happily reading with the sun behind the clouds, I may just swat at it. If the same mosquito were to buzz at my ear when the sun comes out from behind the clouds and I am already becoming uncomfortable, it may provide the impetus for me to go indoors. In this context, we can read the notion of constructing a body without organs as a practice that entails attending to subtle nuances in perception and thought, seeking out small shifts and anomalies in our experience that are but a hint of the range of variation my perceptions and thoughts could take, rather than assimilating them to familiar patterns and representable categories, in order to arrest the automatic repetition of self-sustaining patterns and extend those anomalies along new lines of experience and action.

Attending to the present in terms of its intensities constitutes constructing a body without organs when virtual tendencies of competing lines of possible actualization create a plateau; any one line of becoming is suspended because a number of potential lines could unfold, no one of which has yet reached the threshold point that would exclude the others. Such plateaus can precipitate lines of flight from habitual patterns because they put previously excluded tendencies on equal footing with regularly actualized ones. Rather than close my book and go inside, I could choose to become aware of my sensations, attending to each sensation as it arises, simply observing them without evaluating or reacting to them. Such "mindful" awareness could entail a wider and more subtle range of perceptions that defies habitual expectations and brings me into a state of suspension where I resonate with the intensities unique to that moment. Such an experiential "plateau" could precipitate actions that constitute a break in my routine (I might finally drop my book and go for a walk rather than go inside).

According to Massumi, emotion is "qualified intensity, the conventional, consensual point of insertion of intensity into semantically and semiotically formed progressions, into narrativizable action–reaction circuits, into function and meaning. It is intensity owned and recognized." Affect, by contrast, is unqualified. "As such, it is not ownable or recognizable and is thus resistant to critique" (Massumi 2002, 28). Emotions are subjective states that one can recognize as being like similar states experienced in the past. They can be represented, referred to, named, and discussed. An affect is not yet an emotion. It hovers at the very limits of conscious experience, but has not taken a stable enough form to be recognizable or representable. It is thus, from a phenomenological perspective, the unrepresentable glimmer of emotion that speaks to implicit possibilities of one's present that may or may not unfold. "Affect or intensity in the present account is akin to what is called a critical point, or a bifurcation point, or singular point, in chaos theory and the theory of dissipative structures. This is the turning point at which a physical system paradoxically embodies multiple and normally mutually exclusive potentials, only one of which is 'selected' " (32–33). Like the components of concepts that act as limit points governing the concrete thought movements of embodied thinkers (see chapter 1), affects are limit points governing the concrete emotional states of embodied human beings (among other entities). They insist in subjective states, and the forces actualizing them may intensify—either crossing a threshold and actualizing into a recognizable emotion, or the disorienting state of a novel or "alien" experience, or simply drawing closer to some threshold point without actually crossing it. They are real in the sense that they inform the emotions actually experienced (some people are quicker to anger than others, others may be quicker to "break down" and cry), but they are the unrepresentable condition of manifest emotions and constitute some of the ineffable richness of embodied life. Ahab (a favorite example of Deleuze and Guattari's of someone pursuing a line of flight) was moved by something beyond emotion to chase Moby Dick—affects intimating a nexus of possibilities that were ultimately unrepresentable and yet pushed him into the intense emotions impelling his obsessive and destructive hunt for the great white whale. As Herman Melville puts it: "[E]ver since that almost fatal encounter [when the whale took Ahab's leg], Ahab had cherished a wild vindictiveness against the whale, all the more fell for that in his frantic morbidness he at last came to identify with him, not only all his bodily woes, but all his intellectual and spiritual exasperations" (Melville 1967, 175). Ahab's obsessive search for Moby Dick is motivated by inchoate thoughts and feelings irreducible to a set of representable emotions and articulate beliefs. Deterritorialization from the "normal" emotions and reactions of a whale-hunting captain leaves him in a volatile state that ultimately unfolds a line of flight from behavior that "makes sense" for whale hunters of his time and place.[3]

The subject's conscious perceptions and emotions emerge from the sensorimotor system's selections and combinations of the variations in sensations that are responses to the myriad forces impinging on the body. Unless the interval between perception and action is opened up, perception is likely to be in service to the subject's needs with respect to corporeal and psychic comfort and survival. If I am hot, I throw off the covers. If I lose my job, I may get up and go through my usual routine of getting ready for work, unsure of what else to do and unwilling to relinquish the self sustained through those routines. It will take some reorientation on my part to shift my perceptions of what I need to do next. Variations, intensities, and affects are unrecognizable and unrepresentable. Many if not most of them are not taken up and regularized in the functions of lived experience. I may experience years of discomfort with putting on make-up and being addressed as "she" without ever reaching a decision to become a female-to-male transsexual. Or I may experience years of such discomfort in the form of inchoate thoughts and affects that finally accumulate and qualitatively shift when I become aware that such a transformation could be economically and medically possible, and I come to understand my experience through that possibility. There is a wide range of variations in the capacities of the body to affect and be affected that never emerges into conscious awareness and yet could, through alternative selections and connections, be actualized in ways that allow them to cross into consciousness. Opening consciousness to the present with its unique configuration of intensities—be it through the sensations of the body, an encounter with another, or cultural thought forms like philosophy, art, or science—can precipitate the unpredictable actualizations that occur when lines of becoming come together with other lines of becoming in ways that transform them all. For example, according to Carrie Sandahl, Robert DeFelice, a disabled artist, "queers the crip" when he performs a parody of exercise videos by strutting about in red spandex and discussing his intent to make a video called "Crippled Sluts in Spandex" (Sandahl 2003, 39). Sandahl argues that DeFelice's performance parodies the cultural law that disabled people should "improve" themselves and the subcultural law that gay men be buff, as well as the role of exercise divas like Susan Powter and Jane Fonda (40). DeFelice's crippled body with attire and behavior invoking able-bodied exercise videos constructs a plateau or body without organs with his audience. In the intimate space of the theater the audience encounters a man they might have simply categorized and dismissed as "disabled" if they had passed him on the street. When the audience laughs there is a shared moment of suspension, a gap opened up between perception and typical reactions that induces a circulation of energy and a shifting of intensities that allow new perspectives on the disabled, sexuality, and oneself to emerge.

Our intelligence grants us knowledge of our organs and the functions they need to perform to keep us alive. But the body without organs eludes all such phantasmatic understanding of our bodies. Instead we experience our bodies in direct relationship to the world, in assemblages of which they are a part. Strange experiences are explained by psychoanalysis in terms of an image of the body (ATP 165). It "substitutes family photos, childhood memories, and part-objects for a worldwide intensity map" (ibid.). Deleuze and Guattari are more concerned with what the body can do than how to interpret the body. What we need to watch out for as we explore and experiment with what we are able to do—as we pursue desire to see where it will take us (as opposed to assimilating it to a narrative about a personal self)—is whether the desires that are unfolding lead to "stratic proliferation" or "too-violent destratification," or if they lead to the construction of a plane of consistency (ibid.). The first option is fascist, the second suicidal or demented, but the third could lead to changes with proliferating effects for our lives or larger repercussions on the social field. "How can we fabricate a BwO for ourselves without its being the cancerous BwO of a fascist inside us, or the empty BwO of a drug addict, paranoiac, or hypochondriac?" (ATP 163).

Constructing a body without organs entails releasing desire from its oedipalized identity-based forms in order to allow its immanent unfolding. Attunement to what always exceeds life in its recognizable forms can tap the incipient force of intensities at the expense of the patterns of perception, action, and thought that confirm the identities of the faciality machines. Interpreting the body's experiences in terms of the personal history of a recognizable self misses the ongoing connections of embodied individuals to the surrounding world. These connections do not need to be interpreted but pursued. There is no secret key that can explain them. Interpretations only block deterritorializations from dominant reality by explaining them away. Deleuze and Guattari would instead have us experiment with where such experiences could take us. Despite Deleuze and Guattari's emphasis on escaping the trap of personal identity, however, the narratives through which we attempt to give our identities coherence can themselves act as bodies without organs. A narrative can act as a plateau of meaning—a creative act of self-naming or group-naming that brings together disparate circulations of meaning in a galvanizing way. Thus, intensive selves are evoked that reflect embodied patterns of life as lived orientations rich with the intensities that inflect them. Narratives at the individual and collective levels may emerge that make revitalizing connections among the rhythms and refrains of our heterogeneous durations, but unless such narratives act as plateaus from which new lines of flight can be launched they are liable to become stultifying. It is when our narratives lose their grounding in lived orientations that even new forms of identity are reduced to the regulative norms of faciality machines that would have us merely repeat the recognizable. Then new experiments and new narratives need to be created that are more attuned to the always novel configurations of time's unfolding. Constructing a body without organs may occur spontaneously (e.g., when we are brought up short by new experiences) or we can foster such construction through cultural forms of thought like those of philosophy and art. The next section discusses how philosophy and art can reground us in life as creative evolution (as opposed to the sterile repetitions of the faciality machines).

Philosophy, Art, and Intuition

According to Deleuze's Bergsonian perspective, technological or representational thinking is not something we can or should do away with. We are practical creatures invested in our own survival who develop forms of perception and cognition designed to assure our success. It is the Bergsonian notion of intuition, however, that speaks to the ability we have to go beyond sheer survival and participate in the creative evolution of life by inserting a gap or interval between the perceptions and cognitions servicing the specific forms our individuation currently takes and the actions resulting from them in order to act in keeping with a future that would release new tendencies and capacities (see chapter 1). Representational thought reduces life to what it has already become and thus excludes the tendencies always implicit in it that could unfold to become other than what it is. Thinking allows us to consider some of the implicit potential insisting in the present and to intensify tendencies in order to foster creative evolution in directions that we would like to go. Although Deleuze cannot give a static measuring stick against which to measure such possibilities, he gives us the Nietzschean/Spinozist standard of proliferating joyful passions that allow us to unfold the creative potential within us and extend ourselves in terms of the tendencies inherent to the specific forms we actually take. His "transcendental empiricism" starts from where we are, but takes where we are to be not simply what has been overtly actualized, but also what exists only as implicit tendencies. These tendencies can only be thought in terms of the genetic processes through which they can intensify and unfold. This means we cannot abstract a finalized form of humanity from its surroundings, but must understand ourselves as always in dynamic interaction with a world from which we cannot extract ourselves.

Words, to take but one example of semiotic activity (and Deleuze and Guattari criticize privileging linguistic activity at the expense of semiotic activities of other kinds) generalize over things. I can name a singular happening, a specific configuration of forces that unfold into an actualized state of affairs, but that state of affairs never exhausts the name I give it. I can go in two directions with words: in the direction of the states of affairs to which I attribute the meaning of my words, and in the direction of the variations of meaning in the words I use that move me away from a specific state of affairs to the relations those meanings have with other words and other states of affairs. Insofar as I move toward the latter, I am operating in the space of the event or the meanwhile opened up by thought. It is due to the complexity of our nervous systems that includes the capacity to speak language as well as engage in other forms of semiotic activity, that we are able to open the interval between perception and action that allows us to respond to our present creatively rather than adhering to the restricted repertoire of reactions of solely instinctual organisms. Philosophy, art, and science are the thought-forms Deleuze and Guattari privilege in the opening up and mapping of this interval in a way that allows us to creatively evolve with our lives rather than simply survive. All life-forms creatively evolve, in their view, because even the most reactively instinctual life-forms unfold along diverging paths. Biology itself, in other words, is always a differentiating process where new connections are formed and sustained in the production of new forms of life. But thought-forms like philosophy, art, and science allow us to deepen and extend the meanwhile of specific forms of access to the virtual that allow us to stabilize and orient ourselves to the infinite possibilities of life without becoming lost in them.

The organism, as well as stable notions of the self, require what we could call rules into which the variables of living can be plugged in order to come up with recognizable perceptions and actions. Successful stimulus–response patterns (e.g., at the cellular and organic levels as well as at the level of sentient awareness) need to be repeated if the organism is to survive. Representational thought allows us to isolate and highlight the general patterns of what repeats across the unique confluence of forces unfolding in specific durations. When we think life in terms of the event rather than our representations, however, we can think an excess that goes beyond such rules. Instead of reducing the present to that which lends itself to repeatable patterns, the event hints at the continuous variations of life that lead up to implicit limit points or points of intensity where qualitative (and unquantifiable) changes take place. These limit points are not directly apparent to sense perception. They insist in terms of the intensities one can only intuit at subthreshold levels of representation in terms of tendencies, a tightening, a sense of building toward a change, or a loosening and relaxing that hints at turning away from a specific tendency that could have pushed one state into another. Furthermore, the event hints at these in the context of the event of events—the meanwhile connecting all events—where everything connects to everything else and any connection could be actualized. In specific states of affairs, some tendencies have actualized into overt states with manifest consequences, moving, in turn, some tendencies toward completion as opposed to others. In the meanwhile that can be opened up by thought (e.g., philosophical thought or the stratigraphic time of some forms of cinema), all possibilities can be maintained in superposition, with none being excluded. Such intimations of the event of events (or what one also could call the durational whole or the eternal return) constitute livable approaches to the chaotic creativity of durational time.

Although philosophy and science are both thought forms that approach chaos in creative ways, according to Deleuze and Guattari, their approaches are different. Scientific thought pins down the event with reference to specific states of affairs, things, or bodies; functions refer to specific states of affairs when independent variables are plugged in. Philosophical thought extracts the virtual from states of affairs; concepts are created in light of a principle of consistency that tracks connections of meaning that exceed specific states of affairs. Thus, functions and concepts are "two types of multiplicities or varieties whose natures are different" (WP 127), making the two forms of thought distinct. Additionally, they differ in terms of how time comes into play: Scientific multiplicities are multiplicities of "space, number, and time" that refer to the variable or independent variables, whereas philosophical multiplicities are multiplicities "of fusion" defined by duration that express "the inseparability of variations" (the continuous variations in overlapping meanings of words) (ibid.). Philosophical events occur in the meanwhile of consistency where what matters is how components of thought overlap with other components of thought, whereas scientific functions are instantiated by plugging in variables that allow those functions to refer to actual states of affairs more akin to the linear chronology of spatialized time.[4]

Both philosophy and science approach the virtual, but the "function in science determines a state of affairs, thing, or body that actualizes the virtual on a plane of reference and in a system of coordinates; the concept in philosophy expresses an event that gives consistency to the virtual on a plane of immanence and in an ordered form" (WP 133). Philosophy explores the meanwhile of the event of events—the relations of virtual meaning extracted from the meaning attributed to actualized states of affairs. Philosophical thought pursues with infinite speed the zones of indiscernibility of events of sense in their connection to other events. These events hint at the intensities of lived experience; because events of sense are extracted from perceived states of affairs, they are rooted in lived experience. But insofar as philosophical concepts pursue the continuous variation of components of meaning and pursue the connection of those variations to other variations of meaning, they go beyond the digitized categories of recognizable sense experience as it has been codified and regulated according to the social machines of perception and understanding. The variations of components of sense are pursued from the perspective not of the personal self of the philosopher with her representable memories and beliefs, but the perspective of conceptual personae who give priority to subthreshold variations in meaning rather than the meanings standardized through philosophical discussion (see chapter 1). The conceptual personae of philosophy are "philosophical sensibilia," perceptions and affections of fragmentary concepts through which concepts "are not only thought but perceived and felt" (WP 131).

Constructing a body without organs means suspending the usual social machines at a point of critical juncture where all the possible lines of actualization are at point zero. On this plateau, habitual functioning is suspended and unprecedented lines of actualization are as likely to unfold as habitual ones. Mapping the social field is one way to construct such plateaus of intensity where something new could happen. Thought-forms like philosophy, art, and science, are various means of resonating the dynamic flow of time with cultural representations of the already actualized real in a way that can bring new possibilities to the fore. Such possibilities have always been there, but were excluded by forms of thought and perception that spatialize time and emphasize representable forms of the past at the expense of dynamic tendencies implicit in the present that in tandem with the actual propel reality forward. Mapping where one is on the social field is a way to attend to the conditions of one's actualized situation, extracting from it events of pure becoming. When this is done through conceptual creation, one is not describing one's situation by representing it. One is rather extracting from lived experience in keeping with a plane of immanence peculiar to specific problems, inventing in the process novel perspectives that render perceptible new lines of flight.

Simply abandoning old ways of perceiving and thinking would invite stunned apathy, paralyzing confusion, or psychosis. Creating concepts is one way to approach the chaotic possibilities of the virtual real in a way that allows our lived experience to breathe in more of the intensities of life than it otherwise could. The conceptual personae invented in the process allow perspectives beyond those already actualized to emerge. Furthermore, the more the concepts thus created are in response to problems of the social field—problems informed by the lived experience and ways of thinking of our time and place—the more powerfully their effects will reverberate. Of course, this could have the fascist effect of regimenting a whole culture onto a path of self-destruction. But it could also have the revolutionary effect of furthering our creative evolution in concert with the surrounding life that sustains us.

Whereas philosophy allows deterritorialization from the "commonsense" rules regulating lived experience through the means of a thought-form that makes infinitely fast connections between disparate mental elements via the principle of consistency, art deterritorializes sensation by extracting blocks of sensations—"a pure being of sensations"—from "percepts" wrested from "perceptions of objects and the states of a perceiving subject" and "affects" wrested from "affections as the transition from one state to another" (WP 167). Percepts and affects, like concepts, go beyond the conventions of communicable representations of experience to make alternative connections (than those regulated by "common sense" or opinion) among the virtual relations insisting in sense experience. Percepts are drawn from perceptions and affects, as seen in the last section, are drawn from affective responses to those perceptions not yet consolidated into representable emotions. Both draw from the infinite array of continuous variation in how the elements of processes resulting in conventional perception and affections could be differently selected and combined in the patterns of consciousness. They thus intimate the virtual potential for alternative forms of perception and affection that insists in the present forms conscious awareness takes. The artist creates a "being of sensations" through her chosen medium by raising "lived perceptions to the percept and lived affections to the affect" with a style unique to her (WP 170). The artist's style evokes the rich potential of time without allowing it to be reduced to any one set of representations.

All of being is the event of the eternal return where everything is connected to everything else. Although living creatures like ourselves, as well as other creatures and things, emerge from relatively stable patterns of equilibrium that maintain their forms (if only for a short time) so that they are not swept away in the becoming-other of life, ultimately these boundaries are made by reducing the speed with which they become-other rather than separating themselves from the flow of life entirely. Just like us, continents and insects are in the process of becoming-other, but their processes have been slowed down or sped up with respect to other processes around them, through the stabilization of the specific patterns of material becoming that make them up. But in the event of events where everything is becoming-other, there are zones of indiscernibility where the boundaries between a given state of relative equilibrium and the other becomings within which it is immersed, are always unraveling. According to Deleuze and Guattari, art is a thought-form that attends to those unravelings and makes them perceptible by creating on the basis of "a ground that can dissolve forms and impose the existence of a zone in which we no longer know which is animal and which human, because something like the triumph or monument of their nondistinction rises up" (WP 173).

In *The Passion According to G.H.*, Brazilian novelist Clarice Lispector presents an example of such a becoming with her protagonist, G.H.'s, chronicle of a journey beyond the human and toward life. This journey entails G.H.'s depersonalization and loss of her "human constitution for hours and hours" (Lispector 1988, 4). During this time, G.H. meditates on a dying cockroach and undergoes an experience ultimately beyond language, and yet to which she struggles to give what form she can: "I shall have to painstakingly translate telegraph signals—translate the unknown into a language that I don't know, and not even understand what the signals amount to" (13). In the process of peeling off the layers of facts connected to a personal self, G.H. comes to experience a rapport so profound with the cockroach that we could, from a Deleuze–Guattarian perspective, say it constitutes a becoming-cockroach. Lispector's rendering of this experience could be described as an aesthetic monument of the always present zones of indiscernibility insisting in life as durational whole: "I, neutral cockroach body, I with life that at last is not eluding me because I finally see it outside myself—I am the cockroach, I am my leg, I am my hair, I am the section of brightest light on the wall plaster—I am every Hellish piece of myself—life is so pervasive in me that if they divide me in pieces like a lizard, the pieces will keep on shaking and writhing" (57).

The monuments created by art confide "to the ear of the future the persistent sensations that embody the event" (WP 176). They thus create a monument of the sensory becoming through which things, animals, or people become-other. "The monument does not actualize the virtual event but incorporates or embodies it: it gives it a body, a life, a universe" (WP 177). Thinking the concept entails counter-effectuating what happens, eluding what is in deference to what has not yet been actualized in the states of affairs to which components of thought can be ascribed. Percepts make perceptible the imperceptible forces "that populate the world, affect us, and make us become" (WP 182). It thus gives us access to what has not been actualized but which informs the present as singularities or points of tension that form the imperceptible backdrop to what actually unfolds. Representational thought assumes the clear-cut boundaries of processes that have attained some degree of autonomy from surrounding flows. Monuments intimate the always present becomings unfolding toward thresholds that threaten such boundaries. Just as Susan Stryker challenges us to confront the panic her problematic existence may provoke due to the unrepresentable intimations we may have of the zones of indiscernibility unraveling our own boundaries (chapter 2), so G.H. experiences that unraveling in a profound (and profoundly unsettling) affinity with a cockroach.

Deleuze and Guattari refer to the flesh or figure, the house, and the cosmos as features of monuments of sensory becoming. The being of sensation expressed in the artwork "is not the flesh but the compound of nonhuman forces of the cosmos, of man's nonhuman becomings, and of the ambiguous house that exchanges and adjusts them, makes them whirl around like winds. Flesh is only the developer which disappears in what it develops: the compound of sensation" (WP 183). That is, the artistic monument shows us something about our lives by rendering it perceptible. The forms of human existence that we think of as so stable are but shifting shapes in an ongoing flux where nothing ever stays the same. The human figures that we are emerge from that flux—a compound of nonhuman forces and a process of selection where forces stabilize into regulated patterns that sustain our actual forms. Deleuze and Guattari compare nature to art, suggesting that like art, nature combines "House and Universe, *Heimlich* and *Unheimlich*, territory and deterritorialization, finite melodic compounds and the great infinite plane of composition, the small and large refrain" (WP 186). Stryker presents herself as what we could call, in this context, a work of art. Lispector, as well, by composing percepts and affects out of an experience intimating life beyond its human forms, even if—as her narrator suggests—this entails framing "that monstrous, infinite flesh" and cutting it "into pieces that something the size of my mouth can take in"—creates a monument that constitutes an approach to the virtual. According to Deleuze and Guattari art does not represent reality (WP 193); it creates composite sensations that deterritorialize reality and allow us to perceive some part of the virtual that insists in our present in terms of fleeting sensations and emotions as well as the inexperienceable tendencies that shape the intensities of experience without emerging in covert form.

Whereas Lispector intimates the durational whole through a microscopic unfolding of an encounter with a cockroach, Virginia Woolf, in her novel, *Orlando*, intimates the durational whole in the kaleidoscopic romp of her protagonist through five centuries of British history, various occupations in various locations and a gender-bending shift from being a man to a woman (Woolf 1928). In the impressionistic blur of life rendered from Orlando's perspective, we get a sense of the relentless push of time as well as the zones of indiscernibility emerging among people of different nationalities, cultures, social ranks, occupations, and genders as Orlando transitions from one phase of his or her life to the next. This blurring of boundaries among ways of life created through the rush of time (as well as Woolf's ironic stance vis-à-vis the various mores she depicts) puts any settled account of what it means to be a worthwhile human being—never mind a woman or a man—into doubt and evokes a rich sense of untapped possibility.

Cinema can show us time as an open whole by deterritorializing us from embodied perspectives and showing us a life and time where movement detached from perspective takes priority. This allows a time-image where movement is no longer subordinated to stable entities located in an extended space, and the power of differing takes precedence. Stabilized perspectives are shown to emerge and dissolve in a durational whole that qualitatively shifts as the new emerges, with no one context for selectively stabilizing a reality. Sally Potter's film adaptation of *Orlando* translates the sense of possibility the novel evokes into cinematic form (Potter 1992). Patricia Pisters contends that Potter's film reveals that "to experience the liberating forces of becoming-woman and the ways in which gender identity might escape from the codes that constitute the subject, Chronos [i.e.,, chronological time] must be confused and give way to Aion [the time of the event]" (Pisters 2003, 124). That is, Potter, through the medium of film, is able to present a time-image that reveals its superpositions and thus hints at the empowering possibilities of going beyond a representational understanding of the past in terms of chronological time in order to tap into time as a durational whole.

Every element created on a plane of thought by one of the three thought-forms evokes other heterogeneous elements "still to be created on other planes: thought as heterogenesis" (WP 199). None of the thought-forms can be taken in isolation from the others; the planes created by each are ultimately in contact with one another. The culminating points of these mutually implicating planes can reterritorialize us onto "the opinion from which we wanted to escape" or precipitate us "into the chaos that we wanted to confront" (WP 199). That is, these thought-forms, like other aspects of human existence as well as life itself, can either rigidify our living by reinforcing patterns of life already lived, or they can deterritorialize us too quickly into a chaotic flux of becoming that is ultimately unlivable. At the "meeting point of things and thought" sensation recurs as evidence of its "agreement with our bodily organs that do not perceive the present without imposing on it a conformity with the past" (WP 203). The opinions or clichés of lived experience are necessary for practical living; opinion acts "like a sort of "umbrella," which protects us from chaos" (WP 203). "But art, science, and philosophy require more: they cast planes over the chaos. . . . Philosophy, science, and art want us to tear open the firmament and plunge into the chaos" (WP 203).

It is precisely the ability to break with standardized perceptions and actions that allows the pursuit of the meanwhile opened up by thought to stabilize into new perspectives on the present and past. This is why Deleuze and Guattari prefer to think of philosophy as the creation of concepts rather than a discussion or dialogue that comes to a consensus about the truth. Coming to a consensus about the truth means, for them, to come to an agreement about what qualities we should select and emphasize in relation to a standardized (majoritarian) subject who becomes the paradigm of what a human being should experience from the range of continuous variation in our perceptions. Recalling the example of smelly cheese (recounted in chapter 1), propositions of belief emerge when one extracts a quality (e.g., a foul smell) from a perceptive-affective lived situation (cheese presented at the dinner table) while at the same time identifying oneself as "a generic subject experiencing a common affection" (those who hate cheese) (WP 145). "Truth," then, insists that we make these selections with respect to this self, thus excluding a whole range of other possible selections and other possible selves. This is in keeping with how organisms need to operate to sustain their existence as the organisms they are: Successful stimulus–reaction patterns are sustained in order to sustain life. But this entails a process of selection that reduces what one attends to in perception to what can be computed in a kind of rule of living that matches perceptions and understanding with affections and actions. Human beings with their complicated nervous systems, as well as cultural practices and systems of meaning, have vastly complicated reaction patterns (compared with e.g., the reaction patterns of an amoeba), but these reaction patterns are still highly regulated. The thought-forms of philosophy, art, and science are the approaches we can take as human beings to the chaotic flux of becoming that allow us to access some part of the incredible array of variations that emerge in life in its singular becoming without being overwhelmed by them. A philosophical thought that attends to variations in meanings, creating stabilized oscillations of components in order to provide new perspectives on lived experience, is accessing this fecundity of life that is our birthright and resource with more skill than a discussion that merely repeats old rules of living.

Concepts are intensive in that they make connections among components of thought in keeping with implicit zones of indiscernibility whose meanings could be actualized in multiple ways, rather than with the logical inferences of a proposition. Making logical deductions from a proposition tied to a specific frame of reference constrains thought to the parameters set by representations of lived experience. Pursuing zones of indiscernibility allows one to pursue how a concept can differ internally from itself through the actualization in concrete thought movements of variations in its relations that do not turn it into another concept as well as how it differs from and connects with other concepts on a plane of immanence. Although we are embodied individuals with corporeal reactions to life necessary to sustaining the life-form that we are, thinking allows us to abstract from the life around us in a way that goes beyond our immediate biological (or sociocultural) needs and delay our reactions so that we can intuit relations implicit in our concrete situation that have previously been excluded. Pursuing such relations means intensifying tendencies already implicit in our situation in a way that allows something new to happen.

According to Deleuze and Guattari, the human capacity for creation is part of the creative force of time itself as differentiating becoming. As organisms we participate in the unfolding of the divergent capacity of human bodies. As creatures who have achieved relative autonomy from the environment we affect and are affected in ways that elicit capacities of which we may not have been aware at the same time as we sustain relatively stable configurations of rest and motion. As our nervous systems have become more complicated, and as our cultural systems of meaning unfold, a human capacity is unfolding that allows us to intuit the creative potential in the durational whole of the present. For Deleuze and Guattari, philosophy, art, and science are all forms of thought that nourish the creative evolution of human life. Although we could say that science is a form of representational thought that supports intelligent living, philosophy and art are thought-forms that can intuit the creative possibilities of dynamic becoming. Although in their view the specific forms of humanity we celebrate are no more than temporary durations of equilibrium in the flow of life, it is our capacity to intuit imperceptible potential that allows us to do more than merely react to impinging forces and thus actively participate in creative evolution.

Becoming-Woman and Lines of Flight

The encounters to which the construction of a body without organs as well as other plateaus can open us can lead, if we let them, to experiments in living our subjectivities that diverge from the norm. Deleuze and Guattari's notion of becoming-other is another concept indicating actualization of lines of continuous variation diverging from socially sanctioned patterns of activity. Their notions of becoming-woman and becoming-other bring out the lines of flight insisting in conventional subjectivity and the patterns of signification and subjectification that sustain it.

What Deleuze and Guattari, in *A Thousand Plateaus*, call molar subjects are defined (in the context of human subjectivity) by the binary faciality machines (discussed in chapter 2)—that is, the processes of signification and subjectification that play out through collective assemblages of enunciation and machinic assemblages of desire in ways that reduce us to this or that set of identifications. As a molar subject, I develop and sustain a facialized identity (however conflicted or contradictory that identity may be) that entails more or less suppression of mutant flows of subjectivity in order to carry out the day-to-day patterns of speech, interpretation, and activity of my location on the social field. Identifications in keeping with the faciality machines are signified through binary categories that affirm and amplify those identifications in redundant overcoding. Such overcoding tends to cancel out and constrain the virtual possibilities always implicit in experience to the already familiar habits and routines of conventional cultural life. Additionally, I exist beyond both my molar designations and identifications as a process of individuation that through the particular patterns of physiological, organic, cultural, and social activity I have lived and live constitute a largely nonconscious orientation shaped and informed by those patterns of living. Becoming-woman entails deterritorializing from molar segments organized around the majoritarian (white, male, propertied, heterosexual, Christian, etc.) subject in order to attend to the variations in sensory experience and meaning of my specific line of becoming that elude binary categories. Such variations may amount to no more than minor perturbations of an otherwise completely conventional existence, or they can open up lines of flight toward new connections, new ways of affecting and being affected, and new powers of the body that could produce proliferating effects across the social field.

When Deleuze and Guattari say, "all becomings begin with and pass through becoming-woman. It is the key to all the other becomings" (ATP 277), they are underscoring the importance of the binary machine of sex and gender in sorting out social identity. It is next to impossible to escape this binary machine (although intersexuals and transsexuals, among others, resist such classification in various ways). In a social formation where cultural, political, and historical flows on the social field are reduced to the traumas of personal selves struggling to line up on either side of the phallic divide, a sexed and gendered identity is a required achievement. According to Deleuze and Guattari's account, the little girl who becomes the example of the object of desire for the boy has her becoming taken from her (ATP 276). She has a history imposed on her that tells her who she is and what she should want. For example, she might be told that she is a little girl, not a tomboy and might be discouraged from pursuing the assemblages she could form by unfolding her capacities to affect and be affected by the things around her. The "boy's turn comes next," but "a dominant history is fabricated for him too" (ibid.). The interpretation of his actions in terms of the secret desire attributed to him of wanting to be like his father, instead of the desire to make things happen, intervenes with his experimentation, reducing it to the dominant paradigms of self-hood and the same old tired stories of what it means to have a self. Beneath the thresholds of what is rendered visible by the bifurcating machines that sort all of humanity into either one or the other of proliferating binaries are the variations that form a continuum that exceeds and complicates any such grouping. Like converting analog to digital, shades of grey are not only rendered imperceptible, but they also tend toward being put out of play in terms of the connections that could be made to other fluxes and flows that could unfold lines of variation that sweep away binary categorization of sex, gender, or sexuality.

Deleuze and Guattari suggest that even women can engage in a becoming-woman whereby one emits particles "that enter the relation of movement and rest, or the zone of proximity, of a microfemininity, in other words, that produce in us a molecular woman, create the molecular woman" (ATP 275). That is, by tuning into imperceptible lines of continuous variation in one's mostly nonconscious lived orientation rather than resonating with the molar segments that affirm the majoritarian subject, women can deterritorialize from traditional forms of subjectivity. Becoming-woman entails evading the binary machines of faciality in order to explore and extend virtual tendencies that either/or identity categories obscure or repress. This is not done in opposition or reaction to those categories, but rather by unfolding the refrains that gives one joy. An oedipal subject organizes desire around what she has to have in order to be the person who resolved her familial love triangle. Such a subject needs to continue to be whomever it was that was able to take up a viable position as a worthy person in her family. Her worthiness is measured not simply with respect to the phallus, but with respect to the majoritarian subject; her personal self is elaborated through the identity designations activated in the social practices she engages outside, as well as within, the family. She continually confirms her personal identity by identifying with the "I" constituted in socially sanctioned linguistic and behavioral practices ("I" am a mother who picks up her child at school, "I" am a teacher who passes along useful knowledge to her students, "I" am a philosopher with these particular intellectual commitments).

Becoming-woman is a line of flight from refrains of living organized around the majoritarian subject and its system of identity designations. Becoming-woman orients itself not around the signposts of such identity designations, but rather with respect to the capacities one is able to extend in evolving patterns that may well drift from such reference points. Thus, Thelma and Louise, of Ridley Scott's 1991 film (Scott 1991), start off on a road trip that moves them further and further from molar womanhood. At first intending only to take a vacation, they are drawn down a line of flight that takes them further and further from their daily routines and the recognizable selves who performed them with only inchoate thoughts of resistance. Far from losing themselves in this unmooring from their normal reference points, they pursue an exhilarating line of experimentation where they act as haecceities who become with their surroundings rather than following the scripts of designated identities. That this line of experimentation ended in their joint suicide speaks to the risks such experimentation entails and the problem of finding ways to productively connect lines of flight.

Blocks of becoming are anti-memories because representational memory is organized in terms of a horizontal flow of time (from the old present to the actual present) and a vertical order of time (from the present to the representation of the old present) (ATP 294–95). Recalling Isak Dinesen's story, "Babette," discussed in the first section of this chapter, we could say that representational memories of Babette as a chef at a café in Paris renowned for her cooking contrast with her present situation as a housekeeper for two sisters with little money who are too devout to consider food of much importance. With no insight into the durational whole connecting these two disparate durations, Babette's chronology would seem to indicate that her days of cooking artistry were irrevocably past. If the connections between her past and present had remained subordinated to a representational memory of herself as chef and her present as housekeeper, she would never have had the audacity to use all her lottery winnings to make one glorious meal for an audience she could not expect to appreciate her artistry. But instead of remaining bound by representational memory, she accessed a block of becoming in which the two durations came together in a way that allowed her to develop and extend capacities exercised in the past that still insisted in her present whether or not she chose to actualize them. Representational memories form patterns of frequency and resonance with the present, but the only new connections made are those that are subordinate to the recognizable or representable memory. History, like memory, is a punctual, arborescent, mnemonic, molar, structural system of territorialization or reterritorialization

(ATP 295). Engaging the becoming-other of intensive time allows one to open up to present intensities and extend capacities in keeping with them along new lines of flight.

Blocks of becoming or creative acts are transhistorical, subhistorical, or superhistorical. "Nietzsche opposes history . . . to . . . the Untimely, which is another name for haecceity, becoming, the innocence of becoming (in other words, forgetting as opposed to memory, geography as opposed to history, the map as opposed to the tracing, the rhizome as opposed to arborescence)" (ATP 296). Babette's haecceity entails not simply the state of affairs actualized in Babette's new duties as housekeeper, but the events that "hover" over that state of affairs as the pure becomings that cannot be localized in time or space because they are never exhausted by that state of affairs and yet exist in terms of intensities and affects that may or may not cross the threshold into actualization. These becomings thus insist in the present in terms of virtual tendencies that may intensify to the point of actualizing (hands that know how to hold a knife, sense of smell that knows how to sniff out the best ingredients). The singularities or events making up that haecceity are an aggregate that is what it is through the working parts of a specific situation along with their manifest and incipient tendencies as well as the way those parts function together. Representational memory cancels out the virtual, turns haecceities into representations cut off from virtual reality, and reduces consciousness to recognizable sensations and conceptions. Babette's memory of herself as a chef locates her in a time and place from which she is now removed. Fleeting affects and intensities that are above or below the threshold of conscious awareness and representable memory are thus lost. There is no way to make use of her cooking capacities in her current situation since it is so different from her past. But when instead of representing the past through memory, Babette in a sense "forgets" in order to embody her memories through intensities and affects that she lives in her present, she is able to extend her capacities in the present through a creative evolution of her cooking abilities in a different kind of situation. The magically revitalizing effect her cooking has on people so lacking in cuisinary distinction that they agreed before the dinner to say nothing about the food is a testament to her artistry as it has evolved in a novel convergence of forces.

Becomings, by connecting fluxes and flows in keeping with the continuous variation of experience rather than the arborescent lines of a punctual system, make new happenings that shoot off the grid of localizable points and open up a future that does not amplify the past in redundant resonance with the present. Deleuze and Guattari frequently use aesthetic examples: a musician floats "a sound block down a created, liberated line, in order to unleash in space this mobile and mutant sound block, a haecceity"

(ATP 297). Drawing diagonals "outside points" and making connections that do not amplify already recognizable frequencies and resonances, but instead create mutant blocks of sound connections that are inassimilable to past listening experiences, can shock the listener out of complacent listening habits and bring her to a new sound sensation. Deleuze and Guattari point to Monet as an example of a painter who does something similar with color, creating visual blocks where the line is between points and no longer outlines a shape. The central perspective of more traditional paintings plunges the "multiplicity of escapes and the dynamism of lines into a punctual black hole" (ATP 298). Monet's visual blocks, by defying conventional lines of perspective, release visual lines of flight.

Cinema, as discussed in the last section, can powerfully evoke the virtual by presenting a time-image where perspectives are freed from settled points of view and thus intimate the creative potential conditioning the embodied trajectories of individual lives. Michelle Langford gives a Deleuze–Guattarian reading of Marziyeh Meshkini's film, *The Day I Became a Woman*, that brings out the durational time the film evokes in the context of a becoming-woman that exceeds the various representations of women the film portrays (Langford 2007).

> The film is structured as a set of three episodic narratives, each featuring and named after a central female protagonist. In the first episode, we meet Hava on the day of her ninth birthday, the day she officially "becomes" a woman. She must adopt the Islamic codes of modest dress and will no longer be allowed to play with boys. In the second episode we meet Ahoo, a young married woman attempting to stretch the boundaries of a strictly patriarchal society by participating in a women's bicycle race. And in the third, we meet Houra, an old, unmarried woman who has come to the duty-free island of Kish to buy all the modern household items she could never afford in her youth. (2)

On a gloriously beautiful day, Hava is asked by her friend (who is a boy) to play. At first she is refused permission by her mother and grandmother—it is her birthday and she is no longer supposed to play with boys—but it is finally agreed that she may play until noon since it is only then that she will be officially nine. Her grandmother gives her a stick and tells her that when she sticks it into the ground and it casts no shadow, she must come home. Hava (as well as the audience) knows that when she comes home she will have to put on the veil her mother is sewing, she will no longer be able to play with her friend, she will become a woman and her childhood, in an important sense, will be over. Hava joyfully runs off to find her friend for her final minutes of freedom, but when she comes to his house, it turns out that he must finish his homework before he comes out. Hava waits, putting the stick into the sand and anxiously checking its shadow over and over again. Finally, she runs off to buy some candy and comes back to share it with her friend (who never is able to come out to play with her before she must leave). They take sensual pleasure in passing the brightly colored lollipops back and forth through his window, despite the bars on the window. The bright colors, crisp sounds, and evident pleasure the children take in their candy and one another are in sharp contrast to the impending sense of passing time that will bring that pleasure to an end.

Through most of Ahoo's section of the film, Ahoo peddles in a desperate attempt to win a bicycle race as well as keep ahead of the male relatives pursuing her on horseback who would have her abandon the race and return to her "proper place" by her husband's side. Her fierce determination is apparent in the relentless push of her legs even as she looks back at her approaching relatives or resets her scarf about her head. Even at the end when her brother finally brings her to a complete halt, the camera continues to sweep forward, first drawing back to reveal Ahoo and her brother as small specks against the sweep of road and sand around them and then moving onward, as if time is still pushing forward as relentlessly as Ahoo's legs were, even if Ahoo herself has had to stop.

Although the pace of Houra's segment is slower, it also pushes forward as Houra moves from shop to shop on an insane shopping spree, enlisting more and more boys to push her purchases forward, collecting more and more things, until they reach a beach, where she has the boys put out all her purchases in a bizarre rendition of a bedroom set up on the beach. The segment becomes increasingly surreal until Houra has all her things sent off onto the water where they float off to an unspecified destination with young Hava watching from the beach.

The film's presentation of three stories that are disconnected (the three stories are of three women with different names and situations) and yet connected (the first story of a young girl, the second of a grown woman, and the third of an old woman are chronologically linked; Hava appears on the beach at the end of Houra's story, suggesting that the two characters are connected—or even, as Langford suggests, that all three stories are in Hava's mind) conjures up the irrational gaps of a film that evokes a time-image—a durational whole that can be accessed in multiple ways rather than the seamless whole of a linear chronology. Furthermore, the timeless quality of the children's delight in the sensual beauty of the morning, despite the anxiety produced by Hava's makeshift sundial, the limitless quality of "a seemingly vast desert bordered by an apparently limitless ocean" (Langford 2007, 30) along which Ahoo's bicycle races even as she is chased by men on horses, the "intensive force within her body . . . [that] is her becoming-woman" of Houra's body that has grown old and heavy with time, slowing her down as she sifts "the vast recesses of her memory" (29) in order to remember an item on her list of things to buy that she has forgotten, all evoke an open-ended duration of heterogeneous durations that "bring forth affective becomings-woman between film and viewer" (33) that go beyond any given representation of woman in the film. As Langford points out, despite the constraints placed on the women represented in the film—Hava's approaching womanhood, Ahoo's failed attempt to escape the constraints of a traditional conception of womanhood, and Houra's somewhat pathetic attempts to make up for a life of deprivation by buying all she ever wanted even though she is now past the age of being able to use much of what she purchases (e.g., a wedding dress), there is something exhilarating about watching the film. Langford points out that these heterogeneous durations concern the durations of Iran that include periods of modernization (under the Shah), and the return to Islamic tradition (after the Islamic revolution), as well as "a layering of the "ages" [rather than stages] of a woman's life" (26) as they emerge in the imagination of a young girl contemplating her future,[5] or the layered memories of an old woman:

> [E]ach woman in the three episodes comes to embody a very complex set of temporalities both in relation to the other women and also within herself: each bears within her past, present, and future simultaneously, with complex temporal flows being exchanged between each of them. (28)

Meshkini's film makes the imperceptible perceptible; the depiction of turning points in three lives evokes the multiple connections of a durational whole and creates a plateau with the audience where habitual patterns are suspended. Although one does not know how these lives will turn out, the assemblages of becoming-candy (in Hava's case), becoming-landscape (in Ahoo's case), and becoming-old as the superposition of the heterogeneous durations of one's life (in Houra's case) evoke the present of each as an intensive duration that could unfold as-yet untraveled pathways of perception, action, and thought. Rather than representing a "better future" for women, the film instead precipitates a gap resonant with the multiple interrelations within and among three durations. Rather than depicting a new identity and positioning for woman vis-à-vis the majoritarian subject, the film depicts lines of flight emerging from three durations: a timeless moment of shared sensual pleasure that defies the before and after of Hava's ninth birthday, an alignment with the creative evolution of a landscape unfolding beyond-the-human that defies Ahoo's subordination to male power, and an attunement to multiple durations and a watery expanse that defies the narrowing of desire in Houra's old age (and death) or the exclusion of her multiple selves (and durations).

The selves intimated by the film are not the representable selves of oedipal subjectivity, but are rather selves shown in transitional moments of nomadic subjectivity—subjects in process who rather than deferring to an ideal against which they measure their worth, unfold their power in concert with the intensities of a present that incites open-ended becoming. Thus, Meshkini's film, despite its "failure" to suggest "viable" alternatives for its characters and the hope of a future for each that one can confidently predict, instead evokes the complicated interrelations of heterogeneous durations that suffuse the audience with a revitalizing sense of possibility. Even if new patterns of life have not yet been formed, there is a sense of renewed connection with the vitality and creativity of life itself as well as one's own co-participation in time's unfolding. The forms and meanings one's life takes, from this perspective, can be seen as playful effects (rather than predetermined results) of an infinitely creative whole.

Rosi Braidotti points out that the Deleuze–Guattarian reconception of memory as a vector of deterritorialization as opposed to a "data bank of frozen information" allows us to see memory as "careful lay-outs of empowering conditions which allow for the actualisation [of virtual possibilities] to take place" (Braidotti 2000, 162). This kind of memory connects flows and intensities in new ways that prompt creative responses to the present. Such memories are intensities that can make things happen in contemporary states of affairs by pushing an accumulation of elements over certain threshold points, actualizing singularities in new configurations that defy historical understandings of the past.

Becoming entails entering into composition with something else in such a way that the particles emitted from the aggregate compose something-other as a function of the relation of movement and rest, or of molecular proximity, into which they enter (ATP 274). Becoming-woman entails actualizing the event of "woman" in a way that allows one to deterritorialize from conventional points of reference in being-a-subject. Listening to music can allow me to lose my typical references as a listener attending to music I appreciate and enter a state of becoming-sound. Looking at a painting by Monet can allow me to enter a state of becoming-color where "I" dissolve and become lost in visual lines of flight. Particles are not recognizable; they flux and flow at thresholds beneath the level of conscious awareness. And yet, by attending to the immediacy of lived experience, we can become more aware of whatever it is that intimates something beyond the perceivable, the thinkable, and the doable. At the edges of my emotions are subtle nuances of feeling—affect that is not, strictly speaking, experienceable as such, but which intimates a capacity to be affected on the threshold of actualization. At the edges of my perception are sensations not quite experienced that intimate the virtual potential this moment holds for other ways of perceiving. At the edges of my thinking are the other paths my thought could have unfolded but did not. When I become, I let go of my habitual reference points and allow movement along some of these alternative paths. In an encounter with a human other I do not initially understand, I can enter into a becoming-other where I relinquish my habitual orientations in order to be affected by the lines of continuous variation in human-becoming emitted by the other and compose new lines of flight in thinking, perception, and emotion. Just as encounters with the environment, art, or human others can precipitate multiple becomings, so can thinking constitute a form of becoming-other where I lose myself and my old reference points and allow new orientations to emerge. Thus, I can read Frantz Fanon's phenomenological description of his struggle with racism or Marilyn Frye's characterizations of the arrogant and loving eyes and be dissolved and transformed as my thinking travels lines of flight that would otherwise have been unavailable to me (Fanon 1967; Frye 1983).

Deleuze and Guattari's ontology provides a means for approaching time as a durational whole rather than remaining in the spatialized time of practical existence. This, in turn, allows us to open up intuitive insight into creative solutions to the pressing problems of contemporary life. If the modern era comprised the "age of reason," then it may be that the postmodern era needs to place increasing emphasis on imagination and creative intuition as well as reason in order to find a way past the destructive impasses with which we are now confronted. Philosophy, art, and science all are needed to open up new ways of thinking, but living life can in and of itself be an art that brings new solutions to bear on the difficulties in living. Thus, although theory of various forms, including those of feminism, may still be an important avenue for progressive change, and aesthetic practices, cultural politics, and politically sensitive participation in science will continue to be important, lived experience that breaks with clichés of perception and conventional thinking—the lived experience always so valued by feminism for grounding a new future—also will continue to be an important resource for actively shaping a future we can embrace. In order to deepen our individual and collective access to vitalizing and yet livable flows of dynamic time, we need practices that can continually attune and reorient us to what is always in excess of the familiar patterns of social life. In the next two chapters we consider how this imperative of Deleuze and Guattari's might be conceived as an ethos of becoming that could inspire ethical and political practices suitable to the increasing speeds of life in the twenty-first century.

Chapter 5

Ethics, Trauma, and Counter-memory

Spinoza's Joy and Nietzsche's Gift-Giving Virtue

Bergson's notions of the actual and the virtual (as opposed to the real and the possible), and the interval between stimulus and response that can lengthen from that of an instinctual reaction to that of the intellectual ability to choose between various representable possibilities to that of the intuitive ability to access durational wholes from perspectives beyond those invested in preserving ourselves as the specific creatures we are in our current forms, emerge in new configurations in Deleuze and Guattari's constellations of concepts to suggest an ethics and politics able to unfold with time rather than impose universal principles on shifting circumstances. Humanity, although not unfolding toward any one telos, has, in this view, diverged from a form of life whose power to affect and be affected was limited to a repertoire of instinctual reactions to evolve into a global community of human subjects (each of whom could be conceived as an assemblage in its own right with multiple relations to other assemblages) whose participation in cultural and social assemblages complicate and extend our capacities in ways that now reach beyond the specific perspectives we embody and open up intuitive perspectives on the unfolding wholes of which we are a part. In keeping with Nietzsche's call for completing the nihilistic destruction already under way of transcendental ideals (to which we compare life in order to judge how life "should" be) that would have us crash all such ideals in favor of immanent forms of valuing, Deleuze and Guattari appeal to the immanent criterion, inspired by Spinoza and Nietzsche, of affirming the active and joyous extension of our power for action in the assemblages of which we form component parts.[1] Both Spinoza and Nietzsche embrace what one might call a naturalist ethics and politics—one that is premised on what bodies can do and become. The immanent standard they both put forward is a notion of good and evil that can only hold from specific embodied perspectives rather than any God's eye view.[2] Both Spinoza and Nietzsche not only eschew transcendental ideals, but also diagnose the present state of humanity as one of impeded power, and make positive suggestions for how to interpret our situation in a life-affirming way that will foster humanity's increased power and vitality.

In *Expressionism in Philosophy: Spinoza* (hereafter, EP), Deleuze cites Spinoza's view that finite modes (like ourselves) are "born in conditions such that they are cut off in advance from their essence or their degree of power, cut off from that of which they are capable" (EP 226). The *conatus* (or innate striving) of our composite bodies endeavors to preserve the relation of movement and rest that define them (EP 230), but because knowledge of how to do this initially is derived from the imagination, a faculty that presents us with inadequate ideas about the objects affecting us (and thus of how best to compose the relations of our bodies with the relations of other bodies), our power of action is reduced to clinging to passive joy or warding off passive sadness. Because both these affections are caused by external factors over which we have no control, this leaves us in a reactive position that diminishes our power of action. "Whence the importance of the ethical question. *We do not even know of what a body is capable*, says Spinoza. That is: *We do not even know of what affections we are capable, nor the extent of our power*" (EP 226). It is only when we develop "common notions"—notions of what is common to some external body and our own (EP 283)—and adequate ideas (that extend knowledge of common notions into knowledge of how a singular essence is part of God as infinite substance)—that is, knowledge of what Spinoza calls, respectively, the second and third kinds—that active joy is born and our desires, insofar as they proceed from adequate ideas, become rational (EP 284).[3] Once we have this kind of knowledge, we can better organize our encounters so that we can fully engage our capacities to affect and be affected in confluence with the forces of our durations.

According to Deleuze's reading of Spinoza, bodies encounter other bodies that either agree with them, in which case their power of acting increases, or disagree with them, in which case their power of acting diminishes. When I have an encounter with another body whose relations combine with my own, I have a "good" encounter that produces in me "the idea of an effect which benefits or favors my own characteristic relation," as well as a movement of variation whereby my power of acting is increased and I undergo an affect of joy (Deleuze 1978, 8). A "bad" encounter entails "the idea of an effect which compromises or destroys my own characteristic relation," and produces a movement of variation whereby my power of acting is diminished and I undergo an affect of sadness (ibid.).[4] An idea is "a thought insofar as it is representational" (2). An affection (Spinoza's *affectio*) is "the trace of one body upon another, the state of a body insofar as it suffers the action of another body" (Deleuze 1997, 138). Affection-ideas—for example, sensations or perceptions—give us knowledge of our affections. These ideas

> know [connaissent] things only by their effects: I feel the affection of the sun on me, the trace of the sun on me. It's the effect of the sun on my body. But the causes, that is, that which is my body, that which is the body of the sun, and the relation between these two bodies such that the one produces a particular effect on the other rather than something else, of these things I know [sais] absolutely nothing. (Deleuze 1978, 6)

Affection-ideas are, according to Deleuze, inadequate ideas and constitute Spinoza's "first" kind of knowledge. They are representational ideas that confuse the affect other bodies have on one's own body with something inherently true about the body itself apart from its unfolding relations with the world. Because such knowledge cannot help one actively organize the "good" encounters that will agree with (rather than threaten or compromise) the relations of movement and rest that define one, it is, for Spinoza, the lowest form of knowledge.

Every affection "envelops an affect, a passage" (Deleuze 1981, 7). Whereas an affection can be summed up and described, affects, as seen in chapter 3, concern transitions that are cancelled out by representational thought. According to Deleuze's reading of Spinoza, Spinoza's notion of an affect (Spinoza's *affectus*) is "the lived passage from the preceding state to the current state, or of the current state to the following state" (ibid.). Because these passages always entail shifts in the intensities inflecting oneself and one's situation (i.e., shifts in one's readiness to enter into other states of specific kinds), an affect consists of an increase or decrease of power. Deleuze gives the example of being in a dark room. "You don't have visual affections, that's all. . . . All of a sudden someone enters and turns on the lights without warning: I am completely dazzled" (ibid.). The two states (of being in the dark and of being in the light) are close together, but there is a passage from one to the other "so fast that it may even be unconscious . . . to the point that . . . your whole body has a kind of mobilization of itself, in order to adapt to this new state" (ibid.). This passage is irreducible to the two states and "is necessarily an increase of power or a decrease of power. . . . It is not determined [which it is] in advance" (ibid.). Deleuze continues his example with the possibility that one is in a deep state of meditation that is interrupted by the light. "You turn around, you are furious." If, however, you were looking for your glasses in the dark, the light "would have brought you an increase of power. The guy who turned the light on, you say to him: 'Thank you very much, I love you.' " (ibid.).

> [O]ur present state is always a slice of our duration, and as such
> determines an increase or decrease, an expansion or restriction
> of our existence in duration in relation to the preceding state,
> however close it may be. It is not that we compare the two states
> in a reflective operation; rather, each state of affection determines
> a passage to a "more" or a "less": the heat of the sun fills me or,
> on the contrary, its burning repulses me. (Deleuze 1997, 139)

These qualitative shifts in state cannot be represented in an affection-idea
because affections mark not the shift itself, but an actualized state. Affects,
by contrast, concern the readiness or lack of readiness to unfold into other
states of various kinds—they are the intensities that inflect one's situation
as small changes build toward or draw back from various kinds of threshold
points. They "are passages, becomings, rises and falls, continuous variations
of power [*puissance*] that pass from one state to another" (ibid.).

We experience the transitions among the states of being of which our
sensations and perceptions give us knowledge as nonrepresentational affects
on our duration—pleasure or pain, joy or sadness—that indicate variations
in our power of action.[5] "[T]here is a continuous variation in the form of
an increase-diminution-increase-diminution of the power of acting or the
force of existing of someone according to the ideas which s/he has. . . .
[A]ffectus in Spinoza is variation (he is speaking through my mouth; he didn't
say it this way because he died too young . . .), continuous variation of the
force of existing, insofar as this variation is determined by the ideas one has"
(Deleuze 1978, 4). Thus, in Deleuze's reading, developing common notions
and adequate ideas entails attending to the transitions in one's body that
encounters precipitate. It is only when affection-ideas—ideas that represent
the world in terms of the effects a thing has on one—are surpassed by a
knowledge of the relations between two bodies that produces specific affects
(where affects are understood as variations in one's power of action), that one
can begin to organize "good" encounters. The kind of knowledge required
for such skillful living is thus not that of the imagination or representational
intelligence (which reduces the world to snapshots of the emergent effects
of processes of which one remains largely unaware), but rather an intuitive
attunement to bodies as processes inflected with affects and intensities that
can enhance and diminish other processes in their mutual implication.

According to Deleuze, Spinoza's ethical project requires not suppressing
passion, but rather increasing one's power of action through the passive joy
produced in chance encounters with "good" objects. This, in turn (by virtue of
increasing one's power), aids one to form common notions that can be further
refined into adequate ideas of what is common to two or more bodies (EP
285). This leads to the active joy that comes from being the cause of one's

own increase in power: "The formation of notions, which are not abstract ideas, which are literally rules of life, gives me possession of the power of acting" (Deleuze 1978, 15).

> A man who is to become reasonable, strong and free, begins by doing all in his power to experience joyful passions. He then strives to extricate himself from chance encounters and the concatenation of sad passions, to organize good encounters, combine his relation with relations that combine directly with it, unite with what agrees in nature with him, and form a reasonable association between men; all this in such a way as to be affected with joy. (EP 262)

The second kind of knowledge develops its ideas through attentive awareness of, in particular, what gives us joy, in what Deleuze calls a kind of apprenticeship in which lived experiments are performed in order to determine how bodies can be agreeably composed. Deleuze thus reads Spinoza as developing a conception of knowledge (of the second and third kind[6]) as a knowledge of intensities or affects.

Like the event that inheres or insists in actual states of affairs without being reducible to them, affects "always presuppose the affections from which they are derived, although they cannot be reduced to them" (Deleuze 1997, 140); they are not, themselves, representable or perceptible despite the effects they produce. They are nonrepresentational aspects of awareness that may enter into confused and inadequate ideas or the common notions and adequate ideas one develops as one better understands how one's relations may agree with those of another body or thing. Although representational thought may reduce experience to its manifest outlines (thus stripping it of the intensities that could unfold new forms of experience), experience reduced to one's affections—sensations, perceptions, emotions, and thoughts that one can represent, describe, and explain—strips experience of the affects irreducible to those affections and yet always inhering in them as they are actually lived. Thus, we can see in Deleuze's reading of Spinoza a philosophy of affect that refuses to reduce experience to the actual and instead thinks experience in terms of the intensities inflecting it—intensities that speak to the passage of time and a form of thought and knowledge that goes beyond the representational thinking of intelligence as well as the affections of imagination, and attempts to intuit duration.

Spinoza advocates, then (in Deleuze's reading) a form of knowledge premised on keen attention to what moves us (rather than the reduction of experience to the preconceived categories of conventional experience) with an emphasis on unfolding lines of flight in thinking that orient our living in a joyful direction. Additionally, we could say that what gives us the most joy is not something that can be determined through overarching principles of the good, but only can be determined on a case-by-case basis through pragmatic experiments made by actual individuals. It is only on the basis of attentiveness, then, to experiments in living that thought can come to conceive the notions that will allow us to come into our full power as active organizers of the encounters most conducive to the forms of life that we are. Given Spinoza's view that composing agreeable relations with other human beings like oneself will enhance one's own *conatus*, joyous living will turn out to be premised on (as discussed in the next chapter) the collective living of larger social wholes composed of agreeably related parts.

In his seminar of Jan. 24, 1978, Deleuze comments that when one is enclosed in the world of affection-ideas and "affective continuous variations of joy and sadness," one is separated from one's power of acting: "In other words, I am not the cause of my own affects" (Deleuze 1978, 11). In another seminar session, he suggests that a bad encounter produces a kind of fixation where one devotes part of one's power to investing and isolating the trace left by a disagreeable object. In order to avert the effect of the object on me, I devote a quantity of my power to investing its trace in order to put it at a distance.

> This is what is meant by: my power decreases. It is not that I have less power, it is that a part of my power is subtracted in this sense that it is necessarily allocated to averting the action of the thing. Everything happens as if a whole part of my power is no longer at my disposal. (Deleuze 1981, 10)

Unlike sadness, in which there is "an investment of one hardened part which would mean that a certain quantity of power (*puissance*) is subtracted from my power (*pouvoir*)," the experience of joy entails the composition of the relations of two things into "a third individual which encompasses and takes them as parts." Using the example of listening to music he likes, Deleuze suggests that in such an experience a third individual is composed of which he and the music "are no more than a part" (Deleuze 1981, 11). The increase in power at issue for Spinoza is thus not that of conquest, mastery, or control, but rather of composing relations with other bodies that require no diversion of one's power into warding off the effects of another body on one's own relations of speed and rest. Deleuze goes on to explicitly align Nietzsche with this positive conception of power.

> What Nietzsche calls affect, is exactly the same thing as what Spinoza calls affect, it is on this point that Nietzsche is Spinozist, that is, it is the decreases or increases of power (*puissance*). They

have in fact something which doesn't have anything to do with whatever conquest of a power (*pouvoir*). Without doubt they will say that the only power (*pouvoir*) is finally power (*puissance*), that is: to increase one's power (*puissance*) is precisely to compose relations such that the thing and I, which compose the relations, are no more than two subindividualities of a new individual, a formidable new individual. (ibid.)

According to both Spinoza and Nietzsche, then, in Deleuze's reading, the increase in power they advocate is a power that overcomes the tendency to invest power in averting or resenting what is in order to compose one's relations with the relations of something else by becoming, along with that something else, part of a larger whole.

Both Spinoza and Nietzsche depict the ability to skillfully compose oneself with life as it is (in all its dynamic becoming) as one that requires the ability to read phenomena in terms of duration. Whereas Spinoza conceives of this latter ability in terms of his notions of knowledge of the second and third kind, Nietzsche conceives of it in terms of his notion of a genealogical method that interprets sense and evaluates valuing. Deleuze emphasizes the revolutionary quality of this aspect of Nietzsche's philosophy:

> One of the most original characteristics of Nietzsche's philosophy is the transformation of the question "what is . . . ?" into "which one is . . . ?" . . . The one that . . . does not refer to an individual, to a person, but rather to an event, that is, to the forces in their various relationships in a proposition or a phenomenon, and to the genetic relationship which determines these forces (power). (NP xi)

The event as a configuration of unfolding forces produces states of affairs and bodies that we can represent and describe, but itself comprises as well the shifting virtual that conditions specific states of affairs. Like Spinoza, Nietzsche advocates precise attention to the manifest reality of embodied experience as effects of processes of becoming that can become better known. Whereas in the case of Spinoza what thus becomes known are adequate ideas concerning how relations can be agreeably composed, in the case of Nietzsche, what becomes known are phenomena as the expressions of relations of forces of a certain type (active or reactive) and will of a certain type (affirming or denying):

> In Nietzsche's terms, we must say that every phenomenon not only reflects a type which constitutes its sense and value, but also

the will to power as the element from which the signification of its sense and the value of its value derive. *In this way the will to power is essentially creative and giving:* it does not aspire, it does not seek, it does not desire, above all it does not desire power. It *gives:* power is something inexpressible in the will (something mobile, variable, plastic); power is in the will as "the bestowing virtue," through power the will itself bestows sense and value. (NP 85)

The will to power is proliferating life in its incessant diverging from already created forms as forces attempt to extend to their limit (and so fully "discharge their strength"[7]) in implication with other forces that enhance and impede their unfolding in multiple ways.

To know life in terms of its unfolding rather than in terms of the forms it creates as it unfolds, Nietzsche creates a genealogical method that reads phenomena in terms of the kind of force predominating in its production from the particular embodied perspective of the one evaluating that force. This approach to life interprets phenomena in terms of the active forces (forces that go to their limit) and reactive forces (forces that separate other forces or are separated from what they can do) that give them sense from a particular perspective and evaluates phenomena in terms of the affirming or denying nature of the will to power determining the sense phenomena have along with the value of that sense from that perspective. Nietzsche thus "substitutes sense and value as rigorous notions [for those of the true and false]: the sense of what one says, and the evaluation of the one saying it" (Deleuze 2004, 135).[8] Interpretations, like Spinoza's knowledge of the first and second kind, always relate to the striving of the body giving the interpretation. Such interpretations, like Spinoza's distinction between confused ideas and the common notions that can be developed into adequate ideas, can manifest from a viewpoint that either reduces life to its manifest forms (through a denying will to power that interprets phenomena with respect to transcendent ideals) or interprets life in terms of composable relations (with an affirming will to power that reads phenomena with respect to the unfolding forces of life). Thus, for Nietzsche, human consciousness can be read as a phenomenon (composed of conflicting forces) that derives its sense and value through the differentiating force of will to power.[9] Active forces of all phenomena go to the limit of their power, whereas reactive forces separate other forces or are themselves separated from what they can do (NP 59). As phenomena that at any one time and place are symptoms or effects of processes of becoming, we are particular relations of active and reactive forces determined through a will to power that values life's creative unfolding or values transcendent ideals opposed to such unfolding.[10] Because consciousness tends to be reactive and denying (for reasons Nietzsche's genealogical tale in the *Genealogy of Morals* depicts), so do our interpretations. Representational thought that reduces what is to static states of affairs is reactive because it overlooks how incipient forces could unfold new powers in affecting and being affected.

From Nietzsche's genealogical perspective, representational thought can be interpreted as a reactive force emerging from a denying will to power intent on serving a transcendental ideal rather than life's creative evolution. From this perspective, Deleuze and Guattari's philosophy can be seen as an extension of the Nietzschean impetus to shift toward an affirming mode of thought. Such a mode of thought can link the meaning of phenomena to the embodied perspectives informing how those phenomena are interpreted and evaluate those perspectives with respect to whether they align themselves with or oppose themselves to the divergent becoming of durational time. Instead of assuming the truth of one perspective as the standard against which others are found wanting—a metaphysical ideal of one form or another to which a phenomenon is compared—a Nietzschean physiologist interprets phenomenona as symptoms of active and reactive forces. A Nietzschean artist creates the perspectives from which such interpretations can emerge. The perspective informing interpretations of phenomena with respect to transcendental ideals to which they are compared is one that values in terms of already created values at the expense of the creative evolution of life. The perspective able to affirm life as becoming interprets phenomena in terms of the will to power "as a hidden principle for the creation of new values not yet recognized" (Deleuze 2001, 73). The latter perspective does not assume the perspective of a self-same oedipalized subject with a secure identity able to pass down paternal law, but rather moves among many perspectives, evaluating as noble those able to affirm the value of actively unfolding forces. Thus, a philosophy of the future, instead of discovering the truth, interprets the fragmentary and incomplete "meaning" of a phenomenon and evaluates "the hierarchical 'value' of the meanings and totalizes the fragments without diminishing or eliminating their plurality" (65). We interpret life, given our all-too-human propensity for guilt and resentment at life for not living up to the metaphysical ideals it "should" instantiate, with a "base," "weak," "unhealthy," or "slavish" will to power as opposed to the "noble," "strong," "healthy" will to power Nietzsche would like to help bring about.

> We create grotesque representations of force and will, we separate force from what it can do, setting it up in ourselves as "worthy" because it holds back from what it cannot do, but as "blameworthy" in the thing where it manifests precisely the force that it has. (NP 22–23)

A philosophy able to manifest a healthier will to power would expose all such "forms of baseness of thought" (NP 106).

Consciousness, memory, and habit all are "essentially reactive; this is why we do not know what a body can do, or what activity it is capable of" (NP 41). We are so mired in *ressentiment* and the will's gnashing at the "it was" (Nietzsche 1966b, 251) that we can barely muster up the will to will (Nietzsche 1967, 162). We are so busy denying life that we are unable to affirm the eternal return—that is, to completely accept what is and act in accordance with what is in ways we also can completely affirm. We reduce everything to "concept-mummies" and thus miss the movement of life (Nietzsche 1966b, 479). To return to more Spinozist terminology, the sensations, perceptions, feelings, memories, and thoughts of which we are consciously aware are states representing confused ideas about the impact of chance encounters on our bodies. Insofar as we are ignorant of how the relations of movement and rest of other bodies agree or disagree with those of our own, we are not in control of how we might combine our relations in agreeable ways with others and thus increase our power of action. Our ideas of the things affecting us are ideas concerning the effect they have on us rather than ideas concerning the processes of becoming that lead to those effects.

It takes experimentation, interpretation, and evaluation to begin to better understand what we are capable of. Philosophy's "highest art" is to evaluate "this and that," delicately weigh each thing and its sense, and estimate "the forces which define each thing and its relations with others at every instant" (NP 4).

> Forces can only be judged if one takes into account in the first place their active or reactive quality, in the second place the affinity of this quality for the corresponding pole of the will to power (affirmative or negative) and in the third place the nuance of quality that the force presents at a particular moment of its development, in relation to its affinity. (NP 61)

Reactive forces entail forces that deny active force (the "triumph of the weak or the slaves") and forces that turn against themselves (the "reign of the weak or of slaves"). Active forces entail forces that affirm their difference and make their difference objects of enjoyment and affirmation (NP 61).

Just as Spinoza's project advocates a kind of becoming-active of humanity (in an apprenticeship of life that progresses from accumulating joy in chance encounters to the beatific joy of the fully activated humanity of third knowledge), so does Nietzsche's project advocate a becoming-active of humanity in the form of overcoming *ressentiment* in order to evolve into creatures who enact completely affirming will to power. Deleuze explains the significance of Nietzsche's notion of the eternal return in the context of the transmutation of reactive forces into active ones. Spirits strong enough to prepare the way for the overman destroy the reactive in themselves by "submitting it to the test of the eternal return and submitting themselves to this test even if it entails willing their own decline" (NP 70). Nietzsche's notion of the eternal return entails a double selection: first, an ethical selection where one wills only that which one can also will to eternally return ("to eliminate all half-willing, everything which can only be willed with the proviso "once, only once"" [NP xi]).[11] Second, there is the eternal return as the ontological selection where all that resists becoming is eliminated and only the purely active returns (NP xii).

> To affirm is still to evaluate, but to evaluate from the perspective of a will which enjoys its own difference in life instead of suffering the pains of the opposition to this life that it has itself inspired. *To affirm is not to take responsibility for, to take on the burden of what is, but to release, to set free what lives.* To affirm is to unburden: not to load life with the weight of higher values, but *to create* new values which are those of life, which make life light and active. There is creation, properly speaking, only insofar as we make use of excess in order to invent new forms of life rather than separating life from what it can do. (NP 185)

Insofar as the interpretation and evaluation of life proceeds from an affirming will to power, one does not separate force from what it can do, but rather brings forces to their limit—regardless of the stabilized forms that may be destroyed in the process. This process of bringing forces to their limit rather than separating forces from what they can do in order to repeat familiar patterns, entails a release of force from the patterns that constrain its shifting flows of energy. In the context of Deleuze's ethical notion of becoming worthy of the event (see LS 148–53), it means that rather than uphold already actualized patterns of living sanctioned by established conventions, one releases new actualizations in keeping with the accumulation of intensities leading to new thresholds in meaning and action. Whereas a denying will to power will evaluate life from a perspective more intent on opposing the intensities threatening to shift the established order into new patterns—even though those very tendencies were intensified due to the life it has itself inspired—an affirming will to power evaluates life from the perspective of enjoying the unfolding divergence of life from itself—even when such divergence entails divergence from its own past willing. Becoming worthy of the event entails a transmutation in which the will

> wills now not exactly what occurs, but something *in* that which occurs, something yet to come which would be consistent with

what occurs, in accordance with the laws of an obscure, humorous conformity: the Event. It is in this sense that the *Amor fati* is one with the struggle of free men. (LS 149)

This something yet to come is not something inconsistent or out of keeping with the forces converging in a given time and place, but rather something of that time and place, untimely as it may be, something unrepresentable and yet insisting in what manifests—the propulsive force of time in its differentiating and diverging forward becoming as it pertains to that time and place with its actual states of affairs and the virtual intensities relevant to it from the perspectives of its participants with all their varied investments and interrelations.

Deleuze reads both Spinoza and Nietzsche as interpreting manifest experience—the sensations, perceptions, feelings, and thoughts that we can represent, describe, and communicate—as effects of forces that although imperceptible are in some sense knowable, although this knowledge exceeds and defies the cognitive knowledge of representational thought, whether it be through Spinoza's second knowledge of common notions concerning the causes of agreement among bodies (or his third knowledge of bodies insofar as they are manifestations of the differentiating becoming of God), or through Nietzsche's genealogical interpretation and evaluation of the symptoms of life in terms of active and reactive forces and noble or base will to power. Additionally, Deleuze reads the ethics of each as an ethics whose immanent criterion for the ethical mode of life is that of positive power or active force—a power that unfolds out of what a body can do (rather than through what it is able to dominate), a force that extends to its limit rather than being separated from what it can do. In the context of Deleuze and Guattari's notions of constructing a body without organs and unblocking lines of flight discussed in the last chapter, these readings clarify and elaborate the important emphasis in Deleuze and Guattari's work on an active as opposed to reactive stance to life, as well as the importance of cultivating aesthetic as well as theoretical practices that can tap into the joy of creative evolution and overcome the all-too-human guilt and *ressentiment* pervading contemporary forms of culture. Additionally, Deleuze's readings of Spinoza and Nietzsche give us some additional hints for how to go about the process of transforming and transvaluing conventional values in ways that sustain continuity (if not the continuity of self-identical subjects) and foster the kind of joyous, active living they advocate.

Spinoza's notions of bodies as relations of movement and rest, the composition of relations with other relations as an ongoing process in which all things are engaged (appearing, e.g., in Deleuze and Guattari's notion of the assemblage), the unrepresentable affects that we experience in keeping with the continuous variation in our power of action as joy or sadness, the criterion of (active) joy as an indication of skillful composition, and nonrepresentational forms of knowledge that foster more ethical and joyous living, as well as Nietzsche's notions of the will to power, a genealogical approach to the interpretation of sense (in terms of active and reactive forces) and the evaluation of values (in terms of affirming and denying will to power), and the eternal return as a process of double selection (ethical and ontological) that can bring about a transmutation of reactive humanity into active (beyond-human?) forms of life, resonate and amplify the Deleuze–Guattarian themes of human subjectivity as a process of ongoing connection with the flows of life in which we are immersed and the prospect of positive interventions in that becoming that I have already considered. In particular, they help to answer questions about the kind of experiments, bodies without organs, and lines of flight, Deleuze and Guattari mean us to explore.

In light of hints taken from Deleuze's readings of Spinoza and Nietzsche, we could argue that an ethical approach to tapping the creative force of the virtual would be one that transformed negative, reactive stances to life into affirmative, active stances attuned to life in the pragmatic contexts of its always particular unfolding. In the context of constructing a body without organs, this would mean creating a moment of suspension where instead of simply reacting to life in keeping with past stimulus–response patterns (remembering that on Deleuze and Guattari's view, such patterns include processes that result in our sensations, perceptions, bodily comportment, habitual responses, and habits of meaning, thought, and action, as well as routine reactions we can recognize as such), we attune ourselves to the actual–virtual reality of the present from which we can then unfold active lines of flight. An "ethical" line of flight would entail skillfully composing one's relations of movement and rest with those of others in a way that would increase one's power by requiring less investment in averting traces of objects that have brought one sadness in the past and instead actively bringing about the relations that would bring joy in the present. The active ability to be the cause of encounters that bring one joy (rather than being at the mercy of chance encounters) requires, we could say with the help of Nietzsche, a genealogical interpretation of how interrelating forces produce the specific state of affairs in which we find ourselves. This kind of understanding can be developed through an apprenticeship with life where one deliberately accumulates the kind of joy that increases one's power and prompts one to better understand how to bring about the relations that best suit one's own defining relations of movement and rest in concert with the joyful unfolding of the wholes of which one forms a part.

We could add that given Spinoza, Nietzsche, Deleuze, and Guattari's emphasis on the interrelations that compose individuals and the conception of an individual in terms of relations of movement and rest that prompts an understanding of any relatively stable configuration of forces as an individual in its own right, plateaus or bodies without organs and the lines of flight proceeding from them could be conceived in terms of various kinds of individuals (e.g., an individual community, culture, society, ecosystem, or planet) at multiple levels and durations. On this view, the kind of understanding one needs to develop is not simply that of one's own empowerment, but the empowerment of the many assemblages of which one is part. Skillful composition of relations thus entails intuiting the relations of unfolding lines of flight premised on unfolding the power to affect and be affected in concert with the unfolding capacities of related entities (rather than investment in preventing those entities from being what they are). Clearly, life being what it is, human living can never be completely active, but according to both Spinoza and Nietzsche, the path to empowerment is one where the wholes of which we are a part are as active as possible. A completely activated whole entails activated component parts. Thus, on Deleuze's reading, not only is it the case that the more energy is invested in dominating others or keeping others from doing what is in them to do, the less power of action one (whether "one" refers to an individual subject or collective) has, but the more skillful (or ethical) action would be the action that fostered not just one's own power of action, but the power of action of the others with whom one shares various kinds of assemblages (from a family assemblage to the assemblage of a community or movement to an eco-system or a planet) as well. Being "worthy of the event" is thus premised on intuiting multiple durations and the lines of action emanating from plateaus where multiple relations can come together in ways that empower not only oneself, but the assemblages of which one forms a component part.

With the help of Nietzsche, one could say that the kind of apprenticeship that could help us increase our active power would entail the transmutation of a denying will to power intent on investing traces, or to put it into more Nietzschean terms, separating force from what it can do, into an affirming will that can will forces to go to their limit—even if this entails one's own metamorphosis. Such an affirming will can be exercised and tested by embracing the eternal return as an ethical principle of selection. The ethical selection of thought and actions premised on affirming what is with all its dynamic force and intensity rather than railing against or clinging to what was, can actually affect one's ontological make-up and so precipitate the transmutation of reactive humanity into a creature beyond the human (the overman—or could we add, the evolved-global-community?) who acts out of the giving spirit of an affirming will to power.

With this in mind, we could say that becoming worthy of the event means to engage in the transmutation of sadness into joy, reactive forces into active ones, and denying will into affirming will. This kind of transmutation requires us to continually attune ourselves to the propulsive force of time in its forward movement as it unfolds the particular lives we live in the multiple wholes of which we are parts rather than to fixate on our representations of life. And, as Deleuze emphasizes in his reading of both Spinoza and Nietzsche, we need to affirm our becoming with and through the becoming of what is around us rather than extend our power by making others sad or by separating force from what it can do (whether it be one's own force or the force of others) and thus leading reactive forces to triumph (NP 196).[12] Thus, the transmutation for which Spinoza and Nietzsche call cannot be a cerebral one engaged at the level of the representational thought of intelligence. To bring about changes in affects—which after all, occur below the level of representational thought, in the interstices of conscious experience—one must be permeated with an understanding of life that exceeds any cognitive understanding. To be able to interpret and evaluate from the perspective of a noble will to power, one must get beyond the reactive outlook that pervades the habitual postures of contemporary life and begin to live as someone whose perspective—from the sensations, perceptions, and feelings one has, to the thoughts, memories, and hopes one thinks—is lived as affirming.

    If change is frightening, if an ethics that presents no overarching and unchanging principles is unsettling, it is because we want the "good" life, whatever that might mean, and if we are not sure what it means, we want to have some way to at least approach the question. The answer Deleuze and Guattari ultimately give to this question is one that is premised on a deep faith in the creative fecundity of life in finding active solutions for the problems that arise in what are always very particular circumstances. They endorse Nietzsche's claim that the time for the belief in transcendental ideals is drawing to a close, and the Nietzschean and Spinozist claim that a new kind of ethics is needed—one that entails a new way of thinking along with new ways of being human. This new kind of thinking would go beyond representational thought to a thinking that can intuit duration (of various kinds) and read one's situation and history in terms of multiple wholes and the unfolding force of life as creative evolution. This means not recognizing oneself or getting others to recognize you, but rather to come into one's own power by attuning oneself to the forces moving through and beyond oneself and one's situation. This approach to being-human entails a more active, joyous, flexible, and creative subjectivity able to unfold new capacities in changing circumstances to which one is continually attuned. The ethics of such a being-human would be one of ongoing attunement to oneself, to others, and the heterogeneous durations in which one participates in order to find the creative solutions that could best serve the most joyous (in the Spinozist sense) and active (in the Niezschean sense) unfolding of heterogeneous parts composing multiple wholes.

In the next section I turn to the dilemma trauma presents to conventional conceptions of ethics or morality and the aesthetic solution provided by the writer, Dorothy Allison, to the problem of honoring her own need to unfold a joyful and active line of flight. Trauma often entails a kind of rupture in conventional narratives with their ways of making sense of people, actions, and intentions that presents a disorienting crisis in meaning that needs to be resolved if one is to regain confidence in one's world, oneself, and one's actions. Trauma of different kinds marks lives in ways that create dissonance between lived orientations and the identities proffered by the faciality machines of one's location. Allison's aesthetic project provides a means for interpreting a traumatic situation and creating a solution to the problem of unfolding a life she could affirm. On the reading I give here, trauma, by disallowing a conventional ethics (at least if one is to preserve what is important to one about who one is), can prompt an immanent ethics that exemplifies the kind of attunement to duration Deleuze and Guattari advocate. Although trauma may make the creative work of an immanent ethics more pressing, it may be that the speed of contemporary life is pushing us all to become more attuned to life's ambiguities in our attempts to be ethical.

Trauma and Counter-memory

Trauma can relate to the dissonance of a minoritarian orientation or disequilibrium in subjectivity experienced as painful—a deterritorialization of the subject that makes social living difficult. This demands attention to affects, intensities, and subtle nuances of meaning in defiance of commonsense and representable forms of experience. This, in turn, entails a process of self-transformation that resists majoritarian forms of subjectivity and invites new ways of understanding what it means to be human. The subject is not a thing with an ego that can be damaged, but rather a process that is sustained through social, psychic, and physiological processes. On this view, trauma sets off a shift in the sustaining patterns of those processes that block the ability to develop and extend one's capacities to affect and be affected. What is needed to resolve trauma is to find the points of intensification and the connections that might unblock the flows causing the problem.

Leigh Gilmore, in an investigation of trauma and identity in the context of autobiography, contends that traumatized subjects may need to resort to fiction to tell their stories because "legitimate" modes of telling the "truth" about their lives are inadequate to the truths they want and need to tell. They are unable to represent who they are because dominant modes of self-representation render what is most important about their stories—the subtleties and ambiguities of experiences that defy representation—imperceptible. Gilmore defines a notion of "limit-cases" that test the boundaries of acceptable self-representation:

> Limit-cases carve out a jurisdiction in which illegitimate subjects tell stories in forms marked by elements of fiction. In their exposure of the link between illegitimacy and fiction in self-representational projects, limit-cases expose the conditions in which alternative forms of knowledge about justice are compelled to appear, and how subjects who produce this knowledge are marked. (Gilmore 2001, 135)

Gilmore argues that such limit-cases manifest skepticism about "dominant constructions of the individual and the nation" (136). For example, she points out that Dorothy Allison's novel, *Bastard Out of Carolina*, which features the sexual abuse of a young girl, grapples with the abuse, but in the very specific context of dealing with the difficulties of the class status of poverty and an enduring and loving bond between mother and daughter. Allison, by choosing the novel form to tell her story, works through the intensities of minoritarian memory by composing affects and percepts that intimate the virtual tendencies of her experience rather than reduce that experience to "legitimate" representations. From a Deleuze–Guattarian perspective, the "truth" of her experience lies as much in its intensities and the potential connections of those intensities to as-yet unactualized modes of being as it does in what actually happened. Reducing her experience to what "actually" happened would be to reduce it and herself to snapshots that could be filed away under extant categories without getting at the singularity of the experience itself in all its layers of complexity. As Allison puts it herself in the overtly autobiographical form of her memoir:

> I tell my stories louder all the time: mean and ugly stories; funny, almost bitter stories; passionate, desperate stories—all of them have to be told in order not to tell the one the world wants, the story of us broken, the story of us never laughing out loud, never learning to enjoy sex, never being able to love or trust love again, the story in which all that survives is the flesh. (Allison 1995, 71–72)

Allison refuses to let her experiences be reduced to mainstream narratives—either those of the victim damaged beyond repair by unspeakable trauma or the intrepid survivor who beats all odds by "rising above" her circumstances.

She tells "mean and ugly stories" that fully tap the ambiguity and complexity of becomings unassimilable to the conventional representations of human existence rendered plausible by multiple faciality machines. Instead, she tells some of the gory details of the brutal rape of a twelve-year-old child and the departure of a mother who chose to leave town with the man ("Daddy Glen") who raped her daughter, leaving her daughter behind. But Allison tells this story—without mitigating any of its horrific impact on Bone, the twelve-year-old protagonist of her story—amid a larger tale about the assemblage of Boatwrights (her mother's family) and (to a lesser extent) the assemblage of the Waddells (her stepfather's family) and the assemblage formed by her mother with Daddy Glen. It is the connections and disconnections of these complicated assemblages of working parts of people and places and houses and things that are the story she wants to tell. If the trauma of incestuous rape is, in some ways, a motivating force of the novel, it is because that trauma needs putting in its place. That is, it needs to be rendered rather than represented in terms adequate to its complexities.

Being worthy of the event, in Allison's case, means to evoke it as a block of becoming with all its intensities rather than denying it, explaining it, or trying to contain it in a set of propositions. When Bone sees herself in Daddy Glen's eyes (through a series of events leading up to the rape), she wants to die. Or, to put it in her own words:

> No, I wanted to be already dead, cold and gone. Everything felt hopeless. He looked at me and I was ashamed of myself. It was like sliding down an endless hole, seeing myself at the bottom, dirty, ragged, poor, stupid. But at the bottom, at the darkest point, my anger would come and I would know that he had no idea who I was. (209)

Being worthy of the event means to go beyond any current self-representation to explore the gift-giving power of will as it brings accumulating tendencies out of what has been over threshold points toward the actualization of unanticipated forms of lived experience. This entails taking skewed perspectives that disorient coherent personal selves with their settled habits of perception and thought in order to compose percepts and affects into blocks of sensation that can precipitate the unfolding of new capacities to affect and be affected. To find out who she was, Allison's character, Bone, had to go beyond any settled conception of self to bring together the disparate durations of her life. These durations include the varying durations of her relatives (mother, aunts, uncles, grandparents, sister), each of who had worked out their own solutions to the problems of life, and with each of whom she had formed the working parts of various machines. How does one become worthy of the event of being poor, being a bastard, being from South Carolina, being a Boatwright? Bone (and perhaps Allison herself through her aesthetic rendering of her past) answers this question by refusing the dead ends offered her and instead, tapping the intensities of her rich surroundings in order to create the assemblages that could allow her to affirm her life. For Bone, this entailed making assemblages with her uncles and aunts—particularly her "notorious and dangerous" Uncle Earle who "was good with a hammer or a saw, and magical with a pickax. . . . [and] drove a truck like he was making love to the gears" (Allison 1992, 11–12) and her "reclusive old aunt," Raylene, who had been "kind of wild" in her younger days, working "for the carnival like a man, cutting off her hair and dressing in overalls," and calling herself Ray (180). Although Bone's birth certificate proclaimed her a bastard and the Boatwrights were "trash," while the Waddells owned a dairy and had a son (Daddy Glen's older brother) who ran for district attorney, her own uncle was a charmer with a "relaxed and disarming grin" who was "everything Glen had ever wanted to be" (12). Glen, the black sheep of his own family, had married Bone's mother, in part, to become the man his own family did not think of him as being.

> He would marry Black Earle's baby sister, marry the whole Boatwright legend, shame his daddy and shock his brothers. He would carry a knife in his pocket and kill any man who dared to touch her. Yes, he thought to himself, oh yes. (13)

And her Aunt Raylene "was probably the only person any of us would ever meet who was completely satisfied with her own company" (179).

> "I like to watch things pass," she [Aunt Raylene] told me in her lazy whiskey drawl. "Time and men and trash out on the river. I just like to watch it all go around the bend." She spoke softly, smelling a little of alcohol and pepper, chow-chow and home brew and the woodsmoke tang that clung to her skin all the time. (180)

Clearly, from the perspective of what one might call an ethics of becoming—an ethics premised on transmuting sadness into joy, reactive forces into active ones, and a denying will into an affirming will in order to divest power from resisting what is and instead working with what is in ways that enhance one's unfolding in the multiple assemblages of which one is a part—Bone cannot remain a working part of the assemblage her mother and sister form with Daddy Glen. As a component part of her immediate family, her capacities to perceive, feel, create, and act are so invested in defending herself against someone intent on her psychic and physical destruction that she is on the verge of paralysis. And yet she is very aware of the power of the assemblage formed by her mother, Daddy Glen, and sister. Despite the harm Daddy Glen does to her own process of individuation, the composition of Daddy Glen with her mother and sister empowers, in particular, her mother. Although it is the assemblage of Bone and her mother she would most like to preserve, she is able to let go of that assemblage—and the identities she has invested in it—in order to realign her relations with other members of the Boatwright family in a way that allows all of them to exercise their capacities in a (relatively) joyful way.

Bone's access to the virtualities informing the actual configuration of relations of her family at the time of her rape comes not just from discursive accounts in the form of family stories, but in her intuitive grasp of affect-laden interactions experienced over the course of her life. She reads the intensities of her situation in the nuances of tone, affect, and meaning her mother's response to her request that they leave Daddy Glen evokes. Being worthy of the event for Bone means that she can look her stepfather in the eye and out of the disparate fragments of her life create a plateau from which to access her past as a durational whole—a superposition of representational and nonrepresentational memories, emotions and affect, perceptions and percepts, actual states of affairs and their intensities—that can coalesce in light of the present demanding a response from her and allow her to say (with reference to a mother who, some might say, has just betrayed and abandoned her at a time of extreme need):

> Who had Mama been, what had she wanted to be or do before I was born? Once I was born, her hopes had turned, and I had climbed up her life like a flower reaching for the sun. Fourteen and terrified, fifteen and a mother, just past twenty-one when she married Glen. Her life had folded into mine. What would I be like when I was fifteen, twenty, thirty? Would I be as strong as she had been, as hungry for love, as desperate, determined, and ashamed? . . . I was who I was going to be, someone like her, like Mama, a Boatwright woman. I wrapped my fingers in Raylene's and watched the night close in around us. (309)

New ways of thinking about who we are—as subjects who unfold over time rather than selves with personal identities—can allow us, as Braidotti puts it, to "actualize virtual possibilities which had been frozen in the image of the past" (Braidotti 2006, 168). If we think of ourselves as finished products—the results of a past that played out in a series of manifest states of affairs—then our possibilities are constrained by the actual occurrences of that past. If we think of ourselves as open-ended systems that unfold in a series of metastable states always on the verge of becoming-other in ongoing interaction with others and with their milieus and environments, then who we are no longer seems like the inevitable outcome of a linear causal chain, but instead seems like a delicately balanced dance interpolated with states of relative equilibrium that with small shifts could develop in completely new directions.

Deterritorializing from designated identities can precipitate disorientation when one encounters difficulties in not being able to take up the subject positions available (although this must be weighed against the painful dissonance caused by trying to force oneself to fit in) as well as the hostile responses of others. It is easier to live within designated identities if your memories are representations and you live in the chronological time of dominant reality with its history and shared reference points. Such time supports oedipal and majoritarian subjects because it avoids the in-between by stripping intensities that could unfold in unpredictable ways. The traumatized subject is a subject who cannot live in the chronological time of dominant reality.

Allison revisits her past in a fictional work that evokes a richer sense of the imperceptible forces moving through her durations than, arguably, a "legitimately" autobiographical account presenting itself as factual could do. The latter genre demands that memory be translated into representations that can be inserted into the striated space and chronological time of the mutually reinforcing narratives of mainstream culture. Especially when autobiographies contain traumatic themes that challenge conventional notions about domestic and social life, ambiguity and skewed realities are suspect: The burden is on the writer to "prove" that the events "actually" took place, that the feelings are "real," that the challenge is warranted. From a Deleuze–Guattarian perspective, it is precisely the reduction of lived experience to representational forms of thought that strip it of its intensive potential to create new forms of life. The stories Allison tells in novel form may not be factually true, but they speak to the propulsive force of life where the past unfolds into the present in the creative act of composing percepts and affects—perceptions and emotions in their mutant, mutating forms, forms that merge and emerge from the past as a block of becoming with the present in a celebration of life as creative evolution. To tell these stories as factual narratives would be to diminish that propulsive force and thus the truth she tells: Despite their traumatic overtones, these are songs celebrating life in all its rich variety at the same time that they are investigations into the specific forces informing the singular lives of particular individuals.

A fictional approach that focuses on the concrete details of unfolding lives can allow us to see not what human beings are, but how human beings become over time in keeping with the forces of specific times and places, so that the story becomes bigger than that of Bone, her mother, Annie, or Daddy Glen—it is a story about a duration, a people, a location, a set of circumstances, a whole where the geography and climate has as big a part to play as the people and events, and where each participant is a co-participant in what is the unfolding of collective life. Bone's dilemma is ultimately not simply how to live a life, but how to live a life that honors the durations of which she is a member and a co-participant without destroying herself in the process. How does she preserve herself without damaging those who have helped make her what she is despite the damage that they have done her? How does she transform her pain and trauma into joy? How does she interpret her life in a way that increases her power of action rather than stopping her in her tracks? How does she get past hatred of what has hurt her in order to act out of her own power rather than in reaction to the traces left in her body, heart, and mind of her past? How does she extricate herself from the assemblages of which she is a part in order to form new connections more in keeping with the unfolding of her own capacities? How does she continue to honor those connections that are part of who she is? How does she transform guilt and resentment into an affirmation and celebration of life that does not deny its complexity?

According to Braidotti, becoming that allows the subject to differ from itself as much as possible while in some sense remaining faithful to itself sustains a self that can endure at the same time that its power to affect and be affected is maintained (Braidotti 2006 169).[13] Minoritarian becoming betrays dominant memory and history, but remains faithful to the qualitative shifts of the intensities insisting in the actual presence of durational becoming. Nomadic memory "reconnects to the virtual totality of a continuously recomposing block of past and present moments" (Braidotti 2006, 171). The pure past of the virtual whole is a past that is always being affected by the passing of time. As individuation unfolds, its relations to the singularities and intensities of the present are always shifting as actualizations shift the intensities implicated with shifting singularities. Although emotions are affects already anchored in the recognizable forms attached to personal selves, affects hint at the impersonal, transpersonal flow of intensities that exceeds the already organized self-system (181).

A subject can only perceive, think, do, or become "what she or he can take or sustain within his or her embodied, spatio-temporal coordinates" (Braidotti 2006, 216). Individuals differ with respect to what they are capable of, "the degree, speed and extension of one's power to interact and produce affirmative ethical relations with others" (ibid.). Just as individuals must navigate sustainable thresholds in living, so must collectives of various sorts. This, according to Braidotti, "requires a transversal synchronization of our different modes of interaction with our habitats" (224). We can sustain ourselves by fostering the kind of encounters that are appropriate for the specific "affective speed, rhythm and intensity" of the individuating processes that we are (225). It is through joining forces with others that we can enhance our own enjoyment of life (233). Changes in my own capacities to affect and be affected communicate with everything with which I come into contact. Insofar, then, as I attend to what enhances my own joy and power, I also attend to what will foster empowerment of those most like myself—that is, other human beings—around me. If those with whom I interact become less able to sustain themselves, shut down, or cut off from their capacity to affect and be affected, then I will encounter others who are unable to affect me or be affected by me, thus impeding my own power.

Insofar as I am surrounded by others who are traumatized and thus cut off from their own ability to affect and be affected, their joy dampened, their openness impaired, I am surrounded by others unable to respond to me and unable to provoke, through responsive attentiveness, responses in me that enhance my own becoming.[14] It can only enhance our own joyful becoming to be in connection with systems that are as open-ended as possible. A situation in which most lines of flight are blocked will most likely be a situation in which my own lines of flight will be blocked as well. Despite the concern for the becoming of others I am suggesting Deleuze's conception of a Spinozist and Nietzschean ethics entails, Deleuze and Guattari are not known for promoting the kind of concern and sensitivity to the other that Levinasian-inspired forms of poststructuralist feminism have advocated. In the next section, I consider how to bring out an emphasis in Deleuze and Guattari's work designed to extend its intensities beyond a perhaps overly romantic emphasis on revolutionary novelty. Although their emphasis on prepersonal singularities at the expense of personal identity may seem out of keeping with the sensitivity to the different other that many strands of feminist thought rightfully encourages, I evoke a reading that emphasizes the kind of ethical form of empowerment brought out in my interpretation of Deleuze's reading of Spinoza and Nietzsche.

Witnessing New Territories

Deleuze and Guattari deliberately create a minoritarian style that undermines an authoritarian stance and invites creative encounter. Their notion of the concept as an event that hovers over actualized states of affairs, as well as their emphasis on language as inevitably implicated with the pragmatic contexts of embodied speakers, suggests that it is impossible to think concepts except through the actual embodiment of subjectivity (whatever form that may take) in human living. The perhaps cavalier lack of concern for personal identity Deleuze and Guattari's notion of the nomadic subject indicates, however, could be attributed to the pretension so prevalent in the philosophical tradition for the philosopher to take his own identity for granted by assuming a universal voice that supposedly speaks for all of humanity, as well as an Enlightenment notion of self that privileges its mobility as an indication of its supposed "autonomy" from others. Elizabeth Pritchard argues that the trope of mobility pervading much poststructuralist thought is as guilty of perpetuating an imperialist notion of development as other Enlightenment notions, including those of rationality and autonomy (Pritchard 2000). Deleuze's philosophical experiments, after all, were carried out with institutional support, the recognition of his peers, and the resources of a comfortably bourgeois lifestyle; it is clear that he was able to sustain his personal identity as well as his conceptual personae in ways that are not available in the difficult situations of many of the marginalized subjects with which movements like feminism needs to be concerned. There may even be a strain of Nietzschean elitism in Deleuze and Guattari's work that speaks to those "strong" enough to pursue schizoanalysis without worrying about those subjects too traumatized and silenced to be welcomed or supported by their prose.[15] The subaltern subject yet to give voice, the problematic subject struggling to make affirming sense of the "abnormal" experiences of a marginalized subjectivity, the border-crossing or transnational subject attempting to fit together the lived experience of dissonant perspectives, the traumatized subject attempting to heal ruptures in her sense of a shared humanity, the anxious subject struggling to come to grips with her implication in perpetuating oppression, the raced subject confronting systemic patterns of oppression or entitlement: It is with these subjects that progressive politics must be concerned. All these subject positions need the kind of mapping that will unfold lines of flight toward new ways of life. Any feminist plane of immanence must take it as a nonphilosophical presupposition that what it means to be human is an open-ended project and that a feminist project is one of supporting fledgling forms of humanity, especially as it relates to fledgling, alternative, or resistant forms of being gendered, sexed, or sexual, in order to allow those forms to unfold and develop their capacities.

From a feminist perspective, schizoanalysis is problematic because it does not place enough emphasis on lines of the social field concerning gender, sex, and sexuality, nor does it give much consideration to the problem of giving nurturing and stabilizing support to new forms of subjectivity and collectives and the new territories they require. It is one thing to advocate a thinking and practice that fosters and supports minoritarian becoming—feminine becoming and becoming-woman among them. But the power of a feminist project is that it constitutes a thinking and practice that supports and sustains alternative modes of living one's gender, sex, and sexuality. That is, it makes connections among disparate struggles in order to galvanize coalitional support and new frames of reference for action and it tries to provide a kind of home or reterritorialization that can sustain livable modes of becoming produced through such galvanized action. As Braidotti points out:

> The real issue is conceptual: how do we develop a new post-unitary vision of the subject, of ourselves, and how do we adopt a social imaginary that does justice to the complexity? How does one work through the pain of dis-identification and loss? Given that identifications constitute an inner scaffolding that supports one's sense of identity, how do changes of this magnitude take place? Shifting an imaginary is not like casting away a used garment, but more like shedding an old skin. It happens often enough at the molecular level, but in the social it is a painful experience. (Braidotti 2008, 9)

If one's deviation from the majoritarian subject is relatively narrow, there may be enough territorialization in play that no matter what the rate of one's practice of schizoanalysis, one is unlikely to fully unravel. More marginal subjects, however, less rooted in normative territorializations, subjects who may even be excluded from the support of such territorializations, may need more in order to survive as subjects. Although Deleuze and Guattari's notion of the nomadic subject suggests that insofar as one's subjectivity unfolds in keeping with immanent flows of desire one can achieve the joy of affirmative living, the fact of the matter is that identity and personal selfhood are still inevitable aspects of human life. Just as intelligent representations support our pragmatic projects, so do representations of identity and selfhood support the pragmatic living of everyday life. Although conceptual creation finds inspiration in a confrontation with the virtual, an art of living entails using those concepts as tools that can aid in a project of dismantling strata in a way that does not entirely undermine one's location.

Although claims of Deleuze and Guattari's anarchism (most pronounced after the publication of *Anti-Oedipus*) are exaggerated (they take pains in *A Thousand Plateaus* to point out how careful any deterritorialization from human strata must be if one is to avoid the dead-end of a "botched" body without organs), it is still true that there is an insistent emphasis throughout their work on novelty. Of course, this is not surprising given Deleuze's claim that traditional thought has excluded novelty; it is precisely the emergence of difference (as opposed to a repetition of an inversion of what has already been represented) that he wants to think, for example, in *Difference and Repetition*. But this emphasis is striking in light of feminist work such as

Iris Young's "House and Home" essay where Young contends a gendered bias in emphasizing transcendence of the present toward a new future at the expense of the maintenance of the habitual routines of home (Young 2000). Although Deleuze and Guattari might be more interested in lines of flight that break free, an appropriation of Deleuze–Guattarian thought interested in promoting pragmatic change needs to take into consideration nurturing forms of territorialization that through attunement with marginal flows allow new forms of subjectivity and ways of living to stabilize and mature. I have thus chosen to intensify tendencies in their conception of subjectivity that make it conceivable from the perspective of our embodied situations as we struggle to flourish in the face of what are often painfully dissonant experiences. Putting Deleuze–Guattarian concepts into continuous variation with feminist concepts of nurturing, such as Linda Alcoff's notion of identity as an orientation emerging from collective patterns of corporeal and semiotic activity (see chapter 3), entails shifting the understanding of territorialization as entrapment to considering the question of what is needed to nurture the imperceptible into recognizable existence. This entails questioning the automatic assumption that all territorialization is suspect in order to consider just how and when territorialization can take joyful forms.

Deleuze and Guattari's emphasis on the nomadic is in part due to their view that the danger at our historical juncture is one of the homogenizing spread of globalizing capitalism and a need to ignite a faith in the earth in the wake of the death of transcendental systems of meaning. But if the fear of fascism was a threshold point in their work, it may be that in our time we are as confronted by the growing confusion caused by cultural fragmentation. We need not just to deterritorialize, but to reterritorialize (albeit it in productive ways) as well. Part of the strength of Deleuze and Guattari's work is that it provides more resources for a constructive project than many poststructuralist theories. But if there is a masculinist note struck in their theory, it may relate to how eager they are to emphasize nomadic space over the homier spaces that are our resting points as we continue to unfold. When Young speaks of making a home, or Alcoff speaks of the need for identity, they are in part referring to the need to create territories resonant with the current configurations of our lives. Spaces that sustain us by nurturing the subjects we currently are rather than rushing us on in our becoming-other give us the time we need to attune ourselves to the durational whole. Slowing down the speed of life, particularly in a day and age when everything seems to be going too fast, is a skill to be learned and practiced alongside the ability to creatively evolve. The trick is to find the right speed of life and to know how to slow down as well as to speed up in keeping with the intensities of our current living.

It has been an ongoing concern of feminism to speak to the issues and needs of subjects whose voices require the space and amplification to be heard. Such voices are rendered imperceptible in terms of dominant forms of recognition and uptake for normative subjects. As projects like that of Luce Irigaray suggests, women (or other marginalized subjects) may be heard in mainstream forums only insofar as they strip themselves of difference and speak within and through the normative. This practice, of course, renders what is different about them invisible. Thus, for example, transgender individuals who may manifest differences that defy traditional gender dichotomies are rendered perceptible through social recognition of a problem related to having a gender identity that is different from their biological sex. Such an interpretation of their situation, although it may resonate with the lived experience of some transsexuals, may render a range of variation in defiance of any straightforward bifurcation of humanity according to a gender binary invisible. Although a majoritarian subject may feel comfortable engaging in a practice of schizoanalysis that opens up his subjectivity without undermining it completely, a transgender individual experiencing gender dysphoria and mixed messages that lead her close to the edge of what is considered sane, may need to focus more on reterritorializing some sort of workable identity than to deterritorialize from oedipal subjectivity.

In "The Philosophical Critique," Alcoff gives an incisive overview of some feminist theories with respect to their positions on identity (Alcoff 2006a). She argues that although Hegel launched a radical challenge to the modernist conception of an autonomous self that was carried forward in the theoretical traditions of existentialism, phenomenology, and psychoanalysis, there is a lingering anxiety that goes with the recognition of the self's dependence on the other. This anxiety relates to anxiety about the formative effects of the other on the self, leading to a deflection or diminishment of those effects in most of the theories Alcoff examines. Even feminist theory continues this tradition, according to Alcoff.[16] Although many feminist accounts acknowledge and account for the necessity of the other in the formation of the self, they tend to restrict the other's role in terms of the substantive content it gives the self, or pathologize that role, suggesting that one is free only insofar as one is able to overcome or evade the constitutive effects of the other on one's identity. Thus, the fear of being frozen in the gaze of the other manifest in especially early works by Jean-Paul Sartre lingers in Foucault's equation of subjectification with subjection, Derrida's distrust of identity, and Butler's connections between agency and excess and subjection and subjectivity, as well as, one might add, Deleuze and Guattari's notion of the romantically revolutionary nomadic subject. A shift in emphasis more welcoming to notions of nurturing support for fledgling forms of subjectivity and mapping abstract machines such as that of feminism as one factor in providing that support could mitigate some of the effects of this lingering evasion of the impact of others in Deleuze and Guattari's conception of minoritarian forms of subjectivity.

Although I advocate intensifying refrains in Deleuze and Guattari's thought that can support nurturing fledgling forms of subjectivity without assimilating them to already established patterns, however, I share the skepticism Deleuze and Guattari express for traditional notions of personal identity and recognition. As by now should be clear, directing our attention to aspects of current awareness that lead us to explore desires freed from personal or collective identities suggests an unfolding of the capacities of the embodied subject and specific communities that defies conventional forms of self-understanding. A philosophy that takes the virtual as well as the actual into account is one that looks beyond personal subjects as well as beyond the human in order to conceptualize the differentiating forces from which persons and the human emerge and thus to go beyond the already done and already said to find resonances and points of intensification that could lead to the unfolding of the forces implicit in, for example, sexual difference (Grosz 2005b, 183). Just as appeals to a phenomenological conception of the lived experience of a personal self can sometimes lead to overlooking the intensive effects of time informing conscious experience as it unfolds, so can appeal to a notion of encounter with a personal other sometimes totalize what is a configuration of unfolding forces with only relative autonomy from the forces of my own situation and process of individuation in ways that close off creative possibilities arising in our encounters.

The Hegelian notion of recognition suggests that in order to own or claim our own humanity, we need to have that humanity somehow reflected back to us so that we can internalize it. As Alcoff suggests, this recognition may indicate a shared orientation that validates my epistemological stance in the world. If we put this into the context of theories regarding the Althusserian notion of the interpellation of the subject or the Lacanian notion of becoming a speaker of language by picking up a position in a set of (sexually differentiated) subject positions that precedes one, then it is in part through the recognition of others played out by being introduced to and being allowed to participate in ways of talking, speaking, and acting, that one is affirmed as a subject. The psychoanalytic notion of identity entails exclusion because to be the ideal ego we want and need to be we must exclude aspects of ourselves that do not fit that ideal. Thus Lacan argues that the ego in the mirror stage is set on a fictional direction right from the start (Lacan 1977, 2). And, as Julia Kristeva argues, we abject and project aspects of ourselves onto others that can hold those aspects without forcing us to acknowledge or recognize them in ourselves (Kristeva 1982, 1991).

Kelly Oliver, in an inspiring rereading of psychoanalytic theory, offers an alternative to recognition with her conception of a form of witnessing that is based on responsiveness to the concrete rather than recognition of an ideal identity we want confirmed. Although, like Alcoff, Oliver is not working from a Deleuze–Guattarian-inspired perspective, she presents a form of the feminist concern not to assimilate the other (inspired by, among others, Levinas, Derrida, and Kristeva) that can be provocatively read alongside that of Deleuze and Guattari. Her conception of witnessing evokes the more nurturing aspects of relinquishing static notions of identity in order to attune ourselves to encounters in defiance of faciality machines. Rather than the struggle to the death of Hegelian recognition, Oliver gives love a key role to play in her notion of witnessing, suggesting that love "is an ethical and social responsibility to open personal and public space in which otherness and difference can be articulated. . . . Loving eyes are responsive to the circulation of various forms of energy, especially psychic and affective energy, that enable subjectivity and life itself" (Oliver 2001, 20).

Oliver contests the notion that "the social struggles manifested in critical race theory, queer theory, feminist theory, and various social movements are struggles for recognition" (Oliver 2001, 8). Subjects do not want merely to be recognized or seen. "[T]hey bear witness to a pathos beyond recognition and to something other than the horror of their objectification. They are also testifying to the process of witnessing that both reconstructs damaged subjectivity and constitutes the heart of all subjectivity" (ibid.). Oliver contends that it is witnessing rather than recognition that subjects need; the desire to be recognized "is the desire to become objectified in order to be recognized by the sovereign subject to whom the oppressed is beholden for his or her own self-worth" (24). Thus, the need for a recognizable identity—an identity that can be repeatedly represented—is a need introduced by the oppressive situation itself. The oppressed subject would not want to be an object visible to others if she could sustain her subjectivity in another way. In Deleuze–Guattarian terms we might say that the need for recognition is a need for interpellation by faciality machines. The problem is not so much that she needs recognition as that her vital powers have been blocked; her productive desire has been prevented from making the connections that extends its capacities. Loving eyes facilitate the connections necessary for allowing the circulation of energy that makes things happen. It is not so much recognition that is needed then, as connection. The power of an individual subject cannot unfold without connecting to other energy flows.[17] It is the ability to affect and be affected that allows energy to circulate. It is the double becoming-other of genuine encounters where each allows self-transformation through being open to affecting and being affected by the other that allows new assemblages to form that enhance the power of all the components of the new assemblage.

The deliberate isolation of certain subjects blocks their power by cutting off the connections that allows them to affect and be affected by what is around them, thus blocking the unfolding of their capacities to make things happen.

Oliver characterizes witnessing as the capacity to acknowledge that the experiences of others may be real, despite our inability to comprehend them.

> Acknowledging the realness of another's life is not judging its worth, or conferring respect, or understanding or recognizing it, but responding in a way that affirms response-ability. We are obligated to respond to what is beyond our comprehension, beyond recognition, because ethics is possible only beyond recognition. (Oliver 2001, 106)

Deleuze and Guattari would agree that not everything that is real is recognizable to us. In fact, what is recognizable to us is only what is created in reaction to life—a representation that we can repeat, something we can generalize from moment to moment, thus a selection from experience that allows us to sustain ourselves in a specific form. What is real for Deleuze and Guattari are becomings (as well as actualized states of affairs that we can represent). The movement of becoming "happens behind the thinker's back, or in the moment when he blinks" (Deleuze and Parnet 1987, 1). We cannot always perceive becomings because perception has already selected from our experience that which we need to survive—that for which we already have an established effective response. Becomings involve aspects of life that we do not need to perceive in order to maintain and sustain our present forms. Consciousness allows us to extrapolate from present contexts in order to analogize, generalize, and apply what we learn in one kind of situation to other situations in ways that allow us to try new things and achieve practical goals and thus to creatively evolve. Consciousness also allows us to intuit what is beyond our present needs for survival and so to make connections beyond human need and beyond personal identities. These connections allow us to go beyond pragmatic survival to creatively evolve in an active rather than reactive manner. The real is not just what has already happened, what we can already represent to ourselves, it is also what could happen, the connections that could be made, the capacities that could unfold. These all insist in the present even if they are not perceptible, with increasing or decreasing intensity depending on changing circumstances in ways that we can intuit and to which we can then creatively respond.

Oliver's theory of witnessing provides a way of thinking about how to expand community to include unrecognizable others—those who do not "make sense," those who have experiences we cannot understand—without completely undermining ourselves or the stable patterns of social life necessary to its sustenance. Her notion of working through entails listening to the testimony of others without trying to categorize it according to our own past experiences. "These testimonies that repeat discrimination and oppression by denying differential subject positions and different social situations work to close off the social space necessary for symbolizing affects in an effort to work-through the suffering of being othered and dehumanized" (Oliver 2001, 110). Working through provides a step toward unfolding the capacity of culture to not simply admit subjects by homogenizing their humanity to fit already established forms, but to unfold human capacities in unprecedented ways toward novel ways of being human. Oliver's notion of "response-ability" can be compared with a Bergsonian intuition that moves beyond inversions of what was in order to explore and experiment with the virtual as well as actual aspects of what is.

There will always be new capacities to unfold. But we may choose at times to slow down our unfolding toward the new in order to come into better synchronization with our world and others. That I have a capacity that could unfold at this point in time does not mean that I should unfold that capacity, even if I could take joy in that unfolding. Given the different scales of living and the myriad viewpoints that can be taken, we need to be aware of the ways of life we are blocking or enabling. There are individual human bodies and subjects, but there are social bodies and collectives as well. There also is the body of the earth and the collective life of this planet. To unfold our capacities in the long-term—in the slower time of the evolution of the human race—we need to consider how and when the slowing down of some of our durations may be needed in order to enable the joyous flourishing of bodies that take a different perspective than that of our own or even that of the human race as a whole. It is part of the domains of philosophy, art, and science to be able to provide these different perspectives—perspectives that go beyond that of an individual living organism with its limited take on what it needs to survive as that organism.

The ethical task of thought-forms like philosophy and art is, as Colebrook puts it, "the creation and maximization of becoming against the *recognition* of becoming in any of its actualized terms" (Colebrook 2002, 102). Whereas representational thought tends to stabilize what is into forms of equilibrium by excluding lines of becoming that would metamorphosize being, thus enabling a recognizable world amenable to the habits and rituals of social life, an ethical approach to life would, for Deleuze and Guattari, entail resisting what is recognizable in order to pursue variations of being that could lead to new ways of perceiving, thinking, and acting more attuned to incipient capacities in collective living. In the next chapter I consider how this conception of ethics might be extended through the notion of Spinozist ethology into a collective politics and further elaborate the kind of subjectivity that could support the flourishing of human becoming such an ethology promotes.

Chapter 6

Politics, Subjectivity, and Theory

Spinozist Ethology

Moira Gatens and Genevieve Lloyd present a lucid and inspiring account of Spinozist ethology in their book, *Collective Imaginings*, which explores a Spinozist ethics in keeping with the Deleuzian account given in the last chapter in the context of the "social imaginaries" of larger social wholes. According to Gatens and Lloyd, Spinoza believes that human beings judge things on the basis of past encounters that produced joyful or sad passions as, respectively, "good" or "bad" (Gatens and Lloyd 1999, 104). Such judgments about what will best serve one's *conatus* are "more likely to be based on imagination than on rational reflection" leaving individuals prone to manipulation of their hopes and fears by those in power (92). That is (as we saw in our Deleuzian reading of Spinoza), reason is needed to overcome the "illusions and superstitions of defective imagination" and cultivate a rational understanding of bodily transitions that will allow one to take a more active role in striving to preserve one's being (33). Repeated joyful encounters with other bodies leave traces in the body that prompt ideas in the imagination that become the basis for common notions adequate to understanding how to produce such encounters. "In this way the individual begins to form knowledge of the second kind (*ratio*) as well as knowledge of the first kind (*imaginatio*). . . . human knowledge is embodied knowledge and different ways of knowing always imply correlative ways of being" (104).

Gatens and Lloyd's reading of Spinoza stresses the circulation of embodied knowledge derived through various kinds of encounters—imperfect though such knowledge might be—in the images and narratives of who we are with respect to others and our world that spring up in various forms of cultural production. Human beings, in their striving to preserve themselves, form associations that are more agreeable than not with others whose relations are most agreeable to them (i.e., other human beings). These associations "will create 'parables,' or 'social fictions,' which bind each individual to the collective" (Gatens and Lloyd 1999, 105–06). Over time, some of these fictions will "congeal into institutional forms" (106). Scientific, legal, pedagogical, and religious practices, among many others, will be informed by the "fictions" ultimately derived from the confused knowledge produced in the encounters of specific times and places. In order for a community to survive, a past and a future must be created for it "through which its members can make sense of their lives and deaths, their triumphs and sacrifices" and so become invested in its preservation (125). A sense of belonging and mutual endeavor is produced, for the most part, through the imagination. What Gatens and Lloyd call the "social imaginary" is an open and evolving set of "multiple and overlapping imaginaries" where identity can be re-negotiated in encounters where "significantly different others may open one imaginary to another" (146).[1] It is when we can ground our social imaginaries in a more "rational" understanding of the effects produced by varying compositions of relations that we can compose those relations more effectively and so bring about more joyful communities.

Gatens and Lloyd give the example of an Australian social imaginary that fantasized Australia as a continent devoid of law, society, and history prior to British colonization as grounds for entitlement to land at the expense of its indigenous inhabitants. When claims were taken to the High Court of Australia for legal recognition of traditional ownership of specific territories on the grounds that the land had indeed been occupied and cultivated (i.e., that its indigenous occupants were indeed members of an organized social group, governed by law, and therefore entitled to their land), the legal fiction that Australia was *terra nullius* prior to British colonization was challenged. In 1992, this legal fiction was overturned by the High Court in the *Mabo* judgment and an aspect of a social imaginary premised on the erasure of its indigenous inhabitants was transformed (Gatens and Lloyd 1999, 140–46). In Gatens and Lloyd's view, it is through the imaginative work of all members of society grounded in the experiments of lived experience that we can together create the social imaginaries that can lead to more skillful composition of our relations into collective wholes. Their example indicates how self-representations and narratives (e.g., that of the educated colonial occupying and cultivating uncivilized territory) can ground "feelings of belonging" and "claims to social, political and ethical entitlements" that are then circulated through social institutions (e.g., the legal system) as well as come into conflict with the social imaginary of another group (143). Clashes between social imaginaries can lead to the enhancement of the power to affect and be affected of one group at the expense of the powers of another group, as it did in this case. But such clashes also can be resolved or ameliorated, as it was in this case, by increased insight into how one group's powers were thwarted and how unblocking that group's powers could actually enhance the whole composed of the two groups' component parts.

Caroline Williams, like Gatens and Lloyd, stresses the role of the imagination and the affective nature of the social imaginary in her reading of Spinoza. She points out the positive role given to a materialist conception of the imagination by contemporary Spinozist scholarship: "Exposing the non-rational, imaginative sources of reason and the affective composition of individuals and groups, the contemporary view of imagination is given a much stronger political as well as epistemological sense" (Williams 2007, 350). The mind, according to Spinoza, is "an idea of the body perceived under the attribute of thought. It is a kind of thinking body since each of its ideas have their source in images regarding the affective state of the body" (355). Imagination reflects the traces of the changes brought about through interactions with other bodies retained in the body. Since "the recollection of one experience may trigger imaginative associations with similar ones. . . . imagination, image and memory are intimately tied to our affective and corporeal existence" (ibid.). To return to our earlier example, the conceptions of Australia of both British colonials and indigenous inhabitants emerged from the concrete encounters of bodies engaged in practices that would enhance joy and avert sadness. Sustaining the patterns of activity that successfully empowered one in the past means extending the identities formed in such encounters along with the practices supporting them. The knowledge of how to empower oneself and one's collectives is confused when it rests on past encounters without insight into how those encounters unfold with respect to the dynamic intensities of specific situations. Although knowledge of how one set of effects may be followed by other effects may give rough guidelines for how to transpose knowledge of what was effective in the past to existing situations, more refined knowledge is required to gain more control in harmonizing evolving forces.

As we saw in Deleuze's reading of Spinoza, *conatus* strives to preserve the relations of movement and rest that define our composite bodies (EP 320). Since, as Williams puts it,

> the human body requires many other bodies to preserve and regenerate itself, and . . . the affects are always turned towards others, conative existence is always implicated in the desires and aspirations of others. . . . Thus, every desire is socially mediated, and each conatus will be modified and affected through a process of interaction and communication with others. At the same time, since the desire of each may differ from the desire of another (EIII, P57), so the conatus will give rise to a matrix of psychic and social conflict with important political effects. (Williams 2007, 356)

In this view, desire is better read in terms of flows that exceed any particular individual (rather than as the desire of a personal self). From a Deleuze–Guattarian perspective, we could say that an individual's power to affect and be affected is mediated by the many flows (e.g., physiological, organic, and social) of which she is a part and that the signifying flows of collective assemblages of enunciation and machinic assemblages of desire of a given social field entail empowering as well as disempowering effects for the individuals caught up in them. Imagination embodies knowledge of these effects. A more intuitive understanding of the interaction of unfolding forces manifesting in these effects would provide a form of knowledge that could lead to more skillful interventions in the flows of life with more joyful results for the multiple components of the bodies (of various kinds) involved. According to Gatens and Lloyd, ethology, as a way of thinking that would promote a Spinozist ethics and politics, rather than claiming to know universal values for humanity would, on the basis of observation and experimentation, "provide a sketch of that which aids, and that which harms, a particular being's characteristic relations with its surroundings, along with a description of its desires and aversions" (Gatens and Lloyd 1999, 100). Insofar as ethology is premised on Spinoza's knowledge of the second kind, it is a knowledge that can lead to the production of joyful encounters for the community as a whole.

Gatens and Lloyd's and William's emphasis on the importance of the imagination and the embodied nature of knowledge in Spinoza's account resonates with the interpretation of Deleuze's conception of Spinozist and Nietzschean ethics presented in the last chapter. It seems to me that the answer to the question of the kind of knowledge that can help one to compose "better" relations of speed and rest that pervades the work of Deleuze and Guattari manifests in the Nietzschean terms of "active" rather than "reactive" solutions that exercise an affirming "belief in the earth" and "invention of a new people" rather than the negative turning away from the earth manifest in ethical and political perspectives grounded in transcendental ideals and universal, normative conceptions of the subject. Additionally, the Spinozist emphasis on a theory of affect that would have us attend to the intensities affecting us as well as foster relations that would unfold our joyful participation in life as becoming, suggest ways of elaborating the ethical and political implications of Deleuze and Guattari's notions (discussed in earlier chapters) of mapping, plateaus, the construction of bodies without organs, and lines of flight.

Spinozist ethology amounts to mapping events in terms of the singularities of specific durations (and thus with respect to topographies that change over time) rather than with respect to universals. This requires a nonrepresentational self-understanding—that is, a self-understanding premised on a notion of self as a durational whole immersed and continually connected to other durations—as well as cultural practices that encourage embodied forms of knowing rather than reduce reality to what can be represented by cognitive intelligence. Mapping some part of how objects and subjects emerge from the flow of life, allows us to see not only what elements came together to make the forms with which we are familiar, but also to see how those forms are right now always on the verge of becoming something else. Such mapping entails discernment of how forces with their virtual intensities unfold into the manifest reality of our present as well as discernment of how our conscious experience of that reality is informed by patterns of living that may be predominantly reactive. Additionally, such mapping, by enabling us to think the virtual (always in relation to the actual in which it inheres), suggests creative compositions of relations of speed and rest that can unfold new, more actively affirming, solutions to the problems of living.

In chapter 3 we saw one form mapping can take in the feminist genealogical accounts of the concept of race tracked by McWhorter and Warnke and the concept of disability tracked by Stubblefield. Such analysis of the historical sedimentation of meaning insisting in words we use today with little conscious awareness of the past situations through which those words evolved allows us to become more aware of the intensities inflecting their present use. Such maps can foster new flows of meaning that affect the nonconscious attitudes and assumptions the use of words can carry. If we are concerned with ameliorating the lives of groups oppressed by such concepts, intensifying nuances of meaning can bring out their practical and affective force and suggest appropriate changes. Spinoza's theory of affect as interpreted by Deleuze, Gatens and Lloyd, and Williams, however, entails more than attending to the discursive force of words. It entails attunement to the quickening and dampening of joy as we engage in all the practices of social living. Thus, although discursive analyses, for example of legal precedent, as we saw in the *Mabo* case, can help to track evolving forces involved in legal meaning, the affective force of such meaning (e.g., the identities and the affective investments those identities entail of British descendents and indigenous groups) needs to be taken into account as well. Furthermore, nondiscursive as well as discursive practices may carry affective charges that are not readily articulable; Spinozist ethology takes us beyond the analysis of discursive genealogies, as well as a liberal conception of the public realm as a space of open debate adhering to the rules of rational discourse, to a reconsideration of how multiple forms of expression intimate our shifting capacities and our attempts to honor those capacities in our collective unfolding.

For Nietzsche, interpretations and evaluations spring from embodied ways of being rather than the reactive awareness of cognitive reflection. For Spinoza, reason, to be effective, needs to emerge from experimental encounters attuned to how shifting compositions of powers of affecting and being affected can be harmonized. Both imply that we need a more robust notion of rationality if we are to become more skillful at creating the kind of lives suited for the embodied forms of life we are. Such a notion of rationality must include the opening up of our senses and emotions to full participation in the multiple durations of which we are a part rather than the repetitive and sterile tracings of implications derived from representations of the past denuded of their virtual potential. This suggests a cultural need for multiple forms of thought that refuse to subordinate or assimilate themselves to any overarching pattern that would totalize them into a homogenized whole. We need to make connections among our multiple durations—transversal connections that promote vitalizing flows, maps of overarching and heterogeneous patterns through which we can galvanize new and shifting forms of individual and collective identities, and stories and imaginaries through which we give our lives impetus and meaning. This requires various approaches and strategies that shift over time in keeping with tensions that accumulate over thresholds that lead to new forms of living.

The means by which we transform ourselves into the kind of creatures who can joyously compose their relations with other relations and actualize active forces through the power of affirmative willing requires ongoing counter-actualization of the sense of events so that we unfold the capacities that push us with intensifying force (rather than holding them back from what they can do in order to maintain old patterns of living) toward a future we cannot predict. In order to attune ourselves to intensifying forces (rather than ignoring or thwarting them) we need to open ourselves to the affective effects brought on by the increases and decreases in our power of action as we engage our world and the others in it. And we need to do this in such a way that rather than becoming fixated on what impedes our own increases in power, we affirm what is and become adept at composing our relations to what is in effective ways. Both Spinoza and Nietzsche thought that forms of social life have everything to do with the power of the individuals participating in it; human individuals are assemblages formed through relations that are social (as well as physiological, organic, geographical, and so forth). Both thought that the social life of their day left something to be desired in terms of the forms of human living it engendered. Spinoza diagnosed social life as premised on confused ideas. Nietzsche diagnosed culture as sick and reactive. To enact the immanent ethics they endorse requires a politics as well—a politics of social change that promotes the transformation of not simply an individual, but the collectives through which individuals become as well as the larger wholes through which, in turn, collectives become.

If Deleuze and Guattari's descriptions of the genealogy of the modern subject and its inherent (schizo) alternatives have any resonance, to even think the changes required by a shift to an immanent ethics and politics requires a shift in the very way we experience our world from that of dominant forms of majoritarian subjectivity (premised as the latter is on a reactive, oedipal subject) to that of a nomadic subject able to intuit duration and become with time. To begin to live as the nomadic subject entails deterritorialization from the multiple ways that subjectivity is stabilized and normalized—from the faciality machines of identity that operate at the level of perception, comportment, habitual reaction, emotion, and thought to capitalism as an abstract machine informing the myriad assemblages of which we are working parts in an increasingly globalized community.

William Connolly, in a provocative exploration of what he calls the "neuropolitics" of contemporary life, points out that Deleuze's conception of "affectively imbued thinking" suggests that thinking is "already under way by the time consciousness intervenes to pull it in this or that direction." Deleuze's perspective provokes one "to think about how institutional disciplines, micropolitical movements, and tactics of the self are deployed to move the affective organization of thought and judgment" (Connolly 2002, 95). Connolly suggests that techniques of thought may be required to take us beyond normative thinking. Such techniques would work at levels beyond the cognitive to allow new patterns of being to emerge:

> An ethical sensibility, you might say, is composed through the cultural layering of affect into the materiality of thought. It is a constellation of thought-imbued intensities and feelings. To work on an established sensibility by tactical means, then, is to nudge the composition of some layers in relation to others. You work experimentally on the relays between thought-imbued *intensities* below the level of feeling and linguistic complexity, thought-imbued *feelings* below the level of linguistic sophistication, *images* that trigger responses at both levels, and linguistically sophisticated patterns of *narrative, argument, and judgment.* You do so to encourage the effects of action upon one register to filter into the experience and imagination available on others, thereby working tactically upon a dense sensibility whose layered composition is partly receptive to direct argument and deliberation, partly receptive to tactics that extend beyond the reach of argument, and partly resistant to both. (106)

Techniques are required—for the self and for collectives—that can shift things at levels other than that of representational thought. Cultural practices—art, philosophy, science, among others—work on our bodies and minds at subthreshold levels, levels below the conscious meaning we attach to them. Work like that of Connolly's takes seriously the need for reworking the subjectivity of those already invested in promoting change (as well as of those set against it) when considering how to engage an effective politics. Progressive social change requires insight into how multiple flows in mutually implicating and superposing patterns result in the conscious awareness of individuals in their specific locations. The processes from which we emerge are both shared and diverge in ways that we can map in order to more skillfully intervene and thus foster more vibrant flourishings of the whole of which we all form a part.

In the next section I summarize and elaborate some of the features of a kind of subject more able to engage the kind of immanent ethics and politics a Deleuze–Guattarian conception of Spinozist ethology suggests. This schizo or nomad subject is already with us; it is a possibility and opportunity emerging from the forces and intensities of our own time and place. Imperfect knowledge of this subject embodied in images, stories, multiple aesthetic forms, scientific models, and theory (like that put forth in this book), could contribute to social imaginaries supporting post-majoritarian forms of subjectivity and further insights into how to organize our collective flourishing.

Minoritarian Subjectivity

The normative subject of late capitalism that Deleuze and Guattari describe— the subject who is positioned in terms of its deviation from the majoritarian subject—is a subject who is self-regulating, self-policing, and paranoid. This inevitably lacking subject has a secret shame about her (or his) inevitable failure to be fully adequate—fully human—and is always guilty with respect to an infinite debt to a mysterious father who is the agent and representative of the paternal law that both constitutes who she is as well as blocks other possibilities in becoming. If she could only fill in the hole in what should be a complete subject—through the objects of consumption she buys if not through what she is—she could finally feel worthy. But her desires are ultimately dangerous. If they deviate from the norm, she is perverted, psychotic, or subhuman. It is only by filling in an unfathomable lack that she can finally be what she wants to be—a subject without lack. Thus, she must divert herself from making alternative connections, close herself off from her surroundings, and defer whatever alternative satisfactions might come her way in order to get *the* object that will finally make her whole. If her particular location is relatively unproblematic, then the molar identities of the faciality machines actualized through her patterns of living will be unproblematic reference points for personal identity and life narratives about how she ought to live. Although even in such cases there will be intensities and affects subtending molar identity that could be actualized into lines of flight from dominant reference points, this is more likely to occur when converging flows produce dissonance among her lived orientations and the molar identities she is called on to enact.

Deleuze and Guattari's account of the oedipal subject in *Anti-Oedipus* as well as the molar or majoritarian subject of *A Thousand Plateaus*, suggests that the dominant form of the modern subject of late capitalism is a subject at a critical juncture. Their ethics and politics advocates deterritorializing this subject from a beyond-human perspective that accesses the virtual in order to foster connections that allow humanity to creatively become rather than maintain itself in keeping with already established forms of human life. Tapping the creative resources of the present, in their view, entails what Deleuze calls "counter-effectuating" events of sense (i.e., exploring permutations in meaning by actualizing that meaning in new states of affairs in ways that go beyond how that meaning was actualized in the past), as well as pursuing intensities in sensation and feeling that lead to new forms of experience in order to "become worthy of what happens to us, and thus to will and release the event, to become the offspring of one's events and thereby to be reborn" (LS 149). Deleuze and Guattari's descriptions of this process are helpful and evocative for the process of self-creation undergone by subjects unable to resonate with contemporary norms as well as evaluating when such identity formations can in turn become counterproductive. They are also helpful for those struggling for new ways of coming into ethical harmony with human and nonhuman others as well as the environment as a whole. According to Deleuze and Guattari's view, ethical transformations entail self-transformation. To become worthy of the event we need to extend our capacities, unfolding potentials not yet actualized, inventing a new people and a new earth in the process.[2] With the benefit of the delay we can open up between perception and action we can creatively access the virtualities of our present and create new habits of living in tempo with our changing circumstances.

Human subjects are relatively stable configurations of physiological, signifying, and subjectifying processes. They emerge from self-sustaining psychic and corporeal refrains. These refrains play out in day-to-day routines and habitual ways of thinking, speaking, and interacting with others. These collective practices, along with the physiochemical and neurological processes of organisms like us, are the material basis of our shared humanity. We share a particular speed and duration with human others we do not share with mountains or amoebas. Like any life-form, human subjects and collectives want not simply to sustain themselves, but to unfold their capacities—capacities that are implicit or virtual as well as already actualized and which may or may not become actualized as changing circumstances provide the kinds of situations that will elicit them. Deleuze and Guattari take issue with the psychoanalytic idea that desire is fundamentally the desire to fill in a lack experienced by an oedipal subject in relation to the ideal ego it needs to be in order to get the kind of recognition it wants (and needs to feel whole), and instead emphasize a Spinozist conception of the power of the body and a Nietzschean notion of life as the power to unfold new capacities. A human individual, on this view, comes to know itself not through recognition and identification, but through experimenting with the kind of effects it has on the world and learning how the world affects it. Whereas psychoanalysis posits the necessity of a break with the world (introduced through the rupture of the mother–child dyad) in order for the subject to be able to take up a position vis-à-vis the world as a speaker of language, Deleuze and Guattari's work suggests that the relative autonomy of human processes of individuation can be established through refrains of physiological, corporeal, and semiotic activity. In a process of becoming-other in which the infant and young child embodies various patterns in the multiple assemblages of which she forms a part, meaningful refrains stabilize that can be taken up into the reiterations of speech and institutionalized social practices. The embodied patterns of lived orientations occur in large part below the threshold of consciousness. On this view, identifications with respect to an ego ideal that transcends the ongoing connections of concrete interactions entail reducing the range of possible connections one could meaningfully make to those that "make sense" for that ego ideal (whether those connections are marked "good" or "bad" with respect to the ideal). Thus, the dynamic becoming of a human process of individuation unfolds not with respect to the power to affect and be affected it could extend in keeping with the changing circumstances of life, but rather with respect to a fantasy of wholeness rendered desirable through multiple social machines. What becomes desirable is not to make the affective and meaningful connections available to physiological, corporeal, and semiotic creatures like ourselves, but rather to have a fantasy of wholeness confirmed through procedures of recognition.

The minoritarian subject pursuing lines of flight from majoritarian forms of subjectivity is an intuitive subject who acts in relation to her capacities as they come into play with the capacities unfolding in the impersonal and inhuman flows of life, as well as the social, political, and cultural flows of human life. In the Bergsonian view that is an important influence in Deleuze and Guattari's work, a human being has more choices in action than instinctual reactions allow when a delay or interval between perception and action is filled with the intellectual ability to access representational memories that can indicate viable alternative responses to situations that are similar to ones encountered in the past. The intuitive ability to access the durational whole of time widens the gap beyond that provided by representational intelligence and allows creative resolutions of problems unique to specific durations. The intuitive subject is able to extend new capacities by accessing intensities that insist in the present rather than acting in ways that are analogous to past patterns of action drawn from representational memory. Intuitive action does not require an identity removed from the rest of the world as the basis for first choosing or willing an act, and then carrying it out. Instead, it entails the lengthening of an interval made possible by the nervous system that allows access to virtual relations beyond habitual reactions in ways that enable the extension of new patterns of response.

This view moves away from a conception of the subject as someone who must first represent to herself what it is she must do in order to be able to carry out that act. Instead, the intuitive subject experiments with the intensities of her situation, feeling for resistances and resonances, pursuing new connections (sometimes with the help of philosophical concepts, art forms, or scientific functions) that can induce new forms of experience. Instead of focusing on what she wants to remain the same, she focuses on intensifying affect—even when this means focusing on anomalies and what may resist current paradigms of perception and conception. She works with life, experimenting by testing out various actions in order to register their effects and then moving on to try other actions. Like a seismologist, she sounds out various possibilities, varying the registers she uses in order to play with the intensities of her situation; she does not assume that any situation can be definitively captured or its possibilities adequately expressed in representational thought. She works toward transforming sad passions into joyful ones, and understanding the processes that result in the difference. Such a protagonist acts, not due to envisioning a state of affairs that she can then bring about, but because forces moving through and with her push her toward the future—a future that includes representational thought as one of its effects among others.

From a Deleuze–Guattarian perspective, agency as it is conceived traditionally is an illusion. That an agent can make choices and act accordingly depends on the convergence of forces beyond her control in an actualization of a state of affairs that includes her as an embodied individual with the psychic self and social identity that she has. Subjectivity is an ongoing process of diverging difference, an individuating flux that is always unfolding with and through the fluxes of which it is a part and within which it is immersed; it unfolds in concert with life as creative evolution. Individuation occurs not when a subject or identity is opposed to what surrounds it, but when a flow emerging from other flows is able to sustain its own speed in relative autonomy from the speeds of other durations. Its agency lies not simply in sustaining its current capacities but in unfolding those capacities through its relations to other flows that can affect it and be affected in various ways that further shift what else can unfold. Agency on this view is best engaged not by focusing on what one has already become—that would be to deny the connections to the surrounding world that sustain one's present form as well as the connections that could extend that form into new ways of being. Instead, skillful agency is to unfold one's connections as effectively as possible, and thus to come to know through intuitive insight and experimentation as well as rational reflection what effects produce what other effects, how one can be affected, and how shifts in the social field affect the mutual interactions of communal living. Furthermore, in addition to considering the agency of a human subject as a flow of individuation in its own right, we could consider the agency of other processes of individuation that sustain themselves in relatively stable forms and have varying capacities to affect and be affected by surrounding flows. Human individuals are component parts of multiple assemblages at once that can vary and change over time. Friendship, family, group, community and national assemblages, as well as human-thing, geographical, climatic, and eco-assemblages—all can be considered as individuals in their own right with self-sustaining patterns of activity that can diverge over time into new patterns.

Representative memories constitute a history that block off lines of flight in the present by turning the past into static snapshots and rendering their intensities in the present imperceptible. Anti-memories are blocks of becoming or maps that tap into a past that still insists in one's present in the form of intensities that could unfold if one opens to them in terms of their becoming rather than reducing them to manifestations with no intensity. Phenomenological descriptions can play a role in creating such anti-memories when they reveal nonconscious orientations lived by the human subject at the intersection of organic, signifying, and subjectifying strata. They can thus provide maps indicating counter-narratives and counter-histories that could release new possibilities in the present. The intensive self actualizes intensities from where it is (what experiments do I want to do next?), whereas the extensive self realizes possibilities as they are represented or representable in the categories of dominant memory (who do I want to be?). The minoritarian subject lives her identity otherwise—as an intensification on a line of continuous variation rather than the repetition of molar identities that demand confirming recognition from others. Groups and larger collectives as well, inform their present becoming through the perspectives taken on their past, whether it be through the representative memories of a linear narrative or the anti-memories of shared becomings that invites a more experimental attitude toward the past and future.

According to Deleuze and Guattari, representational identity—like a notion of a body with specific properties—is a representation of a specific duration of being-a-self (or a group or a community) where that state of being was in relative equilibrium. Just as representations of the body can be pragmatically useful, so can representations of the self be useful. The problem comes not in representing the self in terms of a static identity with specific properties, but rather in reducing a dynamic unfolding of individuation to such representations, stripping the creative resources of intensive becoming in the process. Therefore, we could posit, although Deleuze and Guattari themselves spend little time worrying about supportive forms of identity, two notions of identity: the molar identity of the faciality machines that is a reference point for resonating and affirming conventional forms of subjectivity, and identity as an act of self-naming that constitutes a body without organs as a galvanizing plateau where old patterns are suspended and a new configuration intensifying different virtual relations to threshold points could occur. Narratives as well could, from this perspective, take either the majoritarian form of confirming dominant memory in terms of representational snapshots of what it means to be human or the minoritarian form of anti-memories that contest dominant memory and introduce intimations of the virtual into our present becoming.

Ronald Bogue, in a helpful exposition of Deleuze and Guattari's characterization of Kafka as a minor writer, suggests that although the major writer "leaves undisturbed the regular codes and organized practices established in language, seeking simply an adequate expression for a preshaped content," the minor writer induces "metamorphosis of the established forms of the social field" (Bogue 2003, 110). The task of the minor writer is to experiment with a language's collective assemblages of enunciation. The latter actualize specific circuits of power in given social contexts. Minor writing activates "virtual lines of continuous variation immanent within language, which open vectors of transformation toward a people to come" (112). Extending this notion of the minor writer to the minoritarian subject, we could say that the latter seeks a metamorphosis not only of the collective assemblages of enunciation, but of machinic assemblages of bodies as well, and that her work can play out on multiple registers through aesthetic processes of self-formation entailing self-naming along with other experiments in semiotic activity and action. When the identity in question is that of a group or a collective, we can see how the minoritarian subject could precipitate collective metamorphoses (thus bringing about a "people to come") as well as those of individual subjects. Narratives created in keeping with these new identities in various modalities (aesthetic, cultural, political) further elaborate, support, and confirm those identities and the patterns of activity they entail.

Acts of self-naming, like minor writing, other aesthetic practices, philosophy, and the art of living, can all invite transformations of the social field that elicit new forms of individual, group, and collective becoming-human. The minoritarian self is a superposition with different ways of accessing the past in keeping with forces that are always moving toward an unpredictable future. Such a self is always experimenting, trying new things, unfolding new capacities. Her memory lies in the intensities waiting to unfold. Her representational identities are transitory plateaus from which she can unfold new ways of being; they constitute acts of naming particular moments of her becoming-other that can affect the present by intensifying the forces insisting in the present that suspend habitual patterns and provoke new ones. Acts of self-naming create proper names akin to philosophical concepts rather than the normative categories of identity designations: Like a concept they bring together a plateau of component meanings as the singularities or limit points informing a wide range of potential actualizations (see chapter 1). Such identities are not computed by the faciality machines but are a living response to a particular configuration of lived orientations and so reflect a minoritarian response to the faciality machines of her location. For example, Monique Wittig claimed that lesbians are not women because, as Diane Griffin Crowder puts it, "[l]esbians, for Wittig, refuse 'to become or to stay heterosexual,' to enter into or remain in an economic, political, social, or ideological relationship with a man, and are thus 'escapees from [their] class in the same way as American runaway slaves were when escaping slavery and becoming free' ("One Is Not Born a Woman," *SM*, 20; *PS*, 63)" (Crowder 2007, 496 quoting Wittig 1992). Thus Wittig asserts the name "lesbian" (in an act of self-naming that resonated with some of her readers in affirming ways), not in the sense of the binary opposite of "woman" as man's complement with its connotations of being, for example, a "man-hater," but as a name for someone working in the interstices of such binaries. Wittig's novel, *Les Guérillères*, was an audacious stylistic experiment in that she used "*elles*"—the feminine form, in French, of "they"—for the universal, in order to displace a language that always situates woman as the counterpart of a male universal. Furthermore, Wittig was aware of engaging these experiments at a particular point in time. Her hope and her political project were to resist reproducing "the institutions of the heterosexual regime" by performing "a series of repeated daily actions that construct lesbians as not-women and not men" (Crowder 2007, 492). The connotations in meaning her act of self-naming unfolds created certain effects when her work was first published and creates other effects now. Her use of the word "lesbian" neither exhausts nor instantiates that word's meaning, but unfolds with other meanings of the word and other acts of self-naming attuned to a social field that is always evolving.

Such acts of self-naming along with the narratives that support and elaborate them must resonate with the complexities that arise in the subject's process of being the emergent effect of heterogeneous processes if they are to invite creative unfolding. Rather than a subject organized around a personal self, the nomadic subject passes from one state to another in a line of becoming where her identity is never the same, but where her memories accumulate and superpose in an ever richer deepening of symbolic and corporeal patterns that continually shift the actualizations that can occur in the present. These memories are not the reduced memories of representable moments, but the intensities of patterns of activity: the neural and muscular patterns that intensify in learning to ride a bike, the emotional and aural patterns that intensify in appreciating a piece of music, the conceptual and psychic patterns that intensify in coming to understand herself or her world in a different way. They emerge in the interstices of routine living or during practices (such as meditation; participation in art forms like music, poetry, and dance; "genuine" philosophical thinking; communions with nature; extreme sports; communal events such as a political demonstration) designed to elicit plateaus—moments when she is more attuned to the specificities of the present and the incipient capacities of body, heart, and mind they call forth than the automated patterns of living that sustain her life in its familiar forms. With the benefit of intuitive thought-forms like philosophy and various aesthetic practices, as well as the encounters with others (human and nonhuman) from all over the world made possible through high-tech forms of travel and communication, she can intuit multiple durations in complicated ways without losing the grounding of her own embodied duration. Such intensifications in virtual possibilities, whether or not they are completely actualized, leave their traces in the ways they come together with present forces of becoming, creating in the process new thresholds in lived experience. These intuitive experiences and encounters widen the gap between perception and action based in a representational understanding of herself and her past and enable an intensive relation to time where she can unfold previously unactualized tendencies insisting in her present. Groups and communities of various kinds as well can deliberately evoke plateaus in collective practices or find ways to productively resonate unexpected anomalies in habitual patterns back into the processes that sustain them.

The minoritarian subject engages in acts of collective as well as individual self-naming. She knows that insofar as she shares territories with others—habitual patterns of thinking, feeling, speaking, interpreting, behaving, routines of living, strategies of survival, methodologies of knowledge, arenas of activity—she shares orientations of which she may or may not be explicitly aware that inform her perceptions, emotions, cognitions, deportment, and behavior. In order to unfold the becomings she shares with others in defiance of majoritarian norms, she needs to pay attention to the interstices of her experience as well as the experiences of others. Maria Lugones develops a notion of "complex communication" that conceives a kind of communication appropriate to what she calls the liminal spaces of social life (Lugones 2006). Her depiction of a subject willing to undergo self-transformation in response to aspects of experience that resist assimilation to available categories of meaning is a powerful example of one of many forms of minoritarian subjectivity that already exist. According to Lugones, although domination constructs the oppressed subject as invisible, abnormal, inferior, or threatening, oppressed people "have a vocabulary for what the oppressor does to the oppressed, a shared wisdom" that leads the oppressed to "create a clear sense of standing in a dual reality, one in which we use double perception and double praxis" (Lugones 2006, 78). Exercising a double vision that can read reality as multiple and begin to decipher codes resistant to the oppressive reality of domination "can enable genuine coalition and effective resistance to domination" (75). The first step in such a process is to recognize liminality. The limen "is at the edge of hardened structures, a place where transgression of the reigning order is possible" (ibid.):

> To understand that you are in a limen is to understand that you are not what you are within a structure. It is to know that you have ways of living in disruption of domination. . . . [I]f we recognize each other as occupying liminal sites, then we will have a disposition to read each other away from structural, dominant meaning, or have good reason to do so as oppressed peoples. (79)

Recognizing and reading one another as occupying liminal sites requires a form of communication that refuses to reduce, translate, or assimilate experience to the "transparent" monologue of liberal (as well as other forms of) conversation:

> Complex communication thrives on recognition of opacity and on reading opacity, not through assimilating the text of others to our own. Rather, it is enacted through a change in one's own vocabulary, one's sense of self, one's way of living, in the extension of one's collective memory, through developing forms of communication that signal disruption of the reduction attempted by the oppressor. Complex communication is creative. In complex communication we create and cement relational identities, meanings that did not precede the encounter, ways of life that transcend nationalisms, root identities, and other simplifications of our imaginations. (84)

If we think of complex communication "as occurring among intercultural polyglots who are disposed to understand the peculiarities of each other's resistant ways of living," we may be willing to undergo the kind of self-transformations necessary to engage in forms of communication that resist assimilation to the social practices and orientations of mainstream forms of subjectivity (ibid.). Such communication can intensify shared orientations, inducing shared plateaus from which new challenges to oppressive configurations of power can unfold. One could conceive as well group practices inviting complex communication in multiple forms where a body without organs or plateau could be created between two or more groups, thus suspending the habitual routines of each in order to allow relations to form from which new ways of being with one another could emerge.

Deleuze and Guattari's notions of desiring machines and assemblages emphasize the dynamic interaction of the individual with its surroundings through the flows that connect it with other flows. Subjects emerge and are sustained through the repetitive patterns that the processes informing them maintain. The axiomatics of capitalism fosters normative patterns of human living, many of which are ultimately antithetical to human existence. Globalization of this axiomatic is already having frightening consequences in terms of environmental damage and the physical, economic, and cultural impoverishment of variations in human living. In their celebration of the creative fecundity of life, Deleuze and Guattari were most horrified at the thought of reterritorializations of human existence that reduce all human variation to impoverished subjects serving the continuance of capitalism as a specific life-form of its own—a life-form which like any life-form is invested in its survival.[3] At the same time, globalization is intensifying and releasing new forms of human living that exceed and complicate capitalism's homogenizing forces. Although Deleuze and Guattari emphasize prepersonal singularities and the genetic processes through which a subject comes to be what it is, this is not to say that subjects are not formed or experience not deeply felt by living beings with personal selves. Their view encourages us to see ourselves as momentary waves in a flux of biological and social flows, but these waves are experienced by us, in keeping with our pragmatic needs and concerns, as relatively stable things. Implicit in our current experiences, our sense of selves, our ways of doing things, however, is a reality that relates to the power we have yet to unfold in our living. Science allows us to think the virtual possibility of global warming that is now becoming actualized, unprecedented as it appeared to be. It also allows us to think the possibility of walking on Mars and finding new cures for cancer. Art and philosophy also can allow us to approach the virtual in ways that allow us to conceive new modes of perception, affection, cognition, and action. Philosophy can think the virtualities that structure the flows producing our conscious experience and present bodies by thinking the limit points of the processes through which we are what we are. Art can think these flows by composing affects and percepts that intimate perceptions and emotions beyond those of commonsense experience. Feminism, by virtue of intuiting the limit points of conventional understandings of sex, gender, and sexuality, thinks the flows of sex, gender, and sexuality in ways that suggest new concepts of all three and thus can incite actual living to new thresholds. A Deleuze–Guattarian approach is a realist approach that is not "realistic" in the sense of needing to assume that the future will be just like the past. Instead, it invites us to conceive our reality in terms of the dynamic temporality it is, unfolding always in divergence from the actualities of the past in keeping with the singularities that structure the relations composing those actualities along with their future unfolding.

Feminism could be seen as an untimely schizo practice designed to intervene with contemporary configurations of modern subjectivity that involve suppression and oppression of subjects that deviate from a majoritarian norm with the fault lines of sexed, gendered, and sexual identity as its starting point. Deleuze and Guattari provide a narrative about the formation and production of those subjects that suggest critical points of intervention that could move us beyond binary categorization of sex and gender and the oppression it entails. By distinguishing subjectivity as patterns of lived activity from faciality machines that designate identity they give us a way of understanding how we could be subjects without the binary designations that we currently think of as crucial to being any kind of subject at all. But they do not think we can simply choose to leave those binary machines behind. Rather, they recommend carefully mapping where we are in order to find vitalizing paths that extend the tendencies resisting binary designations. And they suggest that rather than be paranoid about the anarchic chaos we imagine moving beyond such binaries could cause, that we consider the capacities we could unfold if we could open up to the impersonal and inhuman flows around us. They present us with alternative conceptions of subjectivity as relatively stabilized patterns of physiological, corporeal, and semiotic activity that mutate over time in keeping with the flows that constitute them and the flows with which they come into contact, but which, as self-organizing systems, and, in particular, human self-organizing systems with the capacity to intuit the durational whole, can consciously participate in their creative evolution. And while such participation does not entail the masterful control of the autonomous subject as conceived by traditional modernity, it does entail ways of being more skilful than others in coming into joyful synchrony with the flows around it.

Deleuze and Guattari could be read as advocating a renewed relation with durational time—one transformed by the spatialized time of modernity that allowed unprecedented technological advances and global networks, but which breaks with the spatialized time conducive to specific forms of social life in order to obtain intuitive access to the flows supporting that life.[4] To learn to be at home in durational time and the becomings that condition the striations of contemporary social life is to learn new skills in social living attuned to alternative aspects of contemporary reality. Deleuze and Guattari give us concepts to actualize events of sense that could shift our intensities to be more open to such becomings. In the next section I revisit the role of theory as one practice among others that can promote the intensification of contemporary tendencies that might push us toward a different way of thinking about who we are and the ethical and political possibilities available to us.

Theory

Theory does not, for Deleuze and Guattari, represent something more or less accurate about a world from which it is removed. Instead, theory unfolds itself in lines of force that converge and diverge with the lines of force of other things in the world to make things happen. Deleuze and Guattari's project entails thinking consciousness as the effect of processes and attempting to extract the virtual relations that condition the specific configuration of forces that one experiences. Because we can think, because we can engage in thought-forms like philosophy, art, and science, that allow us to approach our experience in terms of semiotics or signs as well as material forces, because, that is, we are creatures for whom experience is meaningful and because that meaning plays an importantly structuring effect in our experience of the world, we can, as Bergson would put it, creatively evolve beyond habitual responses and create a human life. Just as life-forms of all sorts creatively evolve as circumstances come together in unprecedented variations in patterns, so can human beings introduce their own variations into the unfolding of life. Deleuze and Guattari's approach thus suggests a kind of continuity between our conscious interventions in life and a larger, more enveloping creative process of which we are a component part. We may not be the masters of a world that we control, but we can attempt to be as skillful as we can be in working with the forces moving through and beyond us in ways that move us or increase our joyful power. We need to listen not just with our minds, but with our hearts and our emotions as we engage in a thinking that is an artful becoming. Just as we experiment with Deleuze–Guattarian concepts, so too we can experiment with concepts created by other thinkers, feminist and otherwise, with whose concepts we can resonate and pursue lines of flight that unfold from the place we are at. Thus, in addition to a tool-box of concepts, Deleuze and Guattari provide a way of thinking about being, about time, and about theory, that allows us to reinvigorate the theories and concepts we already have, putting into play the theories and concepts that we can joyfully encounter, and simply letting go of those that fail to move us rather than wasting energy on judging or condemning them as "bad" or "wrong."[5]

Reducing human beings and their experiences to categories stabilized in past encounters loses the specificity of present encounters. Along with a loss of specificity comes missed opportunities—connections that could be made that could turn small variations in living into viable lines of flight. Any time that a theory imposes a form on lived experience, finer distinctions are lost and connections excluded that might have led to creative evolutions in living. This may have galvanizing effects when it allows a line of flight to emerge from the cacophony of other possibilities, but it can block vital options when it imposes forms at the expense of attending to tendencies that are intensifying past old thresholds. A Deleuze–Guattarian conception of mapping and creative thought entails attending to the anomalies of current situations through varying concepts as well as modulating our sensations, perceptions, and actions, in ways that could unfold toward a future we invent with others. Feminists have always been sensitive to the way theory can impede us—to the point where some feminists have suggested we do without it entirely. What can theory—as the master's tool—do for us, but force our experiences and our thinking into paradigms that consolidate the very patriarchal perspective that has devalued our sex and our contributions?[6] From a Deleuze–Guattarian perspective, theory should not hammer out a consensus about what qualities to extract from sensation with respect to a generic subject (see chapter 1). To insist that our discussions of what it means to be human should reach such consensus would be to insist that we reduce access to the full range of galvanizing tendencies to which we could open our perspectives. According to Deleuze and Guattari, philosophy, by creating concepts related to a dynamic concept of what it means to be human, could unfold an understanding of our lives that could also affect thresholds of perception and conception in ways that could move us toward new ways of being and a future we could affirm. Thinking concepts of gender, sexuality, race, and class (among others) in terms of an encounter with lived experience that attempts to extrapolate the virtualities conditioning that experience could open up not only new approaches to issues related to how to live with others in a world we share, but new ways of experiencing ourselves as human beings. A Deleuze–Guattarian perspective suggests that any theory that would speak to contemporary problems is provoked by the "shock" of living into creating concepts that are active interventions in living our lives.

Feminism makes use of a gendered line of flight that takes off from the minoritarian alternatives to gendered norms. Ultimately it, like other minoritarian struggles, is headed toward unraveling points of stasis that hamper creative unfolding we can affirm. The kind of unfolding we can affirm, on the view being proposed here, is that of capacities rooted in creative becoming in community rather than ego-oriented preservation; it is only when one's own relations are skillfully composed with the relations of others in terms of the multiple wholes of which one is a component part that one's own joy can increase. Unfolding ways of being human in keeping with the intensities of specific bodies, territories, and situations, allows us to remain open to the vitalizing flows that move through us. All such unfolding is a co-participant in the creative flow of life and has a role to play in that unfolding. Everything is seen as connected not through overarching principles that universally apply, but rather through the specific forces that extend through and beyond relatively stable territories exerting effects that cascade (more or less quickly) throughout the whole. Movements and practices interested in fostering positive change can be seen in this context as a form of co-participation in the creative evolution of human life with particular investments.

Deleuze and Guattari's approach invites theorists to continue to proliferate concepts that can suggest solutions to the problems they confront rather than to apply Deleuze–Guattarian concepts by analogy to the problems that provoked Deleuze and Guattari themselves. The diverging activity of forms of thought and practice like that of feminism creatively evolve in their becoming with life. Insofar as the conceptual creation of theory extracts the virtual from the present (rather than trading in the representations of conventional thought—be it the mainstream thought it contests or the dominant forms of thought it, itself, creates), it can tap perceptual, affective, and conceptual resources we might otherwise overlook. From this perspective, theories such as those of feminism are not true or false, but rather more or less able to intensify tendencies in keeping with the increased vitality of individual human beings in all their differences as well as the communities of which these individuals are a part. The kind of Deleuze–Guattarian approach I am advocating allows us to shift away from the subject–object dichotomies that support problematic self–other relations in order to focus on actualizing the virtual potential of humanity as it manifests in individuals and collectives, as well as of humanity as a collective whole. It emphasizes the creative resources of a present that is not reduced to categories derived from the past, fosters an attentiveness to the present that allows us to tap those creative resources, and fosters a holistic approach to concrete situations that allows networks of interdependency and their critical points to emerge. It encourages a conception of theories and practices emerging from disparate problems and investments, all of which are ultimately interconnected through multiple and heterogeneous durations that overlap and connect in different ways depending on one's location and perspective.

Theories invested in promoting human flourishing in its multiple forms constitute an abstract machine with many bridges among their concepts that have not yet been pursued. Rather than reading such theories in opposition to one another, reading them as part of a larger abstract machine of thought with shared as well as diverging investments allows one to pursue the virtual relations of these projects in order to map out new terrain. This in turn could help to unblock energy—the implicit tendencies toward unfolding movements of thought and practice moving between and through various projects—in order to make connections among disparate projects and across disparate topographies and thus provide further impetus for deterritorializations from oppressive forms of thought and cultural practice. Certain feminist projects, for example, are distinct from others—the project of fighting for equal pay for equal work is a different project than that of finding avenues for feminist forms of cultural expression or dealing with racism in a feminist organization. Some of these struggles need to sustain specific forms if they are to solve the specific problems they are meant to address. But to view these projects as all part of the abstract machine of feminism as well as, from other perspectives, abstract machines such as that of progressive social movements as a whole, allows us to foster links and in-between projects responding to not-yet-defined problems without having to legislate or police what counts as a "feminist" or "progressive" project according to any one overarching perspective. Thinking of various projects as concrete machines functioning in keeping with the abstract machine of feminism or progressive practices allows us to unblock potential flows along lines of continuous variation that extend in all directions among these projects. Mapping this abstract machine allows us to perceive connections where before we saw none, thus fostering actualizations of further thought and practice that could allow further variations on refrains invested in promoting the flourishing of all forms of human life.[7]

Conclusion

As capitalism sweeps the globe, undermining the cultures that gave people sense and purpose, we need to find new forms of self-understanding to support the rich variety of human living. Given a process of globalization where information travels at instantaneous speed, population continues to increase, and cultures inevitably encounter the clash of other cultures, we need to find creative solutions to how to own our collective humanity. A Deleuze–Guattarian approach, rather than attempting to paint the world in terms of universal forms underlying all change, thinks the world in terms of self-perpetuating inventive processes that will always outrun our representations. Being as a durational whole is a univocity of multiple, superposing, heterogeneous durations that are constantly unfolding into the entities that we perceive and capture in representational thought. An ontology of becoming that captures the speed of contemporary life can allow us to better work with the changes that push us onward. A Deleuze–Guattarian ontology may be more adequate to the physical reality revealed by contemporary science as well as the social reality of a globally connected world with conduits of information and technological and cultural change more rapid than ever before in the

history of the human race. If we are not to cling to forms fast dissolving in
the approaching tide, we need to find more flexible ways to characterize our
world and ourselves and be able to shift and transform with our changing
situation. Although there is at times a predilection for change for the sake
of change in Deleuze and Guattari's work, their approach helps us to ward
off the all-too-human tendency to desperately hang on to what is safely
familiar even when everything is in flux.

In addition to fostering more effective ways of working with inevitable
change, such an approach allows us to see ourselves as integral members
of the global community of humanity as well as of the world. Rather than
positing human beings as separate individuals, tribes, or races, Deleuze and
Guattari's work allows us to see the differentiations among us as emerging
from becomings that we share. Rather than positing humanity in opposition
to a world that we can master and control, their approach allows us to see
our commonality with other animals and the environment in terms of the
becoming of life from which we all emerge. Seeing ourselves in ongoing
connection to what is around us can suggest new ways of dealing with
nonhuman as well as human others along with the environments that sustain
us. Understanding ourselves as a series of differentiations in an ongoing and
always interconnected flow of multiple and heterogeneous durations can allow
us to maintain a sense of our distinctive humanity less threatened by the need
for self-transformation; instead of defending ourselves against any other that
appears to us to threaten our identities when the boundaries between us are
blurred, we could delineate our ongoing differentiations from others in more
flexible ways on the basis of the becomings we share and thus proliferate
productively creative interactions with both human and nonhuman others
as well as our surroundings.

Schizoanalysis is not just about the destruction of old constraints; it
is about the creation of new ways of being. It proffers a realistic way of
attending to where one is in light of where one could go. It advocates a belief
in the earth and the natural creativity of life that suggests that insofar as we
can own our own creativity as becoming-human we can learn to work with
one another as well as the other becomings moving through and around us.
Deleuze–Guattarian ethics is an ethics of novelty, one that does not look to
the representable past in order to model a future we could implement, but
rather an ethics that sounds out the present through experimental encounter
and that through affective as well as cognitive attunement attempts to unfold
the tendencies of the present most congenial to the living creatures involved.
This is not an ethics that attempts to apply rules or principles that would
hold for a universal subject, but rather an ethics of the event that entails being
as true to the singularity of unique situations as possible and experimenting
with the intensities that might enhance life's flourishing. The resources for

such flourishing are not to be found in already constituted, regulated, and represented subjects, but in the fluxes of life from which those subjects are formed. Social imaginaries that support ways of understanding who we are as human beings and co-participants in multiply superposing durations can foster enlivening access to intensive possibilities cognitive intelligence may obscure. A notion of embodied rationality attuned to the multiple means through which we gain instinctual, intellectual, and intuitive access to the various durations of which we are a part suggests that multiple forms of thought (aesthetic, philosophical, and affective as well as cognitive and scientific) are needed for skillful living. A revitalized belief in our world—belief in the creative fecundity of life as well as our own unfolding powers as we evolve with that life—is perhaps what we need in order to flourish as we face the challenges that confront us.

Notes

Chapter 1

1. Because in this book I primarily draw from *Anti-Oedipus*, *A Thousand Plateaus*, and *What is Philosophy?* I usually refer to Deleuze and Guattari together. The problem of how to distinguish the two thinkers—especially when, like many commentators on Deleuze and Guattari, I am reading their collaborative work through the frame of my reading of the works authored by Deleuze (rather than those of Guattari with which I am less conversant) is one that I do not pretend to have resolved. It did, however, seem preferable to me to refer to the two of them together rather than to elide Guattari completely by referring to the ideas within the collaborative works as those of Deleuze alone. For further discussion of this point see Genosko (2002, 41–49).

2. *Poststructuralism* is a term that covers a disparate array of French theorists with distinct projects, most of whom work out of the philosophical movements of phenomenology (including thinkers like Edmund Husserl, Martin Heidegger, Jean-Paul Sartre, and Maurice Merleau-Ponty) and French structuralism (including theorists like linguist Ferdinand de Saussure, anthropologist Claude Lévi-Strauss, Marxist Louis Althusser, and Freudian psychoanalyst Jacques Lacan).

3. Nietzsche, in particular, is clearly a strong influence in the work of Derrida and Foucault as well. Deleuze's book on Nietzsche, *Nietzsche and Philosophy*, originally published in 1962, was a key factor in the French resurgence of interest in Nietzsche (1983).

4. See Bergson (1991, especially chapter 3, and 1998, chapter 2, 98–185). Also see Grosz for a clear and concise introduction to this aspect of Bergson's thought (Grosz 2004, 163–75, 227–40).

5. When I first encountered the work of Deleuze and Guattari, I was immersed in the work of Luce Irigaray; I found (and still find) her project of considering the cultural logic of contemporary social systems of meaning in light of sexual difference and the human subjects that logic helps to constitute and support (or fail to support) provocatively brilliant and insightful. Although I make little explicit reference to her project in this book, I have addressed her work together with that of Deleuze and Guattari's in the past, and my study of her project influences the reading of Deleuze and Guattari I give in this book (Lorraine 1999). In particular, I am indebted to her for the notion that normative (masculine) subjectivity entails denigrating complementary

(feminine) forms of subjectivity. I am less inclined to prioritize sexual difference in the same way Irigaray does or to conceive it as irreducible.

6. This is not to say that a conception of time as durational was completely eliminated. Kwinter points to the science of thermodynamics in the nineteenth century as an example of the reintroduction of durational time into cultural thought: Scientists became aware that changes in state and qualitative transformations required a view of matter as active. "From the moment a system is understood as evolving over time, what becomes important are the transformations it undergoes, and all transformation in a system is the result of energy—or information—moving through it" (2001, 23). Linear equations assuming a spatialized time "can transmit only a prior or initial motion along a predetermined path." An approach that assumes that time is real (as opposed to a dimension tacked onto space) must track motion in terms of a sensitivity to its surrounding milieu that requires continual updating of its situation from within its unfolding trajectory. Real time "is not a unitary strand distributing homogeneous units of past, present, and future in a fixed empirical order, but is rather a complex, interactive, 'thick' manifold of distinct yet integrated durations" (22).

7. For an excellent presentation of Bergson's notion of intuition see Grosz (2005a, 2005b, 93–111).

8. Foucault's examples of prisons, hospitals, and schools in *Discipline and Punish* also are appropriate here (1979). In the prison, for example, there are linguistic practices enacted by those running it (at various levels), as well as the prisoners who inhabit it. There also are the physical routines enacted by the administrators, guards, and prisoners that constitute various machinic assemblages of desire.

9. See Brian Massumi's vivid description of a soccer game that takes the virtual intensities of its interrelations into account in a compelling and evocative way, for further insight into some of the complexities that emerge from this kind of perspective (2002, 71–80).

10. "In the order-word, life must answer the answer of death, not by fleeing, but by making flight act and create. There are pass-words beneath order-words. Words that pass, words that are components of passage, whereas order-words mark stoppages or organized, stratified compositions. A single thing or word undoubtedly has this twofold nature: it is necessary to extract one from the other—to transform the compositions of order into components of passage" (ATP 110).

11. See, for example, my discussions of Kelly Oliver's notion of witnessing in chapter 5 and María Lugones' notion of complex communication in chapter 6. Feminist theorists like Luce Irigaray (1985) and Gloria Anzaldúa (1987) also come to mind, but these are just a few examples of what has been a pervasive theme in feminist thought.

Chapter 2

1. My reading of Deleuze and Guattari's depiction of various strata in *A Thousand Plateaus* is indebted to Manual DeLanda's lucid account of Deleuze's philosophy with reference to nonlinear dynamics and complexity theory in *Intensive Science and Virtual Philosophy* (2002).

2. See Keith Ansell Pearson's account of Deleuze's conception of evolution as it relates to the organism (1999, 145–52). He cites Brian Goodwin's work (Goodwin 1995) to argue that this account is in keeping with the new biology of complexity theory (Ansell Pearson 1999, 150).

3. Elizabeth Grosz, in a reading of Darwin compatible with the Deleuze–Guattarian depiction of life as creative evolution, emphasizes the self-differentiating activity involved in natural selection. Individuals are propelled into processes of self-transformation "through his or her sexual relations and his or her relations of inventive survival in a world of tension and competition" (2004, 89). Grosz points out similarities in the evolutionary movement of species, cultural and political life, and the conscious life of individual human beings. Although the process may move more slowly in the life of species, "[a]ll forms of life, even the most stable, develop, elaborate themselves, at very different rates, beyond themselves. . . . Life, whether biologically, culturally, or psychically considered, is this movement not only of the self-differentiated, but of a differentiation always directed to elaboration, complication, emergence—to excessiveness, growth, the forward pull of time" (255).

4. "Stratification is like the creation of the world from chaos, a continual, renewed creation" (ATP 502).

5. The presignifying regime is associated with primitive social formations, the signifying regime with despotic social formations, and the postsignifying regime is associated with Moses and the Hebrews' flight from Egypt, but Deleuze and Guattari emphasize that they are not "doing history," but rather are presenting ideal types of regimes that actually manifest in inevitably mixed forms: "at a given moment a people affectuates the assemblage that assures the relative dominance of that regime under certain historical conditions" (ATP 121). Thus, for example, their characterization of a signifying regime applies "not only to the imperial despotic regime but to all subjected, arborescent, hierarchical, centered groups: political parties, literary movements, psychoanalytic associations, families, conjugal units, etc." (ATP 116).

6. See Lawrence Cahoone's book, *Cultural Revolutions*, for an intriguing account of the shift from foundational cultures to the secular reason of contemporary Western culture (which Cahoone argues is itself cultural) that is in keeping with my reading of Deleuze and Guattari's account (Cahoone 2005).

7. Deleuze and Guattari's account is compatible with Foucault's reading of sexed identity as taking on new importance in the circulation of biopower and the management of large groups of people emerging in the eighteenth century. Compare McWhorter's characterization of Foucault's argument that the definition of sex as a concept that "groups together 'anatomical elements, biological functions, conducts, sensations, and pleasures' into a 'fictitious unity' that can be cited 'as a causal principle, an omnipresent meaning, a secret to be discovered everywhere' . . . [is a] definition and deployment of the concept of sex . . . [that] is new in the late nineteenth century" (2004 40, quoting Foucault 1978, 154). People did not understand themselves as fundamentally sexual in nature until "sex emerged as a concept central to our self-definitions and our pursuit of pleasure, self-understanding, and health" (41). Whereas before one's sex had significance in the role one would play and the patterns of social living in which one participated, it was not key to personal identity, on both these accounts, until the emergence of a modern subject with its increasingly interiorized

psychic structure. Also see Nietzsche's account of the role Judeo-Christianity plays in the process of interiorization in *Genealogy of Morals* (1967).

8. "[T]he individual in the family, however young, directly invests a social, historical, economic, and political field that is not reducible to any mental structure or affective constellation" (AO 166).

9. They call this cure an example of schizoanalysis—their preferred alternative to psychoanalysis (AO 167).

10. As Turner puts it, Ihembi's "main endeavor was to see that individuals were capable of playing their social roles successfully in a traditional structure of social positions. Illness was for him a mark of undue deviation from the norm" (1964, 262).

11. Modern subjectivity entails a mixed semiotic including the signifying and postsignifying regimes. The former "develops a kind of 'wall' on which signs are inscribed, in relation to one another and in relation to the signifier" (ATP 133). The latter entails consciousness or love-passion as the doubling and the recoiling of one into the other of the subject of enunciation (the subject who makes the statement) and the subject of the statement (the subject of the statement made) in "a black hole attracting consciousness and passion and in which they resonate" (ATP 133). Deleuze and Guattari's description of the doubling and recoiling of the subjects of enunciation and the statement resonate with a Foucauldian understanding of the production of modern subjectivity and the Althusserian notion of interpellation (ATP 129–30).

12. As Ronald Bogue puts it: "In their analysis, the basic tendency of capitalism is to undo complex social codes that limit relations of production, exchange and consumption and to convert everything into interchangeable units of capital. In traditional societies, codes determine who can produce what, which relations of exchange are permissible, which are taboo, who may consume what goods, who may not. In capitalist societies, the commodity form tends to replace all restrictive codes" (2005, 19).

13. Also see Guattari's discussion in *Molecular Revolution* (1984, 233–35).

Chapter 3

1. The heterosexual, according to McWhorter, did not come into existence until several decades later (2004, 46).

2. McWhorter succinctly articulates Foucault's notion of power as an event. Power is "a kind of tension that emerges when people have different goals or perspectives or conflicting projects" (2004, 42). Situations involving power struggles always entail resistance since in such situations everyone attempts to affect others as well as resist the effects of others to the extent of their ability. Additionally, Foucault insists that such power struggles always involves "bodily actions" and that power is productive since it "posits and produces reality as much as it sets limits on it" (ibid.). When equilibrium among forces is achieved, daily routines are established that repeat events of power that tend to produce certain human types. Furthermore, the designations used to refer to those types tend to be internalized by the people thus referred to. "They come to understand themselves in relation to such categories. They come to be the people they are identified as. Power produces selves, Foucault says. Power makes

us who we are" (43). Deleuze and Guattari state that for the most part they agree with Foucault with the caveat that they prefer to discuss desire rather than power. In their view, power is a stratified form of desire (ATP 531).

3. Also see Bonita Lawrence for an example of this kind of genealogical approach applied to the case of Native American identity in the context of government regulation in Canada and the United States (2003).

4. For example, Deleuze and Guattari point to the work of Fanon as an example of the permutations oedipalization can take in colonialism (ATP 96).

5. "John/Joan" was actually David Reimer. For more information on this case from various perspectives, see Colapinto (1997, 2000, and 2004), Diamond and Sigmundsen (1997), and Money and Green (1969). I am particularly indebted to Judith Butler's provocative rendition of this case that brings out the problem David posed to the people who responded to him by attempting to render him intelligible from competing perspectives as a problem of a humanity that exceeds intelligibility. In Butler's view: "it is precisely the ways in which he is not fully recognizable, fully disposable, fully categorizable, that his humanness emerges" (Butler 2004, 73).

6. David's situation was particularly contentious because there were at least two views of who he "really" was that were being promoted and contested. To oversimplify what were more complicated and evolving positions over the course of a long debate, John Money, a medical psychologist and founder of the Gender Identity Institute at Johns Hopkins University, thought gender identity was malleable and hoped David's case would prove him right (it helped that David had an identical twin—the perfect complement to an experiment in manipulating gender identity through socialization) and Milton Diamond, a sex researcher involved in a long-standing battle with Money, believed gender identity had a hormonal basis. See Diamond and Sigmundsen (1997) and Money and Green (1969).

7. Stryker describes her outfit as "combat boots, threadbare Levi 501s over a black lace body suit, a shredded Transgender Nation T-shirt with the neck and sleeves cut out, a pink triangle, quartz crystal pendant, grunge metal jewelry, and a six-inch long marlin hook dangling around my neck on a length of heavy stainless steel chain" (Stryker 1994, 237–38). There are, of course, social flows involved in transgender identity that are the subject of heated discussion in feminist and transgender debates that I do not here address.

8. Frantz Fanon, to cite another example, presents a particularly vivid phenomenological description of the dissonance experienced by a black, colonial subject in his famous fifth chapter of *Black Skin, White Masks* (Fanon 1967, 109–40).

9. I explore in more detail Deleuze's readings of Nietzsche and Spinoza insofar as they impact the project of this book in chapter 5.

Chapter 4

1. According to Richard Cross, Duns Scotus (an important influence on Deleuze's thought, although Deleuze and Guattari are clearly varying this term in keeping with the problems they address) understood a haecceity to be "not a bare particular in the sense of something *underlying* qualities. It is, rather, a nonqualitative

property of a substance or thing: it is a "thisness" (a *haecceitas*, from the Latin *haec*, meaning "this") as opposed to a "whatness" (a *quidditas*, from the Latin *quid*, meaning "what")" (Cross 2008).

2. Constantin Boundas makes a similar point when he describes perception as conceived by Deleuze as the result of a process of integration of the differentials registered below the threshold of consciousness and the "summation by means of which the mind tends to connect differentials as a single perception" (Boundas 2006, 12). Perception is thus an achievement that always entails, in addition to whatever is perceived, something that cannot be sensed: "This 'unsensed' is not a mere formal condition of the possibility of sensation in general, but the concrete set of differential *petites perceptions*—the necessary elements for the genetic constitution of whatever is actually sensed" (Boundas 2006, 12–13).

Daniel Smith also characterizes this Deleuzian conception of perception as the outcome of an active rather than passive process. Conscious perceptions are not immediately derived from the objects around us, but are rather the result of the integration of minute and unconscious perceptions. "A conscious perception is produced when at least two of these minute and virtual perceptions—two waves, or two voices—enter into a differential relation that determines a singularity, which 'excels' over the others, and becomes conscious, on the basis of my needs, or interests, or the state of my body. Every conscious perception constitutes a constantly shifting threshold: the minute or virtual perceptions are like the obscure dust of the world, its background noise . . . and the differential relation is the mechanism that extracts from these minute perceptions my own little zone of finite clarity on the world" (Smith 2006, 57). William Connolly cites the evidence of neuroscientists like Francisco Varela in support of this kind of view of perception (Connolly 2002; Varela et al. 1991).

3. See my essay, "Ahab and Becoming-Whale" for a fuller discussion of Ahab's trajectory of becoming-other (Lorraine 2007).

4. "Science is not confined to a linear temporal succession any more than philosophy is. But, instead of a stratigraphic time, which expresses before and after in an order of superimpositions, science displays a peculiarly serial, ramified time, in which the before (the previous) always designates bifurcations and ruptures to come, and the after designates retroactive reconnections" (WP 124).

5. "Hava is figured right on the threshold of womanhood, but rather than passing instantaneously and unquestioningly from a state of child to woman, Hava stretches out this moment. In doing so, she demonstrates her virtual capacity to manipulate time, not so much in order to delay her departure from childhood, but so that she may begin to consciously experience her own becoming-woman" (Langford 2007, 30).

Chapter 5

1. Nietzsche's call, most clearly stated in the third essay of the *Genealogy of Morals*, refers to the encroaching nihilism manifest in the "death" of God and a general malaise with respect to faith in transcendent ideals concerning God or anything that might take God's place (Nietzsche 1967).

2. This needs to be qualified in the case of Spinoza because all bodies

ultimately express God, but knowledge comes through embodied perspectives rather than by transcending the body.

3. According to Caroline Williams, "Common notions are deduced from an understanding of the similarity of composition to be found in certain combinations of relation between bodies. They constitute ideas about the shape and value of encounters from which general axioms emerge regarding the nature of the affects and actions generated. The general axioms that are produced here are best understood as 'imaginative universals,' since any apprehension of such shared notions must refer back to the combination of bodies, their affective relations and the images formed of others in the imagination. Common notions thus find their conditions of possibility in the resources of the collective imagination, and their mode of expression within reason. Spinoza claims that common notions may give way to adequate ideas. It is this knowledge that he will associate, in Part V of the Ethics, with a comprehension of the idea and essence of God or Nature, or amor dei intellectualis, and a knowledge of each singular essence as part of an infinite substance. Hence, Spinoza writes that 'the more we understand singular things the more we understand God' (*Ethics* V Proposition 24)" (Williams 2007, 363; Spinoza 1982, 216).

4. In my discussion of Deleuze's reading of Spinoza I draw freely from transcripts of seminars made available on the Web given in 1978 and 1981. His style of speech is thus the more colloquial style of a professor trying to make difficult ideas accessible to his students. In addition to clarifying his interpretations of his two books on Spinoza that came out in 1968 and 1970 (although *Spinoza: Philosophie practique* was published in a revised and expanded edition in 1981), the more informal speech of Deleuze's seminars reveal another side of him (which I personally find endearing) (Deleuze 1978 and 1981). MP3 files of the original recordings from which the transcripts were made are available at http://www.univ-paris8.fr/deleuze.

5. As Deleuze explains in a seminar where he remarks on the similarity between Spinoza and Bergson's notion of duration: "When Bergson tries to make us understand what he calls duration, he says: you can consider psychic states as close together as you want in time, you can consider the state A and the state B, as separated by a minute, but just as well by a second, by a thousandth of a second, that is you can make more and more cuts, increasingly tight, increasingly close to one another. You may well go to the infinite, says Bergson, in your decomposition of time, by establishing cuts with increasing rapidity, but you will only ever reach states. And he adds that the states are always of space. The cuts are always spatial. And you will have brought your cuts together very well, you will let something necessarily escape, it is the passage from one cut to another, however small it may be. Now, what does he call duration, at its simplest? It is the passage from one cut to another, it is the passage from one state to another. The passage from one state to another is not a state, you will tell me that all of this is not strong, but it is a really profound statute of living. For how can we speak of the passage, the passage from one state to another, without making it a state? This is going to pose problems of expression, of style, of movement, it is going to pose all sorts of problems. Yet duration is that, it is the lived passage from one state to another insofar as it is irreducible to one state as to the other, insofar as it is irreducible to any state. This is what happens between two cuts" (Deleuze 1981, 6).

6. I will not pursue Spinoza's notion of knowledge of the third kind here, although I think it resonates with Nietzsche's notion of the eternal return (at least in Deleuze's reading) in a way that could be productively laid out.

7. See chapter 1, paragraph 13 of Nietzsche's *Beyond Good and Evil* (1966a).

8. Sense is, however, "not a principle or an origin," but rather an effect that is produced, "whose laws of production must be uncovered" (Deleuze 2004, 137). "To interpret is to determine the force which gives sense to a thing. To evaluate is to determine the will to power which gives values to a thing" (NP 54).

9. The will to power is "the differential element which simultaneously determines the relation of forces (quantity) and the respective qualities of related forces" (NP 197).

10. "What the will to power wills is a particular relation of forces, a particular quality of forces. And also a particular quality of power: affirming or denying. This complex, which varies in every case, forms a type to which given phenomena correspond" (NP 85).

11. "As an ethical thought the eternal return is the new formulation of the practical synthesis: *whatever you will, will it in such a way that you also will its eternal return*" (NP 68).

12. According to Deleuze, Spinoza denounces those who are interested in affecting others with sad passions: "They need sadness. They can only reign over slaves, and the slave is precisely the regime of the decrease of power (*puissance*). There are people who can only reign, who only acquire power (*pouvoir*) by way of sadness and by instituting a regime of sadness of the type: repent, of the type hate someone, and if you don't have anyone to hate, hate yourself, etc. Everything that Spinoza diagnoses as a kind of immense culture of sadness, the valorization of sadness, all of which says to you: if you don't pass by way of sadness, you will not flourish. Now for Spinoza this is an abomination" (Deleuze 1978, 11).

13. In another evocative statement, also taken from *Transpositions*, of what nomadic becoming, with some caution on our part, could be like, Braidotti says: "Remembering in the nomadic mode requires composition, selection and dosage; the careful layout of empowering conditions that allow for the actualizations of affirmative forces. Like a choreography of flows or intensities that require adequate framing in order to be composed into a form, intensive memories activate empathy and cohesion between their constitutive elements. Nomadic remembering is like a constant quest for temporary moments when a balance can be sustained, before the forces dissolve again and move on. And on it goes, never equal to itself, but faithful enough to itself to endure, and to pass on" (Braidotti 2006, 167).

14. I am indebted here to Simone de Beauvoir who makes a similar argument about the value the freedom of others must hold for those who value their own freedom in *The Ethics of Ambiguity* (Beauvoir 1948).

15. Guattari fit less neatly into bourgeois identity categories and, in addition, deliberately sought out active engagement with various forms of marginalized subjectivity as his extensive work with the mentally ill attests (see Genosko 2002, 1–28).

16. Her examples are Lorraine Code and Susan Brison (Alcoff 2006a, 59–60), and Judith Butler's accounts of the other (Alcoff 2006a, 75–79).

17. See Teresa Brennan's book, *The Transmission of Affect*, for an intriguing perspective on how energy can pass from one person or group to others (2004).

Chapter 6

1. Gatens and Lloyd point out in a footnote relevant connotations of their use of the term, *social imaginary*, with work by Michèle le Doeuff (1989), Jacques Lacan, Luce Irigaray (1985), and Cornelius Castoriadis (1994) (Gatens and Lloyd 1999, 151).

2. "As concept and as event, revolution is self-referential or enjoys a self-positing that enables it to be apprehended in an immanent enthusiasm without anything in states of affairs or lived experience being able to tone it down, not even the disappointments of reason. Revolution is absolute deterritorialization even to the point where this calls for a new earth, a new people" (WP 101).

3. Guattari, in particular, became increasingly concerned with the conforming subjects produced by contemporary forms of social production and ways of releasing singularizing modes of subjectivity (Guattari and Rolnik 2008).

4. In this context, we could say that there is an affinity between Deleuze's project and that of Heidegger's: both point toward the roots of the abstractions of representational thought in the embodied forms of life emerging from processes of which we are mostly unaware. Heidegger conceives of this in terms of a pre-ontological understanding that orients our thematized understandings of Being, and Deleuze conceives this in terms of thinking beyond the image of representational thought to the differing divergence of life from which representational thought is derived. See Miguel de Beistegui for an extended discussion of the relation between the two (Beistegui 2004).

5. See Eve Kosofsky Sedgwick's analysis of some contemporary forms of cultural theory as paranoid and the suggestion that it might be time to move toward more reparative forms of reading: "to read from a reparative position is to surrender the knowing, anxious paranoid determination that no horror, however apparently unthinkable, shall ever come to the reader *as new*" (Sedgwick 2003, 146).

6. See Audre Lorde's classic article, "The Masters Tools Will Never Dismantle the Master's House," in *Sister Outsider* (Lorde 1984, 110–14).

7. Rosi Braidotti provides an inspiring example of one form such work can take with her book, *Transpositions*, in which she deliberately creates connections among what might appear to be disparate theoretical perspectives (Braidotti 2006).

References

Ahmed, Sara. 2006. Orientations: Toward a Queer Phenomenology. *GLQ* 12 (4): 543–74.

Alcoff, Linda Martín. 2006a. The Philosophical Critique. In *Visible Identities: Race, Gender, and the Self,* by Linda Martin Alcoff. New York: Oxford University Press.

Alcoff, Linda Martín. 2006b. Real Identities. In *Visible Identities: Race, Gender, and the Self,* by Linda Martin Alcoff. New York: Oxford University Press.

Allison, Dorothy. 1992. *Bastard Out of Carolina.* New York: Penguin.

Allison, Dorothy. 1995. *Two Or Three Things I Know for Sure.* New York: Penguin.

Ansell Pearson, Keith. 1999. *Germinal Life: The Difference and Repetition of Deleuze.* New York: Routledge.

Anzaldúa, Gloria. 1987. *Borderlands/La Frontera: The New Mestiza.* San Francisco: Aunt Lute Books.

Bartky, Sandra Lee. 1990. *Femininity and Domination: Studies in the Phenomenology of Oppression.* New York: Routledge.

Beauvoir, Simone de. 1948. *The Ethics of Ambiguity.* Translated by Frechtman, Bernard. New York: Citadel Press.

Beistegui, Miguel de. 2004. *Truth and Genesis: Philosophy as Differential Ontology.* Bloomington: Indiana University Press.

Bergson, Henri. 1974. *The Creative Mind: An Introduction to Metaphysics.* Translated by Andison, Mabelle L. New York: Citadel Press.

Bergson, Henri. 1991. *Matter and Memory.* Translated by Paul, Nancy Margaret and W. Scott Palmer. New York: Zone Books.

Bergson, Henri. 1998. *Creative Evolution.* Translated by Mitchell, Arthur. Mineola, NY: Dover Publications, Inc.

Bogue, Ronald. 2003. *Deleuze on Literature.* New York: Routledge.

Bogue, Ronald. 2005. Nomadic Flows: Globalism and the Local Absolute. *Concentric: Literary and Cultural Studies* 31(1): 7–25.

Borradori, Giovanna. 2001. The Temporalization of Difference: Reflections on Deleuze's Interpretation of Bergson. *Continental Philosophy Review* 34(1): 1–20.

Boundas, Constantin V. 1996. Deleuze–Bergson: An Ontology of the Virtual. In *Deleuze: A Critical Reader,* edited by Paul Patton. Cambridge, MA: Blackwell Publishers.

Boundas, Constantin V. 2006. What Difference Does Deleuze's Difference Make? In *Deleuze and Philosophy*, edited by Constantin V. Boundas. Edinburgh: Edinburgh University Press.

Braidotti, Rosi. 2000. Teratologies. In *Deleuze and Feminist Theory*, edited by Ian Buchanan and Claire Colebrook. Edinburgh: Edinburgh University Press.

Braidotti, Rosi. 2006. *Transpositions: On Nomadic Ethics*. Malden, MA: Polity Press.

Braidotti, Rosi. 2008. Affirmation Versus Vulnerability: On Contemporary Ethical Debates. *Deleuze International, Issue #1*. http://deleuze.tausendplateaus.de/?p=27 Last accessed 10-25-09. Originally published in *Symposium: Canadian Journal of Continental Philosophy* 10(1): 235–254, 2006.

Brennan, Teresa. 2004. *The Transmission of Affect*. Ithaca, NY: Cornell University Press.

Brown, Wendy. 2005. Feminism Unbound: Revolution, Mourning, Politics. In *Edgework: Critical Essays on Knowledge and Politics*, Princeton, NJ: Princeton University Press.

Butler, Judith. 1990. *Gender Trouble: Feminism and the Subversion of Identity*. New York: Routledge.

Butler, Judith. 2004. Doing Justice to Someone: Sex Reassignment and Allegories of Transsexuality. In *Undoing Gender*, New York: Routledge.

Cahoone, Lawrence. 2005. *Cultural Revolutions: Reason Versus Culture in Philosophy, Politics, and Jihad*. University Park, PA: Pennsylvania State University Press.

Castoriadis, Cornelius. 1994. Radical Imagination and The Social Instituting Imaginary. In *Rethinking Imagination*, edited by G. Robinson, and J. Rundell. New York: Routledge.

Colapinto, John. 1997. The True Story of John/Joan. *The Rolling Stone*, December 11, 54–97.

Colapinto, John. 2000. *As Nature Made Him: The Boy Who Was Raised as a Girl*. New York: HarperCollins.

Colapinto, John. 2004. Gender Gap: What Were the Real Reasons Behind David Reimer's Suicide? *Slate*, posted Thursday, June 3, 2004, last accessed at http://www.slate.com/id/2101678/ on October 8, 2010.

Colebrook, Claire. 2002. *Gilles Deleuze*. New York: Routledge.

Colebrook, Claire. 2004. *Gender*. New York: Palgrave Macmillan.

Connolly, William E. 2002. *Neuropolitics: Thinking, Culture, Speed*. Minneapolis: University of Minnesota Press.

Cross, Richard. 2008. Medieval Theories of Haecceity. In *The Stanford Encyclopedia of Philosophy*, Spring 2010 edition, edited by Edward N. Zalta. http://plato.stanford.edu/entries/medieval-haecceity/ Accessed 10-8-10.

Crowder, Diane Griffin. 2007. From the Straight Mind to Queer Theory: Implications for Political Movement. *GLQ* 13(4): 489–503.

DeLanda, Manuel. 2002. *Intensive Science and Virtual Philosophy*. New York: Continuum.

Deleuze, Gilles. 1978. Spinoza: 24/01/1978. http://www.webdeleuze.com/php/texte.php?cle=14&groupe=Spinoza&langue=2 Trans., Timothy S. Murphy. Last accessed 7-20-09 from Web Deleuze, Les cours de Gilles Deleuze.

Deleuze, Gilles. 1981. Spinoza: 20/01/1981. http://www.webdeleuze.com/php/texte.php?cle=191&groupe=Spinoza&langue=2 Trans. Simon Duffy. Last accessed 7-20-09 from Web Deleuze, Les Cours de Gilles Deleuze.

Deleuze, Gilles. 1983. *Nietzsche and Philosophy*. Translated by Tomlinson, Hugh. New York: Columbia University Press.

Deleuze, Gilles. 1988. *Spinoza: Practical Philosophy*. Translated by Hurley, Robert. San Francisco: City Lights Books.

Deleuze, Gilles. 1990. *The Logic of Sense*. Translated by Lester, Mark. Edited by Boundas, Constantin V. New York: Columbia University Press.

Deleuze, Gilles. 1997. Spinoza and the Three "Ethics." In *Essays Critical and Clinical*. Translated by Daniel W. Smith. Minneapolis: University of Minnesota Press.

Deleuze, Gilles. 2001. Nietzsche. In *Pure Imanence: Essays on a Life*. Translated by Boyman, Anne. New York: Zone Books.

Deleuze, Gilles. 2004. *Desert Islands and Other Texts 1953–1974*. Translated by Taormina, Michael. Cambridge, MA: Semiotext(e) Foreign Agents Series.

Deleuze, Gilles, and Félix Guattari. 1983. *Anti-Oedipus: Capitalism and Schizophrenia*. Translated by Hurley, Robert, Mark Seem, and Helen R. Lane. Minneapolis: University of Minnesota Press.

Deleuze, Gilles, and Félix Guattari. 1987. *A Thousand Plateaus: Capitalism and Schizophrenia*. Translated by Massumi, Brian. Minneapolis: University of Minnesota Press.

Deleuze, Gilles, and Félix Guattari. 1994. *What is Philosophy?* Translated by Burchell, Graham and Hugh Tomlinson. New York: Columbia University Press.

Deleuze, Gilles, and Claire Parnet. 1987. *Dialogues*. Translated by Habberjam, Barbara and Hugh Tomlinson. New York: Columbia University Press.

Diamond, Milton, and Keith Sigmundsen. 1997. Sex Reassignment at Birth: A Long-Term Review and Clinical Implications. *Archives of Pediatrics and Adolescent Medicine* 151: 298–304.

Dinesen, Isak. 1993. Babette's Feast. In *Anecdotes of Destiny and Ehrengard*, New York: Vintage Books.

Fanon, Frantz. 1967. *Black Skin, White Masks*. Translated by Markmann, Charles Lam. New York: Grove Weidenfeld.

Foucault, Michel. 1979. *Discipline and Punish: The Birth of the Prison*. Translated by Sheridan, Alan. New York: Vintage Books.

Frye, Marilyn. 1983. *The Politics of Reality: Essays in Feminist Theory*. Trumansburg, NY: The Crossing Press.

Garland-Thomson, Rosemarie. 2002. Integrating Disability, Transforming Feminist Theory. *NWSA Journal* 14(3): 1–32.

Gatens, Moira, and Genevieve Lloyd. 1999. *Collective Imaginings: Spinoza, Past and Present*. New York: Routledge.

Genosko, Gary. 2002. *Félix Guattari: An Aberrant Introduction*. New York: Continuum.

Gilmore, Leigh. 2001. Limit-Cases: Trauma, Self-Representation, and the Jurisdictions of Identity. *Biography* 24(1): 128–39.

Goodwin, Brian. 1995. *How the Leopard Changed its Spots*. London: Phoenix.

Grosz, Elizabeth. 2004. *The Nick of Time: Politics, Evolution, and the Untimely*. Durham, NC: Duke University Press.

Grosz, Elizabeth. 2005a. Bergson, Deleuze and Becoming. http://www.uq.edu. au/~uqmlacaz/ElizabethGrosz'stalk16.3.05.htm, last accessed October 23, 2009.

Grosz, Elizabeth. 2005b. *Time Travels*. Durham, NC: Duke University Press.

Guattari, Félix. 1984. *Molecular Revolution: Psychiatry and Politics*. Translated by Sheed, Rosemary. New York: Penguin Books.

Guattari, Félix, and Suely Rolnik. 2008. *Molecular Revolution in Brazil*. Translated by Clapshow, Karel and Brian Holmes. *Semiotext(E) Foreign Agents Series*. Los Angeles: Semiotext(e).

Holland, Eugene W. 1999. *Deleuze and Guattari's Anti-Oedipus*. New York: Routledge.

Irigaray, Luce. 1985. *Speculum of the Other Woman*. Translated by Gill, Gillian. Ithaca, NY: Cornell University Press.

Kristeva, Julia. 1982. *Powers of Horror: An Essay on Abjection*. Translated by Roudiez, Leon S. New York: Columbia University Press.

Kristeva, Julia. 1991. *Strangers to Ourselves*. Translated by Roudiez, Leon S. New York: Columbia University Press.

Kwinter, Sanford. 2001. *Architectures of Time*. Cambridge, MA: MIT Press.

Lacan, Jacques. 1977. *Écrits: A Selection*. Translated by Sheridan, Alan. New York: W.W. Norton.

Langford, Michelle. 2007. Allegory and the Aesthetics of Becoming-Woman in Marziyeh Meshkini's *The Day I Became a Woman*. *Camera Obscura 64* 22(1): 1–42.

Lawrence, Bonita. 2003. Gender, Race, and the Regulation of Native Identity in Canada and the United States: An Overview. *Hypatia* 18(2): 3–31.

Leach, Edmund. 1971. *Rethinking Anthropology*. New York: Humanities Press.

Le Doeuff, Michèle. 1989. *The Philosophical Imaginary*. Translated by Gordon, Colin. Stanford, CA: Stanford University Press.

Lévi-Strauss, Claude. 1971. *The Savage Mind*. Chicago: University of Chicago Press.

Lispector, Clarice. 1988. *The Passion According to G.H.* Translated by Sousa, Ronald W. Minneapolis: University of Minnesota Press.

Lorde, Audre. 1984. *Sister Outsider: Essays and Speeches*. Freedom, CA: The Crossing Press.

Lorraine, Tamsin. 1999. *Irigaray and Deleuze: Experiments in Visceral Philosophy*. Ithaca, NY: Cornell University Press.

Lorraine, Tamsin. 2007. Ahab and Becoming-Whale: The Nomadic Subject in Smooth Space. In *Deleuze and Space*, edited by Ian Buchanan and Gregg Lambert. Edinburgh: Edinburgh University Press.

Lugones, María. 2006. On Complex Communication. *Hypatia* 21 (3): 75–85.

Massumi, Brian. 2002. *Parables for the Virtual: Movement, Affect, Sensation*. Durham, NC: Duke University Press.

May, Todd. 2005. *Gilles Deleuze: An Introduction*. New York: Cambridge University Press.

McManus, Susan. 2007. Theorizing Utopian Agency: Two Steps Toward Utopian Techniques of the Self. *Theory & Event* 10(3): 1–53.

McWhorter, Ladelle. 2004. Sex, Race, and Biopower: A Foucauldian Genealogy. *Hypatia* 19(3): 38–62.

Melville, Herman. 1967. *Moby-Dick*. New York: Bantam Books.

Merleau-Ponty, Maurice. 1968. *The Visible and the Invisible*. Evanston, IL: Northwestern University Press.

Miller, Christopher L. 1993. The Postidentarian Predicament in the Footnotes of *A Thousand Plateaus*: Nomadology, Anthropology, and Authority. *Diacritics* 23(3): 6–35.

Money, John, and Richard Green. 1969. *Transsexualism and Sex Reassignment*. Baltimore: Johns Hopkins University Press.

Nietzsche, Friedrich. 1966a. *Beyond Good and Evil*. Translated by Kaufmann, Walter. New York: Vintage Books.

Nietzsche, Friedrich. 1966b. *The Portable Nietzsche*. Edited and translated by Kaufmann, Walter. New York: Penguin Books.

Nietzsche, Friedrich. 1967. *Genealogy of Morals and Ecce Homo*. Translated by Kaufmann, Walter. New York: Vintage.

Oliver, Kelly. 2001. *Witnessing: Beyond Recognition*. Minneapolis: University of Minnesota Press.

Patton, Paul. 2006. Order, Exteriority and Flat Multiplicities in the Social. In *Deleuze and the Social*, edited by Martin Fuglsang and Bent Meier Sørensen. Edinburgh: Edinburgh University Press.

Pisters, Patricia. 2003. *The Matrix of Visual Culture: Working With Deleuze in Film Theory*. Stanford, CA: Stanford University Press.

Potter, Sally. 1992. *Orlando*. Sony Picture Classics.

Pritchard, Elizabeth A. 2000. The Way Out West: Development and the Rhetoric of Mobility in Postmodern Feminist Theory. *Hypatia* 15(3): 45–72.

Sandahl, Carrie. 2003. Intersections of Queer and Crip Identities in Solo Autobiographical Perfomance. *GLQ* 1(2): 25–56.

Scott, Ridley. Director. 1991. *Thelma and Louise*. Los Angeles: MGM.

Sedgwick, Eve Kosofsky. 2003. Paranoid Reading and Reparative Reading, Or, You're So Paranoid, You Probably Think This Essay is About You. In *Touching Feeling: Affect, Pedagogy, Performativity*, Durham, NC: Duke University Press.

Smith, Daniel W. 2006. Deleuze, Kant, and the Theory of Immanent Ideas. In *Deleuze and Philosophy*, edited by Constantin V. Boundas. Edinburgh: Edinburgh University Press.

Spinoza, Baruch. 1982. *The Ethics and Selected Letters*. Translated by Shirley, Samuel. Indianapolis, IN: Hackett.

Stone, Alison. 2007. *An Introduction to Feminist Philosophy*. Malden, MA: Polity Press.

Stryker, Susan. 1994. My Words to Victor Frankenstein Above the Village of Chamounix: Performing Transgender Rage. *GLQ* 1(3): 237–254.

Stubblefield, Anna. 2007. "Beyond the Pale": Tainted Whiteness, Cognitive Disability, and Eugenic Sterilization. *Hypatia* 22(2): 162–81.

Sybylla, Roe. 2004. Down to Earth With Nietzsche: The Ethical Effects of Attitudes Toward Time and Body. *Ethical Theory and Moral Practice* 7: 309–28.

Turner, Victor. 1964. An Ndembu Doctor in Practice. In *Magic, Faith, and Healing*, Ari Kiev, editor. New York: Macmillan.

Varela, Francisco J., Evan Thompson, and Eleanor Rosch. 1991. *The Embodied Mind: Cognitive Science and Human Experience*. Cambridge, MA: MIT Press.

Warnke, Georgia. 2005. Race, Gender, and Antiessentialist Politics. *Signs* 31(1): 93–116.

Wilkerson, Abby. 2002. Disability, Sex Radicalism, and Political Agency. *NWSA Journal* 14(3): 33–57.

Williams, Caroline. 2007. Thinking the Political in the Wake of Spinoza: Power, Affect and Imagination in the *Ethics*. *Contemporary Political Theory* 6: 349–69.

Wittig, Monique. 1992. *The Straight Mind and Other Essays*. Boston: Beacon Press.

Woolf, Virginia. 1928. *Orlando: A Biography*. New York: Harcourt Brace.

Young, Iris Marion. 1990. *Throwing Like a Girl and Other Essays in Feminist Philosophy and Social Theory*. Bloomington: Indiana University Press.

Young, Iris Marion. 1997. *Intersecting Voices: Dilemmas of Gender, Political Philosophy, and Policy*. Princeton, NJ: Princeton University Press.

Young, Iris Marion. 2000. House and Home: Variations on a Theme. In *Resistance, Flight, Creation: Feminist Enactments of French Philosophy*, edited by Dorothea Olkowski. Ithaca, NY: Cornell University Press.

Index

abstract machine: Butler, 25; capitalism as, 153; definition of, 14–15; of faciality, 53, 59, 78; feminist, 15, 26, 81, 142; of mutation, 16; and theory, 167–68; of overcoding, 52

actual: and the force of time, 48; and reality, 34, 99; and representations, 84; and Spinoza, 119; and the virtual, 3, 28, 115, 142, 151

affects, 84; that accumulate, 94; and emotions, 136; and intensities, 108, 154; as limit points, 93; and micropercepts, 64; and percepts, 85, 99, 101, 131–32, 135, 163; and speeds, 87; and Spinoza, 117–21, 126, 129; and trauma, 130

Ahab, 93, 176ch.4n.3

Ahmed, Sarah, 72–74

Aion, 22, 102

Alcoff, Linda, 4, 70–73, 140–43

Allison, Dorothy, 5, 130–37

Althusser, Louis, 171n.2, Althusserian, 142, 174ch.2n.11

Ansell Pearson, Keith, 35, 173n.2

Anzaldúa, Gloria, 172n.11

art, 10, 83; as a thought-form, see thought-form

assemblage, definition of, 12, 36; collective assemblages of enunciation and machinic assemblages of desire, 13–16, 27, 36–41, 51, 105, 150, 159

Bartky, Sandra, 58, 70

becoming-woman, 5, 55, 102, 105–13, 138

Beistegui, Miguel de, 179ch.6n.4

Bergson, Henri, 1, 3, 6–10, 28, 95–96, 165, 171–72ch.1n.4 and 7, 177ch.5n.5; Bergsonian intuition, 145; Bergsonian view, 156

Beauvoir, Simone de, 70, 178ch.5n.14

Bogue, Ronald, 159, 174ch.2n.12

Borradori, Giovanna, 7

body without organs, 83, 163; as a moment of suspension, 84; construction of, 86–95, 98, 105, 127–28

Boundas, Constantin, 176ch.4n.2

Braidotti, Rosi, ix, 2, 112, 136, 139, 179ch.6n.7

Brennan, Teresa, 178ch.5n.17

Brison, Susan, 178ch.5n.16

Broca, Paul, 61

Butler, Judith, 24–25, 68, 141, 175ch.3n.5, 178ch.5n.16

Cahoone, Lawrence, 173ch.2n.6

cartographies, feminist, 4, 57–66

Castoriadis, Cornelius, 179ch.6n.1

Chambers, Robert, 61

Code, Lorraine, 178ch.5n.16

Colebrook, Claire, 40–41, 145

concepts, the creation of, viii, 12–29, 33, 99, 103, 166–67; dynamic force of, 2; as an event, 18, 22–23; philosophical, 160; as refrain, 18, 21;